The Complete Letters of Henry James

1872–1876

VOLUME 2

The Complete Letters

of

Henry James, 1872–1876

VOLUME 2

Henry James

Edited by Pierre A. Walker and
Greg W. Zacharias

University of Nebraska Press
Lincoln and London

© 2009 by the University of Nebraska Press
All rights reserved. Manufactured in the United
States of America. Set in Janson Text by Tseng
Information Systems, Inc. Book designer
R. Eckersley.

♾

Library of Congress Cataloging-in-Publication Data
James, Henry, 1843–1916.
[Correspondence. Selections]
The complete letters of Henry James, 1872–1876 /
Henry James ; edited by Pierre A. Walker and
Greg W. Zacharias ; with an introduction by
Millicent Bell.
p. cm. — (The complete letters of Henry James)
Includes bibliographical references and indexes.
ISBN 978-0-8032-2225-0 (v. 1 : alk. paper)
ISBN 978-0-8032-2297-7 (v. 2 : alk. paper)
1. James, Henry, 1843–1916—Correspondence.
2. Authors, American—19th century—
Correspondence. 3. Authors, American—
20th century—Correspondence. I. Walker,
Pierre A. II. Zacharias, Greg W., 1958– III. Title.
PS2123.A4 2008
813'.4—dc22
[B]   2008027370

With gratitude to the Gilbert C. Swanson Foundation, Inc.,
of Omaha for their unwavering support of
The Complete Letters of Henry James

Contents

Illustrations

Acknowledgments

The Center for Henry James Studies at Creighton University, Salem State College, grants from the Gilbert C. Swanson Foundation, Inc., a Summer Fellowship and a Fellowship for College Teachers and Independent Scholars from the National Endowment for the Humanities, a Sabbatical Fellowship from the American Philosophical Society, a Mellon Fellowship to the Henry Ransom Center at the University of Texas at Austin, a fellowship from the Bibliographical Society of America, and individual contributions of time and money have contributed to making work on this volume possible.

In addition to the general editors, associate editors, editorial assistants, editorial board, and advisory group of *The Complete Letters of Henry James*, many individuals have contributed to this volume and to this edition. Nelly Valtat-Comet from the Université de Tours and Annick Duperray from the Université de Provence (Aix-Marseille I) assisted with translations of James's French. Rosella Mamoli Zorzi, Università Ca' Foscari Venezia, and Donatella Izzo, Università di Napoli "L'Orientale," patiently answered questions about Venetian Italian. Harriet Carter from the University of East Anglia, Oliver Herford of University College London, and Anne-Claire Le Reste from the Université de Rennes contributed to this volume during their visits to Omaha in 2006 and 2007. Alfred Habegger was always available to answer questions concerning the James family. Millicent Bell donated her considerable talent and expertise in James studies and as a scholar of later nineteenth-century literature to write the introduction to *The Complete Letters of Henry James, 1872–1876*, volumes 1–3. Patrick Phillips wrote the chronology for this volume. Thomas Wortham conducted the volume's review for the MLA's Committee on Scholarly Editions. For all this we are most grateful.

Very special thanks to Susan Halpert, Elizabeth Falsey, Denison Beach, Jennie Rathbun, Tom Ford, Emily Walhout, Rachel Howarth, Joseph Zajac, and Brent Landau of the Houghton Library, Harvard

University, for their continued help and encouragement. Thanks are in order as well to Isaac Gewirtz, curator, and Stephen Crook and Philip Milito of the Henry W. and Albert A. Berg Collection of English and American Literature at the Humanities and Social Sciences Library, New York Public Library, Astor, Lenox, and Tilden Foundations; to Stephen Jones, Louise Bernard, and the staff of the Beinecke Rare Book and Manuscript Library at Yale University; and to Carl Peterson, head of special collections and Colgate University archivist. In addition, we are grateful to the following repositories for permission to publish letters in this volume: the John Hay Library, Brown University; the Bryn Mawr College Archives, Bryn Mawr College Library; the Everett Needham Case Library, Colgate University; the Rutherford B. Hayes Presidential Center; Manuscripts Division, the Library of Congress; the Massachusetts Historical Society; the Harry Ransom Humanities Research Center, the University of Texas at Austin; and Special Collections, Olin Library, Washington University. We are also grateful to Russell Flinchum, archivist of the Century Association Archives Foundation, for providing information about James's election to and membership in the Century Association.

We are always grateful to Steven H. Jobe and Susan E. Gunter for their *Calendar of the Letters of Henry James and a Biographical Register of Henry James's Correspondents* (http://jamescalendar.unl.edu), which helps us and so many others interested in James's letters.

Creighton University has been generous in its support of the letters project and the Center for Henry James Studies. Special thanks go to Rev. John Schlegel, SJ, president; to Christine Wiseman, former vice president for academic affairs; and to Timothy R. Austin, former dean of the Arts College. In addition, Barbara Braden, former dean, and Gail Jensen, current dean of the Graduate School, and colleagues Robert Dornsife, Bridget Keegan, Brent Spencer, Shari Stenberg, Jennifer Ladino, Nina Ha, and Jackie Masker, each in his or her own way, have been generous in support of *The Complete Letters of Henry James*. J. P. Murray, Kendall Kennedy, Susanne Stahl, Patrick Phillips, Julie Kraft, Mathew Carroll, Michelle McGauvran, and AnaMaria Seglie provided important support for the project in the Center for Henry James Studies.

Patricia Buchanan, former English Department chair, and Anita Shea, former dean of Arts and Sciences, both at Salem State College, have been very generous in their support of work on this project. The office of Salem State College's Vice President of Academic Affairs has provided much-appreciated support from the Faculty/Librarian Research Support Fund.

We dedicate this volume to the Gilbert C. Swanson Foundation, Inc., of Omaha, which continues its important support of the letters project and the Center for Henry James Studies at Creighton. The executive director of the Swanson Foundation, Richard E. O'Toole, believed in the project before almost anyone and deserves special thanks. Special thanks too to Lee Fenicle and Alan James for their support.

The University of Nebraska Press continues an unprecedented commitment to *The Complete Letters of Henry James*. Our thanks go to those at the press with whom we have worked and continue to work, especially Alison Rold, Ladette Randolph, and Joeth Zucco. Richard Eckersley, who designed the pages for this edition and whose career as a book designer was long and remarkable, passed away just before the publication of volume 1 of *The Complete Letters of Henry James, 1855–1872*. We are privileged to have been able to work with a person of such skill, thoughtfulness, knowledge, experience, and kindness. We remember him through the beauty and elegance of this edition's design.

Our deepest thanks go to Bay James, on behalf of the James family, and to Leslie A. Morris, curator of Modern Books and Manuscripts, and William Stoneman, Florence Fearrington Librarian, in the Harvard College Library, on behalf of the president and fellows of Harvard College, for permission to publish those letters still under copyright.

Symbols and Abbreviations

Chronology

1873   July, "A Roman Holiday" is published in the *Atlantic Monthly*.
c. 8 July, after two weeks at Bern, HJ departs for Bad Homburg, spending one night each on the way at Basel and Frankfurt am Main. He arrives at Bad Homburg on 11 July.
15 July, HJ writes home to MWJ, thanking her for "enclosing Willy's photograph" in her last letter. While in Bad Homburg HJ begins to take the water cure, claiming that the "mere change of air & escape from Switzerland have not in themselves miraculously altered my condition." Here he meets and spends time with Henry John Wastell Coulson.
17 July, HJ writes to Grace Norton explaining that he has "seen nothing very wise" yet in Bad Homburg but that the English population offers "exhilarating glimpses of solid British truth," of which he has not yet taken part.
23 July, HJ again writes home to his mother with a message of "no especial adventures" but notes that he continues to spend time with Henry John Wastell Coulson as well as Charley Atkinson and a "very queer Englishwoman" named Lady Piggott. He hears from the Tweedys, who are currently at Saint-Moritz, that they plan to spend August in Bad Homburg. Of his daily activities HJ writes, "I drink, I read & scribble, I stroll in the woods & gardens, I ~~think~~ [∧]listen[∧] to the music at the Kursaal."
August, "Roman Rides" is published in the *Atlantic Monthly*.
1 August, HJ writes to AK after receiving a letter from her in late July concerning AJ's and her "departure for the North." "[A]fter three weeks," HJ writes, the waters "don't seem to suit me—<u>au contraire</u>, & shall slow up. But the air & the place itself are excellent & help me to lead a comfortable life." The Tweedys arrive in Homburg, having telegraphed HJ to reserve

rooms for them. HJ receives word from RJ that GWJ will marry in October.

4 August, HJ writes to his parents as their "holiday" begins in Saint John, New Brunswick, where they have joined AJ and AK (MWJ and Sr. arrived at the Hotel Victoria in Saint John on 26 July). The Tweedys have now settled in Bad Homburg and "seem very buoyant and delighted." He apologizes to his parents for recent financial problems with the *Galaxy*, saying, "They are certainly shabby people"; he gives his parents good news, however, about William Dean Howells's acceptance of "Roman Neighborhoods" and another possible publication (probably "The Last of the Valerii").

5 August, HJ writes to WJ that he is "re-reading Turgenieff in German ♂ beginning a review" for Thomas Sergeant Perry and the *North American Review*. HJ encourages WJ to travel abroad, especially to Rome.

14 August, HJ moves from the Hôtel des Quatre Saisons to "a most agreeable little chamber" in a house on Kisseleff-Strasse because "a change in the weather ∧—toward cold—[∧] had made [his] room uncomfortable." He reports that the Tweedys are doing well and that he has taken a walk with Mr. Tweedy to the French-settled town of Friedrichsdorf. "[L]ast week has ushered in a marked improvement in my health," HJ writes, with hopes that it will correspond to a similar improvement in productivity. He regrets having "despatched a tale" to the *Galaxy*, presumably because of the financial problems that submitting to the magazine has presented in the past. He speculates on his future travel plans, concluding that a brief respite in Paris, where he can get his teeth examined, would most likely serve him well before he returns to Italy.

28 August, "Homburg Reformed" is published in the *Nation*.

3 September, HJ writes to AJ, who has just returned from her travels in Canada. He spends times with the Tweedys and reports that "[a] fortnight ago turned up Miss Bessie Ward," who has come to take the water cure for her eyes. HJ sees her quite often at the Kursaal and describes her as "very pretty ♂ charming." The tooth he had broken feels better, so HJ thinks of revising his travel plans, skipping Paris and returning directly to Italy. HJ asks if the cross that he bought for Mary Holton James almost a year earlier arrived.

9 September, HJ writes to Howells, praising his new book,

A Chance Acquaintance, and offering some friendly criticism about its plot. HJ perhaps sees his comments as permissible, since Howells called HJ's "A Chain of Cities" "meager." HJ tells Howells that he has spent a relatively unproductive summer in Germany and that he plans to return to Italy. HJ acknowledges Howells's literary recommendations, saying, "I shall heed your advice about unlaboriousness. I know I'm too ponderous. But the art of making substance light is hard."

15 September, WJ has decided to meet HJ in Europe in the fall. HJ proposes Florence and awaits a reply from WJ, who, with the help of Charles William Eliot, is trying to find a substitute for his Harvard lectureship. The Tweedys have left for "the Tyrol and Vienna," and HJ now occupies his time with the society of "Mrs. Ward & Bessie." He asks WJ to bring a number of books for him, including those of Sainte-Beuve, Musset, Stendhal, Brosses, and Balzac, along with "a supply of Harrison's lozenges & of Davis's tooth-soap." He remarks on the infrequent correspondence from the rest of the family: "I have never heard so little of them & felt so detatched, as this summer."

18 September, HJ leaves Bad Homburg for Bern, traveling via Basel.

22 September, HJ writes home to MWJ from Bern. HJ is beginning to make his way south in the hopes of meeting WJ in Florence, an event he describes to his mother as "a blessing," for he will then have "a 'superior mind' to converse with, after the general Roman rabble."

25 September, HJ finally receives word from home, by way of MWJ, that WJ will soon sail for England. HJ explains the next day that it will be cheaper to meet in Florence but assures WJ that he will have a letter awaiting his arrival in Liverpool at the Adelphi Hotel with "full instructions" for his southward journey.

October, HJ's review of *Meta Holdenis* by Victor Cherbuliez is published in the *North American Review*.

9 October, "An Ex–Grand Ducal Capital" is published in the *Nation*.

11 October, WJ departs New York aboard the SS *Spain* and arrives in Liverpool on 22 October.

c. 12 October, HJ arrives in Florence but takes a brief respite in Siena, where, as he explains later to Sr., he "repaired to

escape the mosquitoes." He returns to Florence around 14
October, for he writes to Sr. from Florence on 26 October that
he has "been back here some twelve days & [has] found the
weather charming & the mosquitoes departed."

18 October, HJ writes to Howells from Florence, enclosing with his letter some recently finished "sketches" — or,
as HJ self-mockingly calls them, "another bundle of hieroglyphics" — that he hopes will be printed in the January issue
of the *Atlantic Monthly*. HJ plans to spend "three or four weeks
in Florence previous to settling in Rome for the winter." HJ
complains that the previous winter in Rome proved a "bad
time for work," but he resolves to return, for "Rome is [WJ's]
goal." HJ proclaims, "I must, can & shall do better now."

26 October, HJ receives a letter from WJ. Sr. returns HJ's
"Turgenieff m M.S." because it needs revisions. HJ responds
with appreciation to his father for returning the manuscript
but is somewhat concerned with its poor reception by T. S.
Perry and the *North American Review*. He writes that "[i]n my
elation I ⬦ offered to do a series of other articles for T. S. P.
It shows how poorly we judge our own performances." (The
Turgenev article would be published in the *North American
Review* the following April.) HJ mentions several other manuscripts that he has out at the time to *Scribner's Monthly* and the
Galaxy, claiming that Howells is too "choked with my wares"
to publish anything else at the time. He tells Sr. that his health
is improving and that, in time, payments for his work will
"completely cover all [his] expenses" and free him from drawing down his father's line of credit. "Meanwhile," he writes,
"short of real inconvenience, bear with me." HJ passes his time
in Florence in the company of Mrs. Lombard, the Andrews,
and the Greenoughs.

29 October, WJ arrives in Florence, having traveled via London, Paris, and Turin.

30 October, "Dumas and Goethe" is published in the *Nation*.

November, "From a Roman Note-Book" is published in the
Galaxy.

2 November, WJ has arrived in Florence and "is very much
charmed with" the city, according to HJ, who is still greatly
preoccupied with explaining his use of Sr.'s account. Recent
news from the *Atlantic Monthly* leads him again to the subject
of finances: "I was very sorry to see that the A̲t̲l̲a̲n̲t̲i̲c̲ had again

played me false. [. . .] I feel as if I had no business to be over here, compromising you in the delay."

12 November, GWJ marries Caroline "Carrie" Cary.

16–17 November, HJ writes home to his parents with positive news about WJ's life in Florence: "He enjoys Florence very heartily and explores the galleries and churches, day after day, like a regular vigorous tourist." HJ and WJ plan to stay in Florence until 1 December, yet HJ longs for a change in climate, saying, "[t]here has been some sharp weather which makes me long for the Roman softness." The two dine with the Greenoughs on the fifteenth and travel to the Basilica di San Miniato al Monte on the sixteenth. HJ again complains of health problems, this time claiming that his "liver is somewhat out of time" with the rest of his improving health.

18 November, RJ's son, Edward "Ned" Holton James, born.

28 November, HJ and WJ leave Florence and arrive in Rome. That night they take a walk to the Forum and the Coliseum. They find "a couple of sun=bathed chambers at the hotel de Russie" yet separate on 2 December after HJ finds a vacancy at his "old ~~quarteer~~ quarters of last winter." HJ assures his father that despite the separation the situation "will amount to the same as our really dwelling together by day."

December, "Roman Neighborhoods" is published in the *Atlantic Monthly*.

3 December, HJ writes to Sr. from Rome, where he and WJ have been "'settled'" for "some four days." HJ reports that WJ's "spirits, on the whole, are very good, & his appearance excellent." They dine with the von Hoffmanns and Sam Ward (Mrs. Ward and Bessy Ward are "laid up with the measles," according to HJ's 10 December letter to Lizzie Boott). HJ tells his father that he has received a "letter from Albany" from a man who desires his autograph. HJ laments: "Such is fame—& such is idiocy."

10 December, HJ's letter on this day to Lizzie Boott more thoroughly catalogs his and WJ's experience in Florence and hints at a much broader social life than the one HJ had initially described. He tells her that they took two walks to Bellosguardo and spent a "rather social time" in Florence with the Greenoughs, the Huntingtons, the Whitwells, the Lombards, the Andrews, "Dr. G. [Gryzanovski] & Karl Hillebrand," and their wives.

22 December, HJ and WJ dine with the von Hoffmanns (*CWJ* 4: 474). HJ receives word from his father that *Scribner's Monthly* declined to publish some of his "notes." The news brings his financial problems to light again, and HJ asks his father to forward the "notes" to the *Galaxy*, explaining, "I don't like the <u>Galaxy's</u> manners & customs, but one can't afford to be too fastidious." He reports that he has sent *Scribner's* "a tale in two parts" and a third installment despite their recent refusal. Mrs. Ward and Bessy recover from their bout of measles, and HJ and WJ dine with the family "a week ago" and plan to "dine again on Xmas. day." HJ has also "paid [his] respects to the Storeys and Terrys" and called upon Miss Crawford but tells his father that he is relieved that he is having a less social winter than the previous year. He receives word of Wilkie's new wife, Carrie; it seems that much of the family is put off by "her diamonds." HJ himself seems affected by his family's representation of Carrie, for he writes, "I had dreamed of offering her the tribute of some modest Roman toy; but the diamonds put me out of countenance, & I think I shall let it slide." Of RJ's new baby HJ writes, "I long to see the wondrous child & pull its cheeks and pinch its legs. (I mean the Baby's—not Bob's.)"

27 December, HJ and WJ return to Florence because of WJ's health. WJ spends a day at Pisa en route to Florence and takes quinine for a mild case of malaria, which, according to his doctor, has "completely broken." HJ catches a "violent cold" on the trip from Rome.

1874   January, "The Last of the Valerii" is published in the *Atlantic Monthly*.

1 January, "The Autumn in Florence" is published in the *Nation*.

8 January, "Howells' *Poems*" is published in the *Independent*.

9 January, HJ complains that, after Rome, Florence seems "a vulgar little village" and writes to Howells that "life [is] not worth the living away from the Corso and the Pincio." Howells remains the editor of the *Atlantic Monthly* despite a change in ownership; HJ doesn't like the "new type as well as the old," even though "the cover and the paper make one feel as if one were ministering to the highest culture." HJ sends Howells the first half of "a tale in two parts" that he had intended to send

to *Scribner's.* He was dissuaded from the latter course upon Howells's encouragement, yet he warns Howells that "it remains true, in a general way, that I can't really get on without extracting tribute from that source. It's a mere money question." HJ has "lately passed an evening" with Lowell.

13 January, HJ and WJ settle together at the Corona d'Italia, a hotel near the Santa Maria Novella train station, where they "each g[o]t a sunny room & no end of food and general comfort." HJ tells AJ that, upon leaving Rome, he "had a disagreeable combination of indigestion & rheumatism" and that he misses Rome tremendously now that he has been forced "to substitute Florence the meagre, for Rome the magnificent." He and WJ "enjoy no great store" of society but see "Gryzanowski frequently" as well as Lowell and the Huntingtons. "All this seems very frivolous, though," HJ writes, "when I reflect upon the sterner stuff with which your ₐlate₍ₐ₎ letters have been filled." Among other things, the family is concerned with GWJ's matrimonial and financial problems as well as "the death of that poor nice Mrs. Agassiz, the Washburns tribulations, the Norton lamentations &c."

14 January, HJ writes to Grace Norton about Charles's "taking America rather hard." "I am afraid that when ₍ₐ₎I₍ₐ₎ go back," he writes of his own return home, "I shall need all my ingenuity to put it into practice."

February, "A Chain of Italian Cities" is published in the *Atlantic Monthly.*

February–March, "Mme. de Mauves" is published in the *Galaxy.*

5 February, HJ writes to his parents that he has recovered from a "stupid malady" that was "an affair chiefly of the <u>head</u> which caused [him] much pain for many days & nights." He includes some other details of his recuperation so as to lessen any "superfluous anxiety" of his parents' "sympathic hearts." He writes that he has "pretty well made up [his] mind to return home ~~in~~ ₐduring₍ₐ₎ the coming spring." HJ's review of *Jean de Thommeray; Le colonel Evrard* by Jules Sandeau is published in the *Nation.*

9–10 February, WJ leaves HJ in Florence, traveling north "to Paris via Venice, Munich and Dresden" (*CWJ* 4: 483). HJ writes later, in his 15 February letter to his parents, that WJ "wrote you, I suppose, that the Tweedies had kindly 'invited'

him to visit them"; WJ, on the other hand, wrote to GWJ that
the Tweedys had sent him a "cheque for 500 francs to pay for
the extra journey" (*CWJ* 4: 483).

10 February, HJ learns from Anna Hallowell that Mary Louisa
Shaw has died. He offers kind condolences to Hallowell, a
close friend of Shaw, describing the latter as full of "sweetness
& patience and firmness, [and a] generosity & tranquil acceptance of better days or worse." He regrets that news traveled so
slowly and that he was not able to send "a line of sympathy or
an offer of assistance."

12 February, HJ's review of *Dernières nouvelles* by Prosper
Mérimée is published in the *Nation*.

15 February, HJ tells his parents that he had originally planned
to leave Europe with WJ but, wanting "a more contemplative
& ceremonious leave," may sail separately. Upon arriving in
Dresden, WJ decides to adhere to his original plan of sailing
in early March but actually sails on 28 February (*CWJ* 4: 485).
Because HJ did not want to leave earlier than mid-March, he
will "start a month or six weeks later," knowing, as he says, "the
propriety of getting home promptly to heat my literary irons &
get myself financially & reputationally on my legs."

27 February, HJ, not aware that WJ is departing the following
day, explains again to his parents that he does not plan to sail
home with his brother. He assures them that his staying on in
Florence will not put them out too much financially because
he has been working and producing quite prodigiously. "I feel
within the last three weeks so well & so competent to work," he
writes, citing as an example his recently completed "chapters
of <u>Florentine Notes</u>," which he posts "to the <u>Independent</u>"
on 1 March. Despite his change in plans he promises them, at
the close of his letter, that he "will return to [them] primed
for immortality!" In addition to his work HJ has "lately been
taking Fanny [Lombard] about to galleries" and is going "to
some theatricals arranged by Miss Whitwell."

28 February, WJ leaves Bremen for the United States on the
Mosel.

9 March, HJ resumes his solitary life abroad, working, re-
cuperating, and socializing. He begins studying "colloquial
Italian" with a young Roman and "expect[s] in a few weeks to
rattle the divine tongue like an angel." He also begins nego-
tiations at this time with the *Atlantic Monthly* (he writes to

Howells the following day) and *Scribner's Monthly* over the serial publication of the presently unwritten *Roderick Hudson*. HJ tells his parents that "[i]t must depend upon the money question," but, because of his allegiance to Howells, he feels that "if the Atlantic will pay as much as the other, I ought, properly, to take up with it." HJ plans to name $1,200 as the price for his story. He attends "an entertainment" given by James Lorimer Graham Jr., the American consul general in Florence.

13 March, WJ's ship arrives in the United States.

22 March, HJ continues a relatively lively social life in Florence even though he assures WJ that he "lead[s] the same quiet life." HJ explains, for example, that he attended a "large party" thrown by Ellen Greenough Huntington and "didn't get home till 3."

Late March, HJ attends an "afternoon party" at Bellosguardo and visits the Halls, where, he says, "I had a lovely visit, & lost my heart both to the villa & its mistress."

April, "An Autumn Journey" is published in the *Galaxy*. HJ's review "*Frühlingsfluthen. Ein König Lear des Dorfes. Zwei Novellen. Von Iwan Turgéniew*" is published in the *North American Review*.

1 April, HJ visits Livorno, "partly to inhale the sea=breeze [. . .] & partly to do a friendly turn to the poor Lombards." He plans to continue his brief respite with "a little tour of observation through Pisa, Lucca & Pistoia" and then return to Florence in a week's time. HJ is not impressed with Livorno, calling it "strangely blank, modern & stupid" (he later tells Lizzie Boott that "[i]t's more American than America"), but says that the "journey is worth making only to see the Mediterranean blue." He learns that GWJ plans to leave the railroad business and go "into the enterprise for working iron."

7 April, HJ leaves Livorno for "Pisa & Lucca."

8 April–c. 12 April, HJ visits Pisa and Lucca.

9 April, "The Letters of Prosper Mérimée" is published in the *Independent*; a review of Victor Hugo's *Ninety-Three* is published in the *Nation*.

c. 12 April, HJ returns to Florence and takes a three-room apartment at 10 Piazza Santa Maria Novella.

18 April, HJ receives word from Howells, by way of Sr., that *Roderick Hudson* has been accepted for publication in the

Atlantic. He writes to Alice: "I shall immortalize myself: vous allez voir."

23 April, "Florentine Notes" is published in the *Independent.*

30 April, another installment of "Florentine Notes" is published in the *Independent.*

May–June, "Adina" is published in *Scribner's Monthly.*

3 May, HJ tells Howells and WJ that his days proceed ever so "solitudinously." He admonishes Howells for failing to write and updates WJ on his Florence social life. HJ dines alone and is "mortally tired of [the] nature *&* conversation" of the Lombards (although he still accepts the invitations to their parlor). He calls Karl Hillebrand "an unmistakeable snob." HJ's letter of credit expires, and he requests an extension "for June, July *&* August" in the amount of £250.

14 May, "A Florentine Garden" is published in the *Independent.*

17 May, HJ describes his attendance at a ball hosted by the jockey club "at their Casino in the Cascine." He says that he "went for information's sake" and found Florentine society extravagant. He anticipates a return home in the fall, even though he knows he "shall not find life at home simpatico." HJ says that his decision is a purely practical one, based on the financial impositions that he is putting on MWJ and Sr.

21 May, a third installment of "Florentine Notes" is published in the *Independent;* "Tuscan Cities" is published in the *Nation.*

June, "Siena" is published in the *Atlantic Monthly.*

3 June, HJ responds to letters from MWJ and AJ, who have apparently sent him "advice" about home and life. HJ writes, "Alice's [advice] that I must not turn up my nose at home things, *&* yours that I take a wife. I will bore a hole in my nose *&* keep it down with a string, *&* if you will provide the wife, the fortune, *&* the 'inclination' I will take them all."

4 June, HJ's review of Flaubert's *Temptation of St. Anthony* is published in the *Nation.*

c. 6 June, HJ leaves Florence "under pressure of the terrific heat."

11 June, "Old Italian Art" is published in the *Independent.*

13 June, HJ arrives at Monte Generoso, near Como, after first traveling through Milan and Ravenna.

18 June, "Florentine Architecture" is published in the *Independent.*

22 June, HJ arrives in Baden-Baden, having left Monte

Generoso on 20 June, traveling northward via "the Splügen pass, Chur & Basel." After staying one night, HJ decides to remain here instead of proceeding to Bad Homburg. His decision is based in part on the frugality of the location and on Turgenev's having lived there.

2 July, "An Italian Convent" is published in the *Independent*.

9 July, "The Churches of Florence" is published in the *Independent*; "Ravenna" is published in the *Nation*.

23 July, HJ's review of *Souvenirs de Bourgogne* by Émile Montégut is published in the *Nation*.

28 July, HJ makes a reservation to sail back to the United States from Liverpool on 25 August. He tells Sarah Wister the following day that he "shall take what comes, make the best of it & dream inveterately [. . .] of going back for a term of years, as the lawyers say, to Italy."

August, "Professor Fargo" is published in the *Galaxy*. HJ leaves Baden-Baden early in the month and travels to England, via the Rhine, Holland, and Belgium.

20, 27 August, "A Northward Journey" is published in the *Independent*.

27 August, "In Holland" is published in the *Nation*.

3 September, "In Belgium" is published in the *Nation*.

9 September, HJ leaves Liverpool on the *Atlas* and returns to Cambridge around the middle of the month.

17 September, HJ's review of *Henry Beyle* by Andrew A. Paton is published in the *Nation*.

October, HJ's reviews of *Théophile Gautier, Souvenirs intimes* by Ernest Feydeau; *Histoire du Romantisme, Suivie de Notices Romantiques, etc.* by Théophile Gautier; and *The Legend of Jubal, and Other Poems* by George Eliot are published in the *North American Review*.

October–November, "Eugene Pickering" is published in the *Atlantic Monthly*.

4 October, GWJ's son, Joseph Cary James, born.

13 October, HJ reports to RJ that "Cambridge has never looked so pretty [. . .] & I have seen nothing in Europe in the way of weather equal to the glory of an American autumn"; but he qualifies these positive comments of home by admitting that "I have become very ∧much[∧] Europeanized in feeling, & I mean to keep a firm hold of the old world in some way or other."

15 October, HJ's review of *The Old Régime in Canada* by Francis Parkman is published in the *Nation*.

November, "Art," on an exhibit at the Boston Athenaeum, is published in the *Atlantic Monthly*.

12 November, "Gautier's Winter in Russia" is published in the *Nation*.

December, "The Drama," on a production of *The School for Scandal* at the Boston Museum, and a review of Julian Hawthorne's *Idolatry: A Romance* are published in the *Atlantic Monthly*.

15 December, HJ attends H. O. Houghton & Co.'s commemorative dinner for the *Atlantic Monthly*.

16 December–13 January, at some point in late December 1874 or early January 1875, HJ moves to New York, settling at 111 East 25th Street.

24 December, HJ's review of Thomas Hardy's *Far from the Madding Crowd* is published in the *Nation*.

31 December, a review of J. W. De Forest's *Honest John Vane* is published in the *Nation*.

1875   January, (the earliest extant letter from New York is 13 January to Howells). HJ's opinions of life in New York differ depending upon his correspondent. To Howells, he "come[s] back to N. Y. [. . .] with a real relish [. . .] feel[ing] vastly at home"; to Sarah Wister and Lizzie Boott, however, he "like[s] New York decidedly less" and still "prefer[s] F[lorence]" and "fancie[s] [. . .] R[ome]." *Roderick Hudson* begins a twelve-month run in the *Atlantic Monthly*. HJ's reviews of Bayard Taylor's *The Prophet: A Tragedy* and William Dean Howells's *A Foregone Conclusion* are published in the *North American Review*; "Art," on pictures by Wilde, Boughton, J. Appleton Brown, Mrs. W. J. Stillman, and Egusquiza, is published in the *Atlantic Monthly*.

7 January, a review of William Dean Howells's *A Foregone Conclusion* is published in the *Nation*.

14 January, "Nordhoff's Communistic Societies" is published in the *Nation*.

14–23 January, HJ visits the Wisters in Philadelphia at some time between these dates.

21 January, "Theology in the English Poets" is published in the *Nation*.

28 January, a note on Charles Kingsley, "Mr. Greville's Journal," and a review of P. V. N. Myers's *Remains of Lost Empires: Sketches of the Ruins of Palmyra, Nineveh, Babylon, and Persepolis, etc.* are published in the *Nation*.

31 January, Osgood publishes HJ's first book, *A Passionate Pilgrim, and Other Tales.*

February, early in February, Lizzie Boott visits New York; she and HJ share a meal at Delmonico's.

4 February, a review of Sir Samuel Baker's *Ismailïa* is published in the *Nation*.

18 February, "Professor Masson's Essays" and "Sainte-Beuve's First Articles" are published in the *Nation*.

March, "Correspondence of William Ellery Channing, D.D., and Lucy Aikin, from 1826 to 1842" is published in the *Atlantic Monthly*.

4 March, "The Prince Consort" is published in the *Nation*.

11 March, "Livingstone's Last Journals" and "Notes on the Theatres" are published in the *Nation*.

18 March, a review of Sir Arthur Helps's *Social Pressure* and "Madame Ristori" are published in the *Nation*.

1 April, reviews of *Ezra Stiles Gannett, Unitarian Minister in Boston, 1824–1871. A Memoir,* by his son, William C. Gannett, Augustus J. C. Hare's *Days near Rome,* and *Bric-à-Brac Series: Personal Reminiscences of [Thomas] Moore and [William] Jerdan,* edited by R. H. Stoddard, are published in the *Nation*.

8 April, "John Coleridge Patteson" is published in the *Nation*.

15 April, "Sainte-Beuve's English Portraits" is published in the *Nation*.

16 April, HJ writes to Caroline Dall, who believes that he "ha[s] charge of the literary department of the Nation." He informs her that he cannot review her most recent book, *The Romance of the Association,* because an anonymous review for the *Nation* is "already in [. . .] type."

22 April, "Thomson's Indo-China and China" is published in the *Nation*.

27 April–27 May, at some point between these dates, HJ moves to 36 Irving Place, New York.

29 April, Osgood publishes *Transatlantic Sketches.* "Macready's Reminiscences" is published in the *Nation*.

6 May, "Taine's Notes on Paris" is published in the *Nation*.

20 May, a review of H. Willis Baxley's *Spain. Art Remains and Art Realities: Painters, Priests, and Princes, etc.* is published in the *Nation*.

27 May, HJ writes to Mary Holton James from 36 Irving Place, New York, apologizing for his "base procrastination" in mailing her copies of his *Transatlantic Sketches* and *A Passionate Pilgrim, and Other Tales* and attributing the delay to his "physical aversion & incapacity to tie up a parcel." A note on George Rignold as Macbeth is published in the *Nation*.

3 June, HJ's note on Frank Duveneck and reviews of Victor Cherbuliez's *Miss Rovel* and George H. Calvert's *Essays—Aesthetical* are published in the *Nation*.

5 June, HJ is elected to the Century Association.

7 June, HJ again corresponds with Caroline Dall about the *Nation*'s review of *The Romance of the Association*.

10 June, reviews of *A Group of Poets and Their Haunts* and *Home Sketches in France, and Other Papers* are published in the *Nation*.

17 June, notes on Paul Veronese and Jean-François Millet and "Lady Duff Gordon's Letters" are published in the *Nation*.

24 June, a note on J. A. Lawson's *Wanderings in the Interior of New Guinea* and "Personal Reminiscences of Cornelia Knight and Thomas Raikes, Bric-à-Brac Series" are published in the *Nation*.

July, "On Some Pictures Lately Exhibited" is published in the *Galaxy*.

1 July, reviews of Ouida's *Signa: A Story* and Andrew Wynter's *Fruit Between the Leaves* are published in the *Nation*.

8 July, a review of Gilbert Haven's *Our Next-Door Neighbor: A Winter in Mexico* is published in the *Nation*.

15 July, a review of Théophile Gautier's *Constantinople* in translation is published in the *Nation*.

Mid-July, "a few days" before 21 July, HJ leaves New York and returns to Cambridge.

21 July, HJ writes to John Hay, an assistant to Whitelaw Reid at the *New York Tribune*, in an attempt to establish a "regular correspondence with a newspaper" upon his return to Paris. In his appeal to Hay HJ cites an "American [. . .] appetite [. . .] for information about all Parisian things" as well as his own "considerable familiarity" with a variety of French topics—manners, people, books, and the theater, among others.

22 July, a review of Harriet Beecher Stowe's *We and Our Neigh-*

bors: Records of an Unfashionable Street is published in the *Nation*.

29 July, "Swinburne's Essays" is published in the *Nation*.

Early August, HJ receives word from John Hay that Whitelaw Reid has accepted HJ's proposition to write for the *Tribune*. The newspaper had agreed to pay HJ "$20. gold" for his contributions. "Benvolio" and "Three French Books," a review-essay of Bornier's *La Fille de Roland*, Daudet's *Fromont Jeune et Risler Aîné*, and Wallon's *Jeanne d'Arc* are published in the *Galaxy*. HJ makes a short visit to the country.

5 August, a review of Albert Rhodes's *The French at Home* is published in the *Nation*.

12 August, a review of Frances Elliot's *The Italians: A Novel* is published in the *Nation*.

18 August, RJ's daughter, Mary Walsh James, born.

24 August, HJ writes to H. O. Houghton & Co. requesting an advance on the remaining four installments of *Roderick Hudson* awaiting publication in the *Atlantic Monthly*, citing his imminent departure for Europe. The company responds by 30 August with full payment, an unusual practice for the firm. HJ writes to J. R. Osgood on 31 August about the timeline for the book's publication.

26 August, a review of *A Christian Painter of the Nineteenth Century: Being the Life of Hyppolite Flandrin* by Henrietta Lear is published in the *Nation*.

30 August, HJ returns to Cambridge after "a week's absence" in "the country."

September, "Mr. Tennyson's Drama" is published in the *Galaxy*.

9 September, HJ's notes about portraits by Frank Duveneck and Copley are published in the *Nation*.

23 September, "New Novels" is published in the *Nation*.

30 September, a review of T. L. Kington-Oliphant's *The Duke and the Scholar, and Other Essays* is published in the *Nation*.

October, "The Letters of Madame de Sabran" is published in the *Galaxy*.

7 October, "Nadal's Impressions of England" is published in the *Nation*.

13 October, HJ finishes the proofs for the *Atlantic Monthly* serialization of *Roderick Hudson* and divides the final (twelfth)

part into parts 12 and 13. He writes to George Abbot James to set up a meeting for 16 October, the day before he departs for Europe.

14 October, a review of Louisa May Alcott's *Eight Cousins: Or the Aunt-hill* is published in the *Nation*.

17 October, HJ leaves Cambridge for England.

21 October, a review of John Latouche's *Travels in Portugal* is published in the *Nation*.

31 October, HJ arrives in Liverpool and boards an "afternoon train" for London.

November, Osgood publishes the book edition of *Roderick Hudson*.

Errata

Errata from *The Complete Letters of Henry James: 1855–1872*. Corrections made to the 2008 printings.

1: 16:
Previous publication of 8 October [1859] to Thomas Sergeant Perry: Harlow 12 *should read* Harlow 239

1: 216n213.25; 1: 348; 2: 480:
in each entry for Sedgwick, Sara Price Ashburner, 1879 *should read* 1877

2: 134n130.28:
Catharine (Kitty) James Prince *should read* Katharine (Kitty) James Prince

2: 390, line 20:
this out country *should read* this our country

The Complete Letters of Henry James

1872–1876

VOLUME 2

1873

MARY WALSH JAMES
15 July [1873]
ALS Houghton
bMS Am 1094 (1810)

5

Homburg July 15
Hotel des Quatre Saisons

Dearest mother: A week ago just as I was leaving Berne I
received your letter of June 17$^{\underline{th}}$, enclosing Willy's photograph— 10
it having been delayed by being directed to Florence. Many
thanks for it; it bore me benevolent company on my journey.
What that journey was my letter posted the day before I started
will by this time have told you. I came hither by Bâle &
Frankfort, spending a night at each place. I have an impression 15
that you & father once came to Homburg & perhaps you
remember enough of it to picture my ~~journ~~ ∧situation.[∧] The
place is very pretty, very cool and very comfortable and if I get
no great help from the waters I shall at least have a very
agreeable residence. Of what the waters are likely to do for me, I 20
can hardly judge yet having drunk them but four days. The mere
change of air & escape from Switzerland have not in themselves
miraculously altered my condition & I have settled down to
taking the waters in the regular way. I of course immediately
went to see a physician (the English one) and am following his 25
directions. The regular "cure" averages five weeks; but for
myself I am philosophic & neither doubt nor ~~hope~~. ∧anticipate[∧].
I am convinced that my aggravation is temporary & that I shall
sooner or later be better again; meanwhile I get through the
days very tolerably & ~~feel~~ ∧am[∧] well enough generally to feel 30
pledged to being eventually well particularly. This prolonged
out=of=sorts condition rather abridges any working powers, but
I can do quite enough and you needn't at all pity me.—Before
long I am confident of giving you better news.—The common

3

way of living here for families ꝏ couples is in lodgings ♦♦ and
dining at the Kùrhaus; but I have fixed myself at this hotel as
cheaper ꝏ pleasanter for a single man. It is very comfortable,
moderate in its prices ꝏ has a table consistent with the use of the
5   waters. The cessation of the gaming here has diminished the
crowd but it is still very great ꝏ consists mainly of English, of a
better sort than the herds of Cook's creatures who swarm in
Switzerland. There seem to be very few Americans ꝏ I have met
no one I know. I consort somewhat with a very good young
10   Englishman staying at this hotel also for his health—a graceful
product of E̶t̶ Harrow ꝏ Oxford ꝏ of heirship to
Northumberland estates. The resources of Homburg are
otherwise sufficiently numerous to help the days to glide by.
From 7 to 9 every one drinks at the Elizabeth Spring in a
15   brilliant crowd to the sound of superior music. Do you
remember the park through which the springs are scattered? It is
quite large ꝏ lovely ꝏ a very pretty lounging and strolling place.
Beyond it stretch away wide woods which cover the low blue
Taunus mountains, and abound in shady walks. The Kùrhaus too
20   has its own gardens with daily shade and nightly music, ꝏ the
Schloss has <u>its</u> gardens w̶i̶t̶h̶ which are pleasantly picturesque.
All this makes a wonderful amount of shade ꝏ as the place is
high (on a low spur of the hills behind it) one needn't especially
suffer from the heat. The air is extremely delightful ꝏ though it
25   has ʼn't "cured" me by magic I relish it more than that of Berne
ꝏ other low parts of Switzerland. At three o'clock I drink again,
at another spring ꝏ at 5 I dine, with my young Northumbrian—
who, by the way, derives a melancholy interest from just having
had his eye shot out ∧—accidentally—[∧] by one of his own
30   farmers. The Kursaal has all the papers and very good music, à
l'Allemande, in the evening—also concerts ꝏ plays in a horribly
hot little theatre which I don't attend.—There's Homburg. You
see I might be worse off.—I heard yesterday from Aunt Mary
who is at St. Moritz where Mr. T. is taking the waters for gout,

which the doctor there pronounces his ailment to be. She speaks
with faint praise of the place—especially of the cold and says
they will not stay after July 31ˢᵗ. I also got a line from
C. Atkinson who was on his way after a 3 week's tour to Zermatt
&c, to join me at Berne. But missing me there, I doubt now if I   5
shall meet him: which as I regret, as it would mitigate his
loneliness, which I think he suffers from.—It's time I should
hear again from home and I am beginning my periodical "wait"
for letters. Continue to direct for the rest of the Summer to
Brown & Shipley.—I mustn't forget to thank you for Willy's   10
photog., which I like extremely. That is its' a success as photos.
go. I stand reminded dearest mother, of my promise to endow
you with my own image; indeed I hadn't forgotten it. But in
Italy during the hot weather, I shrank from exposing myself
under a photographer's glass roof, and here I can get nothing   15
decent. The first moment of the Autumn I shall go and do it.—
In all your home doings & plannings I took my usual exquisite
interest. Willy ~~is pe~~ ₍ᴧ₎has gon got his passes, I suppose & ~~of~~
~~course~~ ₍ᴧ₎perhaps is home again & Alice is rubbing shoulders
with ice-bergs in Nova Scotia. I hope they have ~~all~~ ₍ᴧ₎both   20
prospered in all things. Willy I suppose will go somewhere on
his return—to Mt. Desert again? I wrote him from Glion in
answer to a letter communicating his plan for next winter, & I
hope he will find my answer as favorable as I meant it to be.
Rome I should think, would suit him very well & he could find   25
no place more supplied with such resources as he is competent
to make use of. I hope if he decides to come, he will get ₍ᴧ₎hold
of₍ᴧ₎ some mild virtuous boy. He will have brought you news of
Wilk & Bob, which you must transmit to me.—I'm glad, dearest
mammy, you are going to take a turn before the Summer's over.   30
I hope, most tenderly, that Cambridge is not too uncomfortable.
I have seen the N. Y. papers up to June 27ᵗʰ & they mention no
unusual heat. Love to F. to whom I wrote a week ago. Farewell.
Your loving H.

No previous publication

∾

3.12 benevolent • benevo= | lent

3.18 comfortable • com= | fortable

3.32 out=of=sorts • out= | =of=sorts

4.1 ◊◊ and • [an *overwrites illegible letters*]

4.11 ~~Et~~ Harrow • [H *overwrites* Et]

4.12 Northumberland • Northum= | berland

4.12 Homburg • Hom= | burg

4.21 ~~with~~ which • [hic *overwrites* wit]

4.25 ʹn't • [*blotted out*]

5.4 Zermatt • Zer= | matt

5.7 suffers • suf= | fers

5.13 forgotten • for= | gotten

5.16 moment • mo= | ment

5.18 ~~gon~~ got • [t *overwrites* n]

5.24 favorable • favor= | able

∾

3.6 Homburg • HJ would spend ten weeks in Bad Homburg; see also his travel essay entitled "Homburg Reformed."

3.14–15 Bâle & Frankfort • That is, Basel, Switzerland, and Frankfurt am Main, Germany.

3.16 you & father once came to Homburg • MWJ and Sr. may have visited Homburg when they were looking at schools for WJ and HJ in Frankfurt, Heidelberg, and Wiesbaden during 1859–60.

3.25 a physician (the English one) • Murray's 1877 *Handbook for North Germany* identifies "Dr. Lewis" as "the resident English physician" (361).

4.2 the Kùrhaus • The Kurhaus or Kursaal (p. 4.30) was a magnificent building on Homburg's main street. It was built between 1840 and 1843 by the Blanc brothers, who moved to Monte Carlo to run the casino there after gambling was prohibited in Homburg. It was the center for gambling (while it was still authorized) and cultural activities in Homburg, containing a theater, restaurant, café, smoking rooms, and a reading room "where

English and foreign papers and periodicals are taken in" (Murray, *North Germany* 362).

4.5 The cessation of the gaming • When Prussia annexed the region in 1866, the casino was forced to close.

4.9-10 a very good young Englishman • Henry John Wastell Coulson (b. 1848) attended Harrow and Exeter College, Oxford, and became a member of the Bar at the Inner Temple in 1876. See HJ to parents, 9 November [1875].

4.14 Elizabeth Spring • The Elisabethenbrunnen, or Elizabeth Spring, Homburg's most significant medicinal spring. Its discovery in 1834 launched Homburg's success as a nineteenth-century spa. Murray's *North Germany* observes that the water of this spring "contains more carbonic acid than any other saline spa known, and on that account sits lightly on the dyspeptic stomach" (361).

4.20-21 the Schloss • The castle of the landgraves of Homburg, actually a seventeenth-century Baroque palace built on the site of a medieval castle. Later in the nineteenth century, Kaiser Wilhelm II used it as a summer residence.

4.30-31 à l'Allemande • German style.

4.33-34 Aunt Mary [. . .] Mr. T. • Mary and Edmund Tweedy (pp. 91, 92).

5.4 C. Atkinson • Charles Atkinson.

5.10 Brown & Shipley • HJ's London bankers.

5.19-20 Alice is rubbing shoulders with ice-bergs in Nova Scotia • AJ and AK were vacationing in Quebec and Canada's maritime provinces; Sr. and MWJ would join them in August at Saint John, New Brunswick.

5.22 Mt. Desert again • WJ recuperated on Maine's Mt. Desert Island in the summer of 1872 following a bout of "philosophical hypochondria" (*CWJ* 1: 167).

5.22-23 I wrote him from Glion in answer to a letter communicating his plan for next winter • HJ to WJ, 18 June 1873 (*CLHJ, 1872–1876* 1: 319-22).

5.33 Love to F. to whom I wrote a week ago • Possibly HJ to Sr., 29 June [1873] (*CLHJ, 1872–1876* 1: 322-34).

GRACE NORTON

17 July [1873]

ALS Houghton

bMS Am 1094 (897)

5

Homburg bei Frankfort

July 17ᵗʰ

Dear Grace—

Your letter of June 19 which came to me yesterday was

10 an ample satisfaction of all the affectionate wonderment I have
been devoting to your unrecorded fortunes for these six weeks.
It gave me very great pleasure ɑ I thank you heartily for making
time to write it so soon ɑ so long. It was eloquent both in all it
said ɑ all it suggested—all it didn't quite say, ⫽ ɑ expresses ɑ

15 quite what I imagined for you—only much better than my
imagination phrased it. I take an immense satisfaction in
thinking it very philosophically cheerful ɑ I feel that your'e
taking things in the right way. You say excellently that your
country is yours very much as your body is and that though you

20 may like it little better you feel a necessary confusion between
its being, its future, ɑ your own. This it is—as you must so often
have felt—that sets a kind of impassable limit (which ~~you~~ ₐweₐ
hardly know whether to accept or to resent) ~~between~~ ₐtoₐ all
our perception, contemplation ɑ enjoyment of the things of this

25 old world; and offers as a last resort a kind of rest ɑ fixedness in
the sense of our own native atmosphere—a something in which,
in spite of pains and distastes, we yet vaguely expand and aspire,
as over here, in spite of pleasures and appreciations ineffable, we
yet, beyond a certain point, contract, congeal ɑ fall out of step.

30 Considering that in this wondrous world opinion, decision
preference ɑc, are rather hard (in their more absolute forms,) it
is a relief ɑ a blessing to have some big absolute thing prescribed
to us by downright nature herself—as you ɑ I ɑ our's have in big
chaotic America ɑ her big uninteresting light. Your remarks

8

about the light by the way, went to my heart of hearts ♃ I do
indeed see you standing there among our brittle breezes—in a
great room without a ceiling. But I am glad with you
nevertheless that you do stand there for better ♃ worse (in their
respective measures) with the weary sea and the painful arrival   5
no longer staring at you between the crannies of present
experience. Of what the change must be for the children I can
easily imagine. To see them in such happy conditions must be a
vast satisfaction—and must indeed help you to reflect that if
America is a good place for children it can't be absolutely   10
worthless for grown people. But perhaps you don't generalize so
far ♃ content yourself with saying that Ashfield is good for them
in the summer of 1873. May it nevertheless be good for them to
the end ♃ in all coming summers. ~~Of w~~ What your mother feels
in finding herself at home after such a gulf of experience, she   15
would probably smile at me, very forgivingly, for saying that I
can understand. Say to her at any rate, with my most affectionate
remembrances, that I ~~do rejoice with her in it~~ have ~~sufficientl~~
sufficient elderly wisdom to rejoice with her in it most heartily.
Your account of your neighbors and their manners is very   20
pleasant and yet I can easily understand that it should give a sort
of uncomfortable twist to your answering good=will to compare
them with your mediaeval Sienese.—Your cares and duties and
problems are very vividly shadowed forth in your account of
Sally's ♃ Lily's ~~sol~~ social aspirations and circumscriptions. I'm   25
afraid that in your place I should be rather puzzled as to the line
of the longest-sighted wisdom: but in any other place I should
appeal to you of all people in the world, for light ~~and~~ ʌonʌ the
subjects ♃ I ~~a♢♢~~ resign you to your opportunities with a most
affectionate blessing on the patient constancy of your   30
inspiration.—Of myself there are no great things to relate; it
being not a particularly immense thing to begin with, that I am
here in German Homburg, drinking the healing waters. I left
Italy more than a month ago, ʌby the Simplonʌ spent some

three weeks in Switzerland (one at Montreux) and two at
Berne—which if you come to Europe again or rather—hideous
<u>if</u>!—<u>when</u> you come, you must spend a few days in and see a
place with a really intense physiognomy—a very charming place
indeed) & then, feeling much more out-of sorts than I cared to,
came hither took a hard look and felt it was Germany and—in
fine, found your letter yesterday in the P. O. and sat and read it
under some cool green German trees in the park. Homburg, is
very pretty (you know the general value of the epithet in
Germany) very agreeable as to climate & position, very well
furnished with shady wood=walks on the low Taunus mountains
which rise behind it and show you the indifferently charming
plain of Frankfort, and less frivolous I believe than of yore,
before the gaming was stopped. I have seen nothing very wise
here yet, but a good third of the population of England are
gathered here and if I were on speaking terms with any of it,
I might have exhilarating glimpses of solid British truth. As it
is I drink not at that well, but at another where a band plays (at
7 a.m, in this land of music & early rising) where all Homburg
assembles & the water tastes of sulphur. Don't waste a moments
emotion on my being out of sorts. I don't mean to be forever
and am so tired of it that I ~~do~~ shall never be again, with my own
concurrence. Little by little we learn some of Nature's secrets &
keep hoping to be on tolerable terms with her. I have been on
excellent ones for a year past & shall be soon again.—I think a
great deal about Italy & seem to myself to love it better than
anything in the world. Altogether why, I don't think I could say,
but I believe that is always the case in a great <u>tendresse</u>. If I feel
the better for Homburg I shall probably cross the Alps again ~~at~~
early in September and spend next winter there. Where I don't
quite ~~no~~ know; I'm afraid in Rome. I say <u>afraid</u>, because Rome is
such an infernal compound of seductions & repulsions. But yet
awhile longer the ~~se~~ former prevail and I shall probably succumb
to them. I didn't see ~~Fl~~ Siena on my way up from Rome, because

I left Italy very hastily; but if things go well I hope to spend a part of the autumn there. I feel as if I had a partial impression of it however; for I spent a week at Perugia and I imagine Siena a sort of magnified Perugia. At any rate I shall see & I can promise you to pay a very pious pilgrimage indeed to the Villa Spannochi.—I have been having ever since you sailed a great many things to say to you; but between what is unspeakable in its essence and what is unspeakable for lack of means and time & opportunity, our relations seem sometimes—even those we would fain make most constant—~~seem~~ ~~t~~ ~~sometimes~~ to shrivel to a narrow stream. I would like to add here what I have to say to Charles & Jane. Give my kindest love to Charles and tell I wish greatly I could have some Ashfield walks & talks with him. I can imagine what he misses in Ashfield; or rather, I cannot, but of that especially we might talk. I at any rate very often think of it. Did he & Jane get each a note from me, the last thing before sailing?—It matters little, for before long I shall write another.—I hope Jane & you are gradually getting rest & that even American cares have a tendency to simplify themselves. For the present dear Grace, farewell, with every grateful & hopeful wish.

Yours most faithfully H. James jr

Please remember me very kindly to Mr. Curtis—if to do so doesn't force his memory of one of his own kindnesses.

No previous publication

8.10 affectionate • affec= | tionate

8.11 fortunes • for= | -tunes

8.14 say, ~~&~~, & • [*both commas inserted;* & *overwrites* &,]

8.14–15 ~~a~~ quite • [q *overwrites* a]

8.16 satisfaction • satisfac= | tion

9.10 absolutly • [*misspelled*]

9.14 ~~w~~ What • [W *overwrites* w]

9.17 affectionate • affec= | tionate

9.18–19 ~~sufficientl~~ sufficient • [t *overwrites* tl]; suf= | ficient

9.22 uncomfortable • uncomfort= | able

9.25 ~~sol~~ social • [c *overwrites* l]

9.25 circumscriptions • circum= | =scriptions

9.29 ~~a◊◊~~ resign • [re *overwrites* a◊◊]

9.29 opportunities • opportuni= | =ties

10.1 Montreux • Mon= | treux

10.1 ⟩ • [*blotted out*]

10.4 physiognomy • phys= | iognomy

10.8 Homburg • Hom= | burg

10.11 wood=walks • wood= | =walks

10.22 ~~do~~ shall • [sh *overwrites* do]

10.29–30 ~~at~~ early • [ea *overwrites* at]

10.31 ~~no~~ know • [kn *overwrites* no]

10.32 repulsions • repul= | sions

10.33 ~~se~~ former • [fo *overwrites* se]

10.34 didn't • did= | =n't

10.34 ~~Fl~~ Siena • [Si *overwrites* Fl]

11.10 ~~seem t sometimes~~ • [s *overwrites* t; seem sometimes *struck through*]

11.23–24 Please remember [. . .] <u>own kindnesses</u>. • [*written across the letter's first page*]

෴

9.12 Ashfield • The Nortons' summer residence (see HJ to Grace Norton, 5 November [1872], *CLHJ, 1872–1876* 1: 133, 136n133.33).

9.25 Sally's *&* Lily's • Charles Norton's eldest daughters.

10.28 <u>tendresse</u> • <u>attachment</u>.

11.5–6 Villa Spannochi • The Nortons' residence in Siena during the summer of 1870.

11.23 Mr. Curtis • George William Curtis (1824–92), critic and travel writer, author of the Editor's Easy Chair column for *Harper's New Monthly Magazine* and articles for the Lounger column at *Harper's Weekly* and editor of *Harper's Weekly* after 1863. Like the Nortons, Curtis had a vacation home in Ashfield, Massachusetts.

MARY WALSH JAMES
23 July [1873]
ALS Houghton
bMS Am 1094 (1811)

5

Homburg July 23<u>d</u>
Dearest of mothers.

 Three days since came to me your letter of July 1<u>st</u>, written
just after packing off A. K. & Alice. I wrote you about a week
ago and though I have had no especial adventures since, I want
you to know that all is well with me. I told you I think that I
likeed Homburg & thought it a very happy inspiration to have
come here. The place improves on acquaintance & I feel very
contentedly fixed here for the summer. The climate &
atmosphere are singular delightful & in themselves can't fail to
do one good; indeed I think I prefer them to any I have ever
known. For the waters, I am quite prepared for slow and gradual
results. I have been drinking only ten days—a period under
which a person starting very much out of sorts can ◇◇ hardly feel
as if he had begun. The Doctor assures me they are "just the
thing for me," & I hope he is ~~write~~. ∧right.[∧] Meanwhile I am
comfortable enough, & have plenty of mental & physical
occupation, as well as enough society to keep me afloat. ~~M~~ With
my young Englishman ∧whom I mentioned in my last,[∧] I have a
daily gossip & stroll; & for the last couple of days Charley
Atkinson has been here—his errand being to pick up Miss
Loring & escort her to England, whither he is now bound. He
seems very much the better for his three weeks Swiss tour
(Zermatt, the Oberland &c) & indeed quite happy & hearty. He
sends a great deal of love to W<u>m</u>, whom he thanks extremely for
his letter and would fain write to if he could. He wishes me to
make a point of giving this message. I see a good deal of a very
queer Englishwoman (staying in this house)—Lady Piggott by
name, a noted breeder of bullocks & taker of prizes for the same,

10

15

20

25

30

who combines with agricultural propensities the cultivation of
an artificial complexion ⅋ fearful ⅋ wonderful "sketching" ⅋c.
She isn't edefying, but she helps one through ~~tab~~ the table
d'hôte. — Now too I have the prospect of the Tweedies, having
5   heard from A. M. at St. Moritz that they will probably come
here for the month of August. The St. Moritz waters have
helped Mr. T., ⊕ but they seem to dislike the place greatly, ⅋ the
doctors have recommended a course of Homburg. I suppose
they will appear shortly. — I drink, I read ⅋ scribble, I stroll in
10   the woods ⅋ gardens, I ~~think~~ [ʌ]listen[ʌ] to the music at the
Kursaal; I think of the tremendously fine things I shall certainly
do when I am better, I dream perpetually of my sweet parents ⅋
I wish them in their venerable loneliness every comfort and
blessing that they can conceive. — I suppose I ought to be
15   ashamed of myself; but, somehow, Homburg is reconciling me
to Germany. I like the country, the people ⅋ the atmosphere
generally. Such an expansion of mind is in itself a gain. — But
enough about myself. Your tidings of Alice ⅋ A. K, ⅋ of Willy
had all my sympathies. I am most happy to hear of Alice's well-
20   being ⅋ hope what she is now in the midst of will pile it up
beyond the reach of any future disaster. — They must be seeing
queer places and things ⅋ I should like extremely to have the
history of it all. But I hope it has all been truly pleasurable.
What a godsend they must have been to my poor old Miss
25   Lanes! By the time this reaches you, you will have started in
pursuit of them, ⅋ I suppose, ⅋ perhaps will read it with the
white bears and walruses jumping about at a safe distance. Your
Cambridge month can't have been lively, but I hope it has been
comfortably cool. I see as yet, nothing about abnormal heat in
30   the American papers. — I felt sad over Willy's failure to get
helped on ~~hs~~ his journey to the West. But I hope he is making a
comfortable summer of it according to the programme you gave
me. It sounds pleasant enough. I fully understand his position ⅋
feelings as regards next winter, ⅋ he shall have all my co-

operation ∉ in getting every possible benefit from coming
abroad if he decides to do so. What I wrote him about Rome
would, I should think tend to make him so decide. I see nothing
to make me understate my strong impression that Rome
(especially if it's a "fine" winter) would help him greatly to lead   5
such a life, for six months, as he proposes. With a companion
ₐor two,₍ₐ₎ this Homburg would suit him quite peculiarly in the
summer. If he decides to try it, I hope he can make an agreeable
"arrangement," ₰ I hope my letter, written in answer to his,
seemed to him as encouraging as I meant it should. —I have a   10
very confident hope of being, by October 1ˢᵗ, (or before) my
better self again—the better self that I have been any time these
last two years—if not a better one still than that: ₰ so being able
to receive him, if she should come, in a suitably robust
manner. —Many thanks for your information about my MS. I'm   15
glad Howells is likely to print my Albano paper. My Carnival
never reached me. Could you ₐi.e. father,₍ₐ₎ (for safety) cut it out
of an old mag. ₰ enclose it in an envelope. I suppose father will
send (all to B. S. ₰ Co.) the Roman Rides. I lately sent H.
another, which I hope he can use. I never got the Galaxy tale   20
either. Could that be cut ₰ sent in an envelope too? —Farewell
dear parents. Believe in my affection, my zeal ₰ my ultimate
prosperity. Love to all the rest. Your affectionate
    H. J. jr.
Always now B. S. ₰ Co London.   25

No previous publication

ॐ

13.10 adventures • adven= | tures

13.12 likeed • [*misspelled*]

13.15 singular • singu= | lar

13.19 ◆◆ hardly • [ha *overwrites illegible letters*]

13.23 M̶ With • [Wi *overwrites* M]

13.26 Atkinson • At= | kinson

13.26 errand • er= | rand

13.32 message • mes= | sage

14.1 propensities • pro= | -pensities

14.3 ~~tab~~ the • [he *overwrites blotted* tab]

14.7 ⊕ but • [b *overwrites illegible letter*]

14.8 recommended • recom= | mended

14.15 Homburg • Hom= | burg

14.16 Germany • Ger= | many

14.19 sympathies • sym= | =pathies

14.26 ∉ I • [I *overwrites* ɟ]

14.31 ~~hs~~ his • [i *overwrites* s]

14.32 summer • sum= | mer

15.1 ∉ in • [in *overwrites* ɟ]

15.14 should • [l *inserted*]

15.20–25 <u>Galaxy</u> [. . .] <u>London</u>. • [*written across the letter's first page*]

൙

13.8 your letter of July 1ˢᵗ • MWJ to HJ, 1 July [1873].

13.9–10 I wrote you about a week ago • HJ to MWJ, 15 July [1873] (pp. 3–5).

13.24 my young Englishman • Henry Coulson.

14.5 A. M. • Aunt Mary Tweedy.

14.7 Mr. T. • Edmund Tweedy.

14.24–25 Miss Lanes • Operators of a boardinghouse at 44 ½ Anne Street, Quebec (see Anesko 85n7; MWJ to HJ, 1 July [1873]; and Moore, "The Letters of Alice James," pt. 1, 32).

15.16 my Albano paper • "Roman Neighborhoods."

15.16 My <u>Carnival</u> • "A Roman Holiday."

15.19 B. S. & Co. • Brown, Shipley and Co.

15.19 the <u>Roman Rides</u> • "Roman Rides."

15.20 the <u>Galaxy</u> tale • "The Sweetheart of M. Briseux."

CATHARINE WALSH
1 August 1873
ALS Houghton
bMS Am 1094 (1328)

5

Homburg August 1ˢᵗ 73.
    Hotel 4 Saisons
Dearest Aunt—
    Your letter, written just before your departure for the
North came to me some ten days ago, & I shortly afterwards
heard from mother that it had prosperously taken place. I have
had no news of you since, but I hope all has gone well from the
beginning & that constant pleasure & increased health has been
the daily lot of all of you. To Be in ignorance of all this for a
whole month is rather tormenting (h Mother's letter was of July
1ˢᵗ)—but I am in hourly expectation of a letter, forwarded from
Switzerland. I was especially gratified to hear of Alice's being
physically well disposed toward the journey. May it leave every
vestige of malady & weakness at last without a leg to stand on. I
can think of nothing better for her & wish her nothing better,
than another journey under your devoted care. I am very glad
she is having so well-chosen a companion as Helen R. I have
ₐInₐ a letter I got from her after her visit to N. Y. she spoke as
if she had taken a great fancy to her; I trust these weeks together
will happily confirm it. I should think H. R. would wear very
well. You are seeing strange things I suppose, & no Lyntons,
Wellses, Grindelwalds & Cadenabbias; but I hope they have a
charm of their own & of course they are cool ◊ at least & rural₍,
₍ₐ₎& have the wild freedom of our native land.₍ₐ₎ I should like
extremely to know just what they are & what you have seen &
done, & hope that Alice & you, between you, especially if A is
invigorated, will give me a "brief synopsis."—Of course you
know all about me, as I have written home regularly & my letters
I suppose have been imparted. You know by this time of my

withdrawal from Switzerland, & even of my 1ˢᵗ impressions of
Homburg. I have now been here three weeks, & these have been
agreeably strengthened. Switzerland seemed pleasant enough,
but, somehow, it didn't seem ~~salubru~~ salubrious, & in a happy
5   hour I bethought me of this place, of which, as you remember,
we heard last summer such good accounts from A. M. T. & I
(more lately) from Chas. ~~Ato~~ Atkinson. It has so many
advantages that I feel as if I ₐhad₍ₐ₎ made quite a precious
discovery. I have been trying the waters "under medical
10   advice"—quite as British as the phrase—& after three weeks feel
free to judge them. They don't seem to suit me—<u>au contraire</u>, &
I shall slow up. But the air & the place itself are excellent & help
me to lead a comfortable life. It is turning out a fiercely hot
summer in Europe, & I'm afraid it isn't blissfully cool with you.
15   The heat here is great, but it is much more endurable, I am sure,
than at any other German bath (they are all buried in hot holes)
or anywhere indeed but a mountain top. Homburg stands high
on the spur of a low mountain, with a great plain before it,
where the air can circulate, & charming ₐgardens &₍ₐ₎ woods
20   behind it where there is perpetual shade. The play is over & its
glory is supposed to have departed, but there are plenty of
people (lots of English) & the Kursaal of an evening when the
band plays, is animated enough to be quite amusing. The
lodging-houses here are prettier & more numerous than ₐany₍ₐ₎ I
25   have ever seen; but they are dear and I live very comfortably at
this hotel in a little ground-floor, room in a dépendance, looking
on the garden, with ₐa₍ₐ₎ window smothered in Virginia creeper.
I have enough society, charming strolls in the ₐKur₍ₐ₎park &
~~gardens~~ ₍ₐ₎woods,₍ₐ₎ & if I stop the waters, shall probably linger
30   on till the middle or the 20ᵗʰ of the month. In an hour, I expect
to have an accession of society in the ~~person~~ ₐarrival₍ₐ₎ of the
Tweedies who telegraphed to me this ~~am~~ A.M. from Heidelberg
for rooms. They left St. Moritz a week ago, & from a letter I also
got from A. M. seem to have suffered everything from the heat

on their journey—the more so as they ∧had[∧] found the
Engadine very cold. At Stuttgart their thermom. was 93° I have
done nothing but thank fortune that our journey of last summer
befell when it did ⅋ not now. Had we undertaken it this year, I'm
afraid the Meyringen episode, the Thusis episode ⅋ the various
other episodes would have ~~left~~ ∧been[∧] more serious matters.
Meyringen must be charming ~~th~~ just now, ⅋ I confess I am very
glad I am not in Thusis. I ~~hope~~ ∧expect[∧] to be there, however,
(if things go well ⅋ I do as I desire) the last of this month, en
route for Italia via the Splügen. I got a letter from
Mrs. Lombard a day or two since (you will have heard I saw her
at Thun, in a quiet pleasant pension, with Mrs. Waring (of
Newport₁), looking poorly, but very cheerful ⅋ courageous. She
appeared to great advantage—as also—in a moral way—did poor
Fanny. I have since heard from her that she was to leave Thun ⅋
join Mrs W. at a pension in Luçerne. She expects to go in
September into Italy ⅋ to winter in Florence. I felt very sorry
for ∧her[∧] ⅋ hope she will thrive. Thy had evidently suffered
much from ~~L~~ loneliness but their equanimity is wonderful. I
have seen no one else of any importance. In this hotel are chiefly
English people of the usual kind.—I rejoice in the thought that
about this time, f. ⅋ m. will have started to join you; ⅋ I try and
imagine you all harmoniously grouped together on some
northern shore with the breezes playing about you ⅋ white bears
jumping around at a convenient distance.—Willy, I hope, has
been able to carry out his programme ⅋ has prospered thus
far.—I must start for the station to meet the T.'s; but will add a
word on my way back. x x x x x x I have just fetched the Tweedies
up from the Station and lodged them in this hotel—jaded,
rather, with travel, but well ⅋ happy. They met Charlotte King
at some railway station the other day en route for München—
almost blind. I have been very glad to see them—they bring
back those days of Rome.—I got yesterday a very pleasant note
from Bob, telling me that Wilky marries in October. Is this even

so, and are there any new developments about Carrie? I wish
them all serenity. — But I must close, dear Aunt, & take a wash
before dinner. I have been thinking every day the last two
months of some anniversary of our last summer's doings —
5 always with deep emotion. My kind love to Alice, to whom I will
speedily write. ⋄ Much love to C. H. & H. R. I haven't forgotten
my letter to the latter — she shall have it yet. Farewell dearest
Aunt; may all repose & bliss be yours. Write always for the
present to Brown Shipley & Co. — Ever your affectionate nevvy
10 H. J. jr.
    P.S. Excuse my scrawling & sprawling hand. It is too hot to write
close.

No previous publication

∾

17.14 To • [*inserted*]

17.15 tormenting • tor= | =menting

17.15 h̶ Mother's • [M *overwrites* h]

17.17 especially • espe= | -cially

17.26 suppose • sup- | pose

17.28 ⋄ at • [a *overwrites illegible letter*]

17.28 ⱶ, • [, *overwrites* .]

17.32 invigorated • invigor= | ated

18.2 Homburg • Hom= | burg

18.4 s̶a̶l̶u̶b̶r̶u̶ salubrious • [i *overwrites* u]

18.5 remember • re= | member

18.7 A̶t̶⋄ Atkinson • [k *overwrites illegible letter*]

18.26 ground-floor • ground- | floor

18.32 a̶m̶ A.M. • [A *overwrites* am]

19.7 t̶h̶ just • [j *overwrites* th]

19.13 ⱶ) • [) *overwrites* ,]

19.19 L̶ loneliness • [l *overwrites* L]

20.6 ⋄ Much • [M *overwrites illegible letter*]

20.11–12 P.S. [. . .] close. • [*written across the letter's first page*]

∾

17.15-16 Mother's letter was of July 1ˢᵗ • MWJ to HJ, 1 July [1873].

17.22 Helen R. • Helen Ripley.

18.6 A. M. T. • Aunt Mary Tweedy.

18.26 dépendance • annex.

19.5-6 the Meyringen episode, the Thusis episode & the various other episodes • HJ was more than his sister's and aunt's guide during AJ's European tour in 1872. He had been entrusted to help AJ get well and to comfort his sometimes difficult sister even as he worked hard to establish his own career. He assumed, in effect, the role of eldest brother. Thus, he reports both AJ's good days and her bad ones. Though Edel does not attend closely to the evident shift of HJ's status within his family, he remarks, "It was as brother and nephew, rather than as writer for the *Nation*, that Henry James sailed for Europe in May 1872" (2: 63). HJ thus reports not only the status of AJ's health but, at the same time, the status of his success as her caretaker. Regarding AJ's "episodes" and her improvement following them, see 24, 28 July [1872] to WJ, 5 [14] August [1872] to MWJ, 11 August [1872] to Sr., 13 August [1872] to Elizabeth Boott, 18 August [1872] to HJ's parents (*CLHJ, 1872–1876* 1: 54, 65–66, 73, 79–80, 84). Letters that indicate HJ's role as caretaker include the following to his parents: 28, 29 June [1872], 5, 6 July [1872], 13 July [1872] to MWJ, 21 July [1872], and 31 August, [3 September 1872] (*CLHJ, 1872–1876* 1: 33–36, 38–42, 42–47, 49–53, and 94–98).

19.11 Mrs. Lombard • Cambridge family friend.

19.12 Mrs. Waring • Probably Virginia Clark Waring (b. c. 1835), wife of George E. Waring (1833-98).

19.15 Fanny • Fanny Lombard, daughter of Mrs. Lombard.

19.22 f. & m. • father and mother.

19.30 Charlotte King • MWJ's first cousin.

20.1 Carrie • Caroline Cary.

20.6 C. H. & H. R. • Cousin Helen Perkins and Helen Ripley.

HENRY JAMES SR. AND MARY WALSH JAMES
4 August [1873]
ALS Houghton
bMS Am 1094 (1812)

5

Homburg Aug. 4$\underline{th}$

Dearest parents:

I haven't written to you for more than my usual time; but I
wrote a few days since to A. K., & she will probably impart my
10   letter. I had been waiting longer than usual for something from
you—which came, at last, per Brown & Shiply, in the shape of a
combined letter from both of you, enclosing a note from W^m; &
a letter from W. himself, from the Isles of Shoals. I haven't
[∧]likewise[∧] just recd. Bob's letter forwarded by Father to
15   Thusis. All this was a feast of reason, & I thank you for
everything. I found especial satisfaction in W$\underline{m}$'s good acct. of
his the effect of his holiday. May it have lasted! By this time your
own well=earned holiday will have commenced & I hope will
have been greatly enjoyable. St. John's N. S., suggests to me
20   nothing very conceivable, & I am anxious to hear your report of
it. I hope you'll bring both yourselves & Alice home as stout and
elastic as filial & fraternal affection can wish you. You must
expatiate as much as possible on your adventures & her's.—You
see I'm still at Homburg, in my 4$\underline{th}$ week now, very contented &
25   well to be here & likely to remain for the rest of the present
month. It's a most blessed little place & I'm more & more glad to
have hit upon it. My experiment with the waters has not been
brilliantly successful—they seem in fact ∧quite[∧] to nonsuit he
me; but my getting into a better order is merely a question of
30   time. Be patient and don't think me utterly incorrigible & I will
be a credit to you yet. With each bad season I learn more about
my self, & I have learnt much this time which I shall profit by.
Meanwhile I am in very excellent & convenient circumstances
for working up to a better level again. You should see ◇ me

sitting here in my little garden-room with the light filtering in
the ₍ₐ₎to₍ₐ₎ window through a framework ₍ₐ₎veil₍ₐ₎ of rank green
vines.—The Tweedies arrived here three days since ⅋ are
established in very pleasant lodgings. Mr. T. is very well indeed
⅋ ⅋ they seem very buoyant and delighted with Homburg. They   5
will probably finish the month, ⅋ they talk of <u>Dresden</u> for the
winter.—There is no one else here that you know or care about.
I lately got a very good ₍ₐ₎pleasant₍ₐ₎ and sensible letter from
Mrs. Lombard, who certainly makes the best of the drearinesses
of her position. She had been joined at Thun by the Andrew   10
family <u>en masse</u>—desperate to know what to do with themselves.
That was a dreariness indeed!—Bob's letter said that Wilky
meditated marriage in October. But as you don't mention it,
perhaps the report is premature. I am very sorry father had a
particle more bother about the wretched <u>Galaxy</u> money. I wish   15
he had taken the $100 simply, from the 1ˢᵗ. They are certainly
shabby people; but with such, I suppose, � is the fat lot of
authors cast. I am delighted Howells took my Albano paper. I
sent him another (a 4ᵗʰ) which I trust he has rec'd. Farewell
dearest authors of my being, ⅋ thanks for all your tender   20
messages. Write always ₍ₐ₎to₍ₐ₎ B. ⅋ S. Love to A. ⅋ A. K. Your's
ever H.

No previous publication

   ∾

   22.10 something • some= | thing
   22.17 h̶i̶s̶ the • [the *overwrites* his]
   22.20 conceivable • con= | ceivable
   22.24 Homburg • Hom= | burg
   22.24–25 ⅋ w̶e̶l̶c̶ to be here • [to be h *overwrites* ⅋ *and blotted* welc]
   22.25 remain • re= | main
   22.28–29 h̶e̶ me • [m *overwrites blotted* he]
   22.29 a̶ better • [b *overwrites* a]
   22.34 ⬦ me • [m *overwrites illegible letter*]

23.5   *&* *&* • *&* | *&*

23.5   delighted • de= | lighted

23.11   themselves • them= | selves

23.17   *+* is • [is *overwrites* —]

23.17   ~~fat~~ lot • [lo *overwrites blotted* fat]

∾

22.8–9   I wrote a few days since to A. K. • HJ to Catharine Walsh, 1 August 1873 (pp. 17–20).

22.13   a letter from W. [. . .] Isles of Shoals • WJ to HJ, 14 July [1873] (*CWJ* 1: 214–17). The Isles of Shoals include nine small islands about ten miles off the shore straddling the border of New Hampshire and Maine.

22.19   St. John's N. S. • The Jameses were vacationing in Saint John, New Brunswick; see MWJ to HJ, 4 August [1873], and Sr. to HJ, 8 August [1873].

23.10–11   the Andrew family • Family of the late Massachusetts governor John Albion Andrew.

23.18   my Albano paper • "Roman Neighborhoods."

23.19   another (a 4ᵗʰ) • After "Roman Neighborhoods," the next piece HJ published in the *Atlantic Monthly* was "The Last of the Valerii."

23.21   B. *&* S. • Brown and Shipley.

23.21   A. • AJ.

WILLIAM JAMES

25   5 August [1873]

ALS Houghton

bMS Am 1094 (1955)

Bad Homburg, Aug 5ᵗʰ

30   Dear Wᵐ—I don't mean to write you a letter—(I wrote yesterday to F *&* M. *&* a few days before to A. K.;) I want simply to thank you for your letter fr. the Steamboat *&* the Isle of Shoals. I am glad my report of Rome struck you as favorable—I

have seen ~~to~~ ₍ₐ₎no₍ₐ₎ reason since to think it was ₍ₐ₎too₍ₐ₎ high colored. — Your decision for the winter I can of course say nothing to illuminate; & I am so anxious to have you decide the matter on simply discretionary grounds that ₍ₐ₎I₍ₐ₎ even hesitate to express the muchness of my desire to see you. — It was a ~~pleasant~~ pleasure at any rate to read of the happy influences of your holiday and your loafings by the sea. Limited as they were I hope they have substantially helped you. Every word you say about Nature & the "normal life" has an echo in my soul. ⋄ I enjoy them more the older I grow & acquire a fatal facility in sitting under trees & letting the hours expire without particular fruits. Homburg is excellent for this & for much else beside — a lovely little place which is insidiously reconciling me to Germany, which I have been hating ever since I came abroad, on the evidence of travelling Germans. I have been taking the waters with indifferent results, & feel better for stopping them. I have ~~been out of sorts~~ ₍ₐ₎touched bottom I think₍ₐ₎ in this particular episode of insalubrity & shall gradually rise to the surface again, & after that I think I can almost pledge myself to keep afloat. Meanwhile I am very well "located" for being either better or worse. I have for two years (up to May 1ˢᵗ last) been so well & ~~am~~ ₍ₐ₎have₍ₐ₎ now in spite of everything such a standing fund of vigor, that I am sure time will see me through. I have no especial ideas or anecdotes to communicate. I am re-reading Turgenieff in German & beginning a review for T. S. P. The German goes very easily. I lately sent a Homburg letter to the Nation by which you will judge me a Teutomaniac. I'm not — but what's the good of writing except imaginatively? Here, at any rate, one feels as if one lived in an Atmosphere with a present living force playing into it — which you don't in sweet Italy, smiling in her sleep. — The Tweedies are here, very well & preferring Homburg to anything in Europe. I see no one else except (in my hotel) Dr. Parkes, the persecutor of the Boston homeopaths & a good Englishman, the partner of my loafings,

"afflicted" like my self, but "benefitted" by the waters. A
"gentlemanly" English mind wears well for daily
companionship.—You offer, if you come, to bring books &
"furniture." I should like 2 or 3 boxes of Harrison's Lozenges. I
brought with me a box & ½, & in 14 mos. have only used the ½,
which testifies to my hitherto well being—this being the only
med. I have taken. Also 3 or 4 cakes Davis's toothsoap, & in the
way of books, <u>chiefly</u> Ferrari's <u>Revolution</u> & Valery's Voyage en
Italie.—I am with you all ~~&~~ ∧in[∧] spirit & desire. I trust your
∧subsequent[∧] summer has been useful & happy. I shall be here
till Sept 1ˢᵗ, but write always to B & S. Ever yours H. J.a jr.

Previous publication: *CWJ* 1: 217–18

෧

    25.5 express • ex= | press

    25.6 ~~pleasant~~ pleasure • [ure *overwrites blotted* ant]

    25.9 normal • nor= | mal

    25.9 ⋄ I • [I *overwrites illegible letter*]

    25.11 <u>particular</u> • <u>par=</u> | <u>ticular</u>

    25.24 communicate • communi= | cate

    26.3 companionship • com= | panionship

    26.9 & ∧ • [∧ *overwrites* &]

    26.11 J.a jr. • [j *overwrites blotted* a; *period following* J *inserted*]

෧

    24.30–31 I wrote yesterday to F & M. & a few days before to A. K. •
4 August [1873] to parents and 1 August 1873 to Catharine Walsh (pp. 17–
23).

    24.33–34 your letter fr. the Steamboat & the Isle of Shoals • WJ to HJ,
14 July [1873] (*CWJ* 1: 214–17).

    24.34 my report of Rome • See HJ to WJ, 18 June 1873 (*CLHJ, 1872–
1876* 1: 319–20), and WJ to HJ, 14 July [1873] (*CWJ* 1: esp. 214–15).

    25.25 beginning a review • "*Frülingsfluthen. Ein König Lear des Dorfes.
Zwei Novellen. Von Iwan Turgéniew*," which would appear in the *North
American Review*.

25.25 T. S. P. • Thomas Sergeant Perry.

25.26–27 a Homburg letter to the Nation • "Homburg Reformed."

25.33–34 Dr. Parkes, the persecutor of the Boston homeopaths • Possibly Dr. Edmund Alexander Parkes (1819–76), British physician and professor at University College and Army Medical School.

26.4 Harrison's Lozenges • John S. Harrison's "peristaltic lozenges" were reputed to be effective for the treatment of dyspepsia, costiveness, piles, and other complaints (see, e.g., Swingle 252).

26.8 Ferrari's Revolution • Giuseppe Ferrari (1811–76) wrote *La révolution et les réformes en Italie* (1848), *Machiavel juge des révolutions de notre temps* (1849), and *Filosofia della rivoluzione* (1851).

26.8–9 Valery's Voyage en Italie • Antoine-Claude-Pasquin Valery (1789–1847) wrote *Voyages historiques et littéraires en Italie* (1825), *Voyages en Corse* (1837), and *Curiosités et anecdotes italiennes* (1843).

26.11 B & S. • Brown and Shipley.

SARAH BUTLER WISTER
10 August [1873]
TLC Bryn Mawr College Library   20

Homburg, Germany.
        Aug 10th
Dear Mrs. Wister—

It seems long ago now that I answered the excellent letter you   25
were so good as to send me at Rome. It's not really so very long,
but it seems long because everything connected with that
blessed place has melted away into a kind of misty fabulous past.
If I may say this, I suppose you can with even better reason, and
yet I should be sorry to think that my poor letter had become so   30
utterly a thing of the past as to have lost all chance of
resuscitation in one of your leisure hours & your kindliest
moods. I think you expected America to bring you a great many
of the former—& I defy it altogether, at its unimaginable

worst.—to rob you of the latter. I really haven't in the least expected you to write to me. I am very sure you have had more urgent duties—& I hope keener pleasures. But I only want momentarily to assume that you <u>might</u> have written, as a pretext
5 for sending you a few lines—which I beg you will think of answering only at your perfect convenience. I remember by the way that I don't at all know your American address; but I suppose I shall be safe in trying <u>Germantown</u>. The little fact [*proves*] that I have heard very little about you since your letter
10 came to me. Nothing at all, in fact: I left Rome very soon after, saw no one who could give me news of you & was left to imagine you in London, imagine you at sea, & at last imagine you looking your native land—a trifle grimly in the face & settling down to your tête-à-tête with it. But now I confess that though my
15 imagination demands no more congenial topic than you & your fortunes. I long for a little plain certainty You <u>have</u> crossed the sea, you <u>are</u> at home I suppose, & you have taken the measure of the situation. Give me a sketch of it, I beg you, & send me a hint of your impressions of everything. If I thought it would be
20 anything of a bribe to you, I would relate my own histoire intime since we parted—or, since I left Rome at least; for I didn't feel as if I had really parted with you till I had done that, too. But the topic has little intrinsic interest & I have had very few adventures. The summer is melting away (melting, alas,
25 literally) very fast & I feel rather blue when I think of the meagre sum of its contributions to my experience. I lingered on in Italy till about the tenth of June & then came doggedly over the Simplon and spent three or four weeks in Switzerland. I have been at Homburg a month, having come here, out of sorts, to
30 attempt a "cure" with the waters. I have ceased to drink them— the "cure" not responding to my appeal; but I am staying because I like the place & have a constitutional shrinking from fleeing to ills I know not of. Do you know Homburg at all? It's very pretty—German pretty—& is cool and shady & comfortable

generally, & still amusing enough, in spite of the death & burial
of the gaming. The Kursaal stands there like a great cavernous
tomb—a tomb however in which they have concerts, a reading
room and a cafe. I have seen no old friends all summer & made
no new ones who have caused me any particular emotion. I have   5
heard nothing of any of our Roman associates—save the
Tweedies, who are here—not a word about Mrs L & Miss B., to
whom, however, I have lately written.—I feel as if I might
sentimentalize inordinately about Rome, if I gave myself leave,
but you probably do your own sentimentalizing, & better than I   10
can. Some of my published attempts in this line you may lately
have seen—a couple of things in the Atlantic & a thing in the
Galaxy—wh. latter however is probably not yet out. There are
to be a couple more Italian scribbles in the Atlantic, which I
know I can trust your friendship for both theme & scribbler to   15
read kindly. You will recognize an allusion or so in the rather
high-falutin Atlantic Rides & in the Galaxy piece. Enjoy them &
forgive them according to need. You will see—I had to make up
for small riding by big writing. But what's the use of writing at
all, unless imaginatively? Unless one's vision can lend something   20
to a thing, there's small reason in proceeding to proclaim one
has seen it. Mere looking every one can do for himself.—I
actually have been seeing something in Germany—a thing I
never expected—& let my imagination dance a little jig on it the
other day for the Nation. I take a voluptuous pleasure in putting   25
you thus au courant of my literature.—not having had speech,
these three months, of any one to whom it—or anyone else's—
the least bit mattered. I don't quite venture to say to myself that
I shall go to Rome for the winter, but I venture still less to say I
shan't. It would be an immense help to know that you were to   30
have a fireside there by which I might sometimes sit in that
before dinner dusk. Has Miss Lowe, by the way gone home? I
met her at Asissi, uncertain & attended by the painter Bellay. I
heard afterwards that it was a case for a more suggestive word

than that I have just used: but isn't this vile gossip to send across the sea? Have you had further news of ce bon Lefêvre? This is a small specimen question of a hundred I should like to ask you. But they mustn't crowd into the particular inquiry I wish to make about Dr. Wister & the friendly message I wish to send him. I hope he is a quite well man & not too much bothered as a new settler. Pray give him my kindest regards. For yourself, I have more good wishes than I have left room for. Do show me that you have guessed some of them by finding a leisure half-hour some day to write to me — Care Brown Shipley, London. Yours always, dear Mrs Wister, most faithfully

    Henry James, jr.

Previous publication: *HJL* 1: 398–400

∾

28.9 [*proves*] • [*The copy text does not transcribe this word; the bracketed insertion is taken from the published version in* HJL. *It is possible that Edel used both manuscript and TLC to prepare this letter for his edition.*]

29.32 Lowe • [*copy text reads:* Lane; *probably transcriber's error*]

29.33 Asissi • [*It is not possible to determine whether the misspelling is HJ's or the transcriber's.*]

30.9–12 that you [. . .] Henry James, jr. • [*written across the letter's first page, according to the copy text*]

∾

27.30 my poor letter • 9, 11 May [1873] to Sarah Butler Wister (*CLHJ, 1872–1876* 1: 286–91).

28.20–21 histoire intime • personal history.

29.7 Mrs L & Miss B. • "Mrs L" is unidentified. However, *L* may be a transcriber's error for *S*, in which case HJ would have referred to Alice Sumner and Alice Bartlett, both of whom were HJ's companions with Mrs. Wister in Rome. See also HJ to Sarah Butler Wister, 9, 11 May [1873], and HJ to Elizabeth Boott, 23 May 1873 (*CLHJ, 1872–1876* 1: 288, 299).

29.12 a couple of things in the <u>Atlantic</u> • "A Roman Holiday" and "Roman Rides."

29.12-13 a thing in the <u>Galaxy</u> • "From a Roman Note-Book."

29.14 a couple more Italian scribbles in the Atlantic • "Roman Neighborhoods" and "A Chain of Italian Cities."

29.24-25 a little jig on it [. . .] for the <u>Nation</u> • "Homburg Reformed."

29.26 <u>au courant</u> • <u>up to date</u>.

29.32 Miss Lowe • Elena Lowe.

29.33 the painter Bellay • Possibly Charles-Alphonse-Paul Bellay (1826-1900), son of painter François Bellay, who died in Rome; Charles Bellay painted Roman scenes.

30.2 ce bon Lefêvre • this good Lefêvre; composer Charles-Edouard Lefebvre (1843-1917).

HENRY JAMES SR. AND MARY WALSH JAMES   15
14 August [1873]
ALS Houghton
bMS Am 1094 (1813)

   · Homburg v.d. Hohe   20
     Kisseleff-Strasse
       Aug. 14$^{\underline{th}}$
Dearest parents.

     Less than a week ago came to me your combined letter of July 20—& 22$^{\underline{d}}$, written apparently just before your intended   25
departure for the North. It seemed to indicate a comfortable & agreeable state of things & was fondly read & re-read. The time is coming round again for me to begin to look for a letter from some point or other of your journey. I hope this has been uninterruptedly prosperous & that I shall hear of everything that   30
befalls you. I thank you kindly for all the expressions of yearning affection in your letters & respond to them with all the enthusiasm of my nature—both in their sentimental and material aspects. I should like to sit between you on the sofa,

holding a hand of you apiece—& I should like also to sit between
you at dinner, putting your generosity to the test by my inroads
into salmon & peas, corn and tomatoes, melons and ice=cream—
luxuries unknown to this ꜰ ponderous land of sodden veal &
5   odorous cabbage.—I wrote to you about a week ago—something
more, & to W͟m a few days later, and I suppose my letters are
safely arriving. Aunt Mary T. who is lodged below me here, told
me yesterday that she was writing to mother. I don't know what
news she gave of me, but she related at any rate that I had
10 become ⬦⬦ their fellow lodger. I quitted my hotel yesterday
(where a change in the weather ₍ᴧ₎—toward cold—₍ᴧ₎ had made
my room uncomfortable) & took up my quarters in this house
where I luckily discovered a most agreeable little chamber at a
most agreeable little price. I go still ⬦ to the hotel for my meals,
15 as I don't like, like the Jacksons, to eat alone & economise the
society of the Tweedies for more desperate hours. They are very
well & happy—more so than I had yet seen them in Europe—&
more and more delighted with Homburg. ~~I too~~ ꜰ ₍ᴧ₎But₍ᴧ₎ A. M.
will have told you everything in her letter. I too remain on
20 excellent terms with H., which has been surpassing itself these
last days in the way of delightful & salubrious air. The weather
which had been ~~cool~~ ₍ᴧ₎intensely₍ᴧ₎ hot for some time lately
changed to cold—with a good deal of wet; but the cold & the
damp themselves are of a most delightful quality—& so free
25 from sharpness that they cushion you about like great soft,
supporting bolsters. I took a long walk through the charming
spreading Hardtwald the other day with Mr. Tweedy, to the little
old French village of Friederichsdorf—founded 200 years since
by a colony of Huguenot refugees & French as ever to this day.
30 The woods and the air seemed full of the breath & brilliancy of
an American autumn; & I could have been homesick, if I hadn't
reflected that I ought to be contented with enjoying American
sensations among old world privileges. The woods here are an
immense blessing & stretch away and away ₍ᴧ₎for miles,₍ᴧ₎ in their

green interior stillness all traversed by wandering paths and
half-cleared grassy vistas. For people with whom a little of the
everlasting Kursaal goes a great way, they are quite the making
of Homburg. — This is all very well, but what I have chiefly at
heart to descant upon is the fact that the last week has ushered in 5
a marked improvement in my health & that I have distinct
previsions of being better and better as more weeks and months
and years elapse. Now at last, physically, I think I understand
myself. It has taken me long to learn, blind & erring mortal that
I am, but I shall preserve the knowledge in the most sacred 10
recesses of my soul. If I were at home I would cease mother
round her delicate waist and lift her to ethereal heights in
celebration of this ~~fact~~ latest. As it is I can only bid you be
happy with me in your still parental hearts and count upon the
now (I trust) less and less obstructed development of a graceful 15
activity! — Your principal home-news was that of Wilky's
intended marriage. I can imagine he shouldn't enjoy waiting &
yet I hope he isn't doing anything irredeemably imprudent. As
mother says, a single year's probation is less than very many
couples submit to. But it is perhaps not for me, disengaged, to 20
cast the stone. — I mentioned, I think, in my last my letter from
W<u>m</u> whose injoyment of his holiday can hardly have been
greater than mine ~~in~~ of his account of it. — Now, I suppose, you
have "connected" with A. K. & Alice & are perhaps looking over
the Atlantic from some breezy northern shore and exhaling soft 25
sighs toward Homburg. Perhaps these ~~art~~ arctic emanations are
the cause of our late <u>refroidissement</u>. I hope you found Alice &
A. K. at any rate, perfectly blowsy with health, & with appetite
for whale's blubber, rein-deer steaks & all other local
delicacies. — I rec'd. of the 2 Atlantic's you must have sent only 30
the one containing the Roman Holiday. It's strange what became
of them. But you needn't bother about the other, as I've sent for
it to London. — With improved health, I look forward to more
work. I yesterday despatched a tale in III-parts to [∧]the[∧]

Galaxy—with regret, as it is the best written thing I've done. But it was the only thing I could do. ~~I~~ One must approach English organs on some other basis than American subjects—unless they are very "racy" & of the Bret Harte & Joaquin Miller

5   type.—I expect to stay on here at least three weeks more, after which my plans are unformed. I did ₍ₐ₎think₍ₐ₎ of making straight back ~~for~~ ₍ₐ₎to₍ₐ₎ Italy; but I have had unpleasant developments with my <u>teeth</u>, now unvisited for more than a year, which make the assistance of a 1<u>st</u> rate dentist urgent. I am thinking of

10 finding it wise to go straight (<u>via</u> Cologne) to Paris & having it out with Burrage. It won't hurt me, I suppose, to keep out of Italy till time has assured me that I'm as much better as I believe. ~~I therefore~~ ₍ₐ₎But I₍ₐ₎ give you no new address till I next write. My blessings on all. Yours ⬦ ever, dearest parents— <u>H. J</u> jr

Previous publication: Horne 54-57

ᔕ

31.25 apparently • appar= | ently

31.26 departure • de= | parture

31.27 reread • re- | read

31.30 uninterruptedly • unin= | =terruptedly

31.31 expressions • expres= | sions

31.34 material • ma= | terial

32.3 ice=cream • ice= | cream

32.4 ᵽ ponderous • [p *overwrites* r]

32.6 suppose • sup- | pose

32.10 become • be= | come

32.10 ⬥⬥ their • [th *overwrites illegible letters*]

32.12 uncomfortable • un= | comfortable

32.13 discovered • discov= | ered

32.14 ⬦ to • [t *overwrites illegible letter*]

32.18 ᵽ ₍ₐ₎But₍ₐ₎ • [t *overwrites* r]

32.31 American • Amer= | ican

33.7 previsions • pre= | =visions

34

33.13 ~~fact~~ latest • [lat *overwrites* fact]

33.15 obstructed • ob= | structed

33.16 principal • princi= | pal

33.20 perhaps • per= | haps

33.23 ~~in~~ of • [of *overwrites* in]

33.26 ~~art~~ arctic • [c *overwrites* t]

33.26 emanations • ema= | =nations

34.2 ~~I~~ One • [On *overwrites* I]

34.14 Yours [. . .] <u>H. J jr.</u> • [*written across the letter's first page*]

34.14 Yours • [s *inserted*]

34.14 ⬦ ever • [ev *overwrites illegible letter*]

∾

32.5 I wrote to you about a week ago • 4 August [1873] to parents (pp. 22–23).

32.6 to Wᵐ a few days later • 5 August [1873] to WJ (pp. 24–26).

32.7 Aunt Mary T. • Mary Tweedy.

32.27 Hardtwald • Forested area in Bad Homburg.

32.28 Friederichsdorf • Friedrichsdorf, village adjoining Bad Homburg to its north, founded by French Huguenots in 1687 under the protection of Homburg landgrave Friedrich II.

33.21–22 my last my letter from Wᵐ • WJ to HJ, 14 July [1873] (*CWJ* 1: 214–17).

33.27 <u>refroidissement</u> • <u>drop in temperature</u>.

33.31 the one containing the Roman Holiday • The July 1873 *Atlantic Monthly*.

33.34 a tale in III-parts • The next story by HJ to appear in the *Galaxy* (in two installments and nine numbered sections) was "Mme. de Mauves."

34.4 Joaquin Miller • American writer Joaquin Miller (Cincinnatus Hiner Miller [1837–1913]).

34.11 Burrage • Murray's *A Handbook for Visitors to Paris* lists among "American Dentists" "Dr. Burridge, 35, Boulevard des Capucines" (189).

ELIZABETH BOOTT
15 August 1873
ALS Houghton
bMS Am 1094 (509)

5

Bad Homburg
12 Kisseleff Strasse
Aug 15<u>th</u>'73.

10   Dear Lizzie—

If your letter from Beverley hadn't come to me yesterday I
think I should ∧have[∧] written to you: in fact I know I should,
for I had had it greatly at heart to do so, for a long time past. As
it was, the day was given up to reading ᵼ re-reading your own
15   document, meditating on it ᵼ delighting in it generally. Yes, I
owed you a letter, ~~or~~ ᵼ your father at least a postscript; for your
two notes of farewell, just before sailing, reached me duly at
Berne. I had heard of course of your presence in the flesh ~~at~~ in
our native latitudes ᵼ of your transitory apparition at
20   Cambridge; but I was impatient to hear the note of your own
voice, under the pressure of these circumstances ᵼ it was
angelically good of you to feel this ᵼ not stand upon the order of
my writing first. I don't know that I can tell you very precisely
why I haven't written before but I think that if you had been ~~Ŧ~~
25   spending the summer just as I have, you would understand it. It
has been very hot indeed, ᵼ I have been very seedy ᵼ have been
dosing myself with ∧the[∧] waters here whose peculiar property
is to reduce you to the extremest depths of depression, languor ᵼ
despair—with a view of ultimately letting ∧you[∧] rebound to the
30   7<u>th</u> ⊕ heaven of salubrity. The ebb has prosperously taken place
with me, but the flow hangs fire; ᵼ meanwhile I have been a
poor correspondent.—Seriously speaking, I lately stopped the
waters: since when I feel much better, ᵼ in my exhilaration, had
planned that letter to you, which your own bedazzled me, so to

speak, into the necessity of postponing. You know, more or less,
by this time, I suppose, how my summer has been spent—& how
I fled from Switzerland, even as we dreamed of doing last year. I
spent nearly three weeks at Berne, which ⬧ would have been
pleasant, ~~if not~~ ∧except∧ for the excessive heat. There was no   5
one there I knew, but I took solitary walks, explored a good deal,
& found the circumjacent country charming beyond compare. I
⬧⬧ found also a treasure of a hotel—the Bellevue—where we
ought to have lived last summer. I went for a day to Interlaken to
see Miss L. Shaw, but she was ill & invisible & I conversed with   10
the ∧Miss∧ Hallowells, who were "fine" as ever. I came straight
hither, & having ⬧ now been here five weeks, feel as if I knew
Homburg à fond. But I expect to be here some three or four
more, from which you may infer that I like it. I do vastly,
Germany though it is; for it is Germany with many mitigations.   15
I continued till I came here, to maintain on general grounds that
it you erred—that you indeed almost <u>sinned</u>—in going home; &
then I took it up on particular ones. You ought to have come
here; Homburg was made for your father. Coolness, excellent
coffee, lovely shady woody walks, capital reading room, excellent   20
orchestra (partial to Italian music) twice a day, table d'hote at
4 frs. (with dishes passed twice) rooms at 3 frs., delicious
Ludwigsbrunnen giving innocuous refreshment to those not
drinking the other springs—all this you might have enjoyed.—
But, at Beverley, with ∧all∧ your fine friends, I suppose you   25
have few regrets.—But, in some desperate hour, remember
Homburg & its merits for the future.—Your impressions of
home were interesting—& I'm delighted they make it seem
natural to you that it should natural to me to prefer Rome.—
À propos of Rome, dear Lizzie, why ~~so many~~ ∧those∧ fiercely   30
epigrammatic ~~taunts about~~ ∧comments on∧ my innocent prose?
& apropos of "prose"—why those dark innuendoes & invidious
comparisons? Let Mrs. W. repose in her chosen (or, I'm afraid,
her endured) Germantown. I compared no one of my fair

<u>compagnes</u> with another; I only compared them collectively, with those of every other cavalier. To me the poetry; to them the prose. But explanations are superfluous. (I have just received the <u>Rom. Rides</u> & find them as usual, horribly misprinted.—) But I

5 thank you tenderly for your relish of them.—I've heard nothing all summer of any of our Roman friends—save from Mrs. Tweedy, of the Terrys who write her from the Baths of Lucca, very ~~doel~~ doleful with the heat. Of Mrs. W. I have heard nothing—nor of Mrs. S. & Miss B. But I have come to an end of

10 time & paper.—I'm very glad to hear you have a roof for the winter—a very good one I should think. I am not at all certain of going to Rome, but I have a great mind to, in order to make you distractedly envious.—The Tweedies are here, below me, in this charming lodging house—well, happy & charmed with

15 Homburg, whose climate ~~Mrs~~ Mr. T. finds perfect. They talk of Dresden for the winter.—The Mrs. Pattison you met at Oxford was a friend of <u>mine</u>, too; & I was lately told by an Oxonian here, famous for her Platonic friendships with handsome young men. I don't give this from my experience, but his testimony. Much

20 love to your father & all sympathy in American pains & pleasures. Friendly remembrances to <u>Anne</u>—I shall write you often, yes; but shall expect eye for eye & tooth for tooth. Yours always   H. James jr

No previous publication

∾

36.11 Beverley • Bev= | erley

36.16 ~~or~~ & • [& *overwrites* or]

36.17 farewell • fare= | well

36.18 ~~at~~ in • [in *overwrites* at]

36.24–25 ~~T~~ spending • [s *overwrites* T]

36.27 peculiar • pecu= | liar

36.28 languor • lan= | guor

36.30 ◇ heaven • [h *overwrites illegible letter*]

36.34 planned · plan= | ned

37.2 suppose · sup= | pose

37.3 Switzerland · Switzer= | land

37.4 ◇ would · [w *overwrites illegible letter*]

37.8 ◇◇ found · [fo *overwrites illegible letters*]

37.12 ◇ now · [n *overwrites illegible letter*]

37.15 Germany · Ger= | many

37.19 Homburg · Hom= | burg

37.21 d'hote · [*misspelled*]

37.33 comparisons · compari= | =sons

38.5 tenderly · ten= | -derly

38.8 ~~doel~~ doleful · [le *overwrites* el]

38.15 Homburg · Hom= | burg

38.15 ~~Mrs~~ Mr. · [r *overwrites* rs]

38.18 handsome · hand= | some

38.20 American · Ameri= | can

38.20–23 can pains & pleasures [. . .] H. James jr · [can *completing* American *from ms. p. 8; the remainder of the letter is written across the letter's first page*]

38.21 remembrances · re- | membrances

∾

36.11 Beverley · Beverly, Massachusetts.

37.10 Miss L. Shaw · Mary Louisa "Loulie" Shaw.

37.11 the ∧Miss[∧] Hallowells · Anna Hallowell was Loulie Shaw's companion.

37.13 à fond · thoroughly.

37.23 Ludwigsbrunnen · Another of Bad Homburg's medicinal springs (see 15 July [1873] to MWJ, p. 7n4.14), discovered in 1808. The water here is described by Murray's *Handbook for North Germany* as "a mild harmless water like Seltzer, but more saline, which anyone may drink" (361).

37.33 Mrs. W. · Sarah Butler Wister.

38.1 compagnes · companions.

38.4 Rom. Rides · "Roman Rides."

38.7 the Terrys · The family of Luther Terry.

38.9 Mrs. S. & Miss B. · Alice Sumner (Mason) and Alice Bartlett.

38.16 Mrs. Pattison · Emilia Pattison; see also HJ to WJ, 26, 27, 29 April [1869] (*CLHJ, 1855–1872* 1: 302n297.25).

ALICE JAMES
3 September [1873]
ALS Houghton
10   bMS Am 1094 (1568)

    Bad-Homburg Sept 3ᵈ
     5 Kisseleff-Strasse.
Dearest Sister—I hear you mean to write to me; indeed I
15   suppose your letter is actually on the way—so I'll generously
answer it before it arrives. This news was conveyed in two
letters, from F. & M. respectively, written at St. John's & received
one some ten days since, ө & one only yesterday. Father's of
Aug. 8, was the 1ˢᵗ & mother's of 4 days before, strangely
20   enough, only reached me yesterday—having consumed 27 days
on its journey. But better late than never, & I have had great
satisfaction in its cool, calm picture of your situation. I myself
have not written for a longer spell than usual, for divers reasons:
1ˢᵗ I was waiting for your own letters; 2ᵈ I was busy, mornings,
25   doing an art. on Turgenieff for the N. A. R. which I have sent
off, I trust in time; 3ᵈ that my last had given you good accounts
of my improved health which I wished to have the warrant of
experience to reiterate. You see there is a method in my
madness; & I have not waited in vain. My article, which is
30   perfectly splendid & very long, has been sent; your letters have
arrived, & my health is steadily more & more promising. This
time I think I have nailed it, & shall never again let it budge from
its vantage.—You see I am still in this blessed cool, comfortable,
~~inhabita~~ [ʌ]pretty[ʌ] Homburg—by this time one of the oldest

40

inhabitants. The season & the seasoners are ebbing away, but I
still linger, waving the charm of these first mildly, deliciously,
autumnal days. I expect to be here a fortnight more. I have dwelt
on the Homburg air in my former letters: but for these three last
weeks it has been surpassing itself, & it seems so charged, in
every pulse, with health-giving influences that I can't bear to
m'y soustraire. The great heats which prevailed up to Aug. 10th
have been succeeded by rapturous coolness, & these last ten
days especially have had a finished, old-world picturesque
refreshingness which would hardly suffer me to read, write or
think, for looking out the window at clouds & light & air and
wanting to go into the woods & lie on the edge of a clairière &
waste existence in the mere rudimental consciousness of it—a
consciousness infinitely sweetend by the sense of improving
heath. I'm glad St. John's N. B. was so cool, so and handsome &
wholesome; but I don't believe you have had at St. John's N any
of our soft, grey, covered days with the breezes wandering
about—to the music of the rustling woods—like couples gently
walzing in a ball-room roofed with dove-color and silver.
Father's & mother's letters date back to so long ago that there
are ∧is∧ nearly a month of your life & adventures still to
account; F for. St. John's, at any rate, I trust, wore well to the
end; and ∧I∧ am daily expecting the rest of the history. To day,
I suspect, you are back in Cambridge, exclaiming over home
plates, table-cloths, victuals, & other luxuries. I wish I could
have a go at the victuals! Mother & father both speak of you as
very robust, which is a good thing. Mother mentioned a letter of
A. K.'s from Quebec which I had never received, & the idea of
losing which filled me with bitterness. I rushed off to the P. O.,
made them ransack their stores & lo! it was produced. Thank
A. K. for it much, & tell her I wrote to her about a month
since—rather less. She told me what you meant to do, but little
what you had done, & father & mother don't go into the
geography of the matter, so I'm reduced to ∧a∧ strange

confusion on the subject. You seem to have scoured the Arctic
regions quite à la Dr. Franklin, & your 4 days at sea are
prodigious to think of. After this, you ought to be toughened ~~for
any of th~~ [∧]up to the "rudest"[∧] pitch of health—& I should
think might fear to find a Cambridge winter relaxing and
demoralizing. I hope at any rate you have copiously retailed your
<u>impressions</u>.—The Tweedies are still here, lodged below me, &
"whirled round in earth's diurnal course" at very much the same
rate as ever. They talk of leaving, & doing the Tyrol, but like
Homburg so much & feel it such a triumph not ~~be~~ to be ill or
hot, or dusty, or packing, or "examining" anything, that they
stay from day to day & I imagine will leave the Tyrol alone, as an
unbraved danger.—A fortnight ago turned up Miss Bessie Ward,
come to drink the waters under the tutelage of a German family
with whom she had been placed ∧at Berlin[∧] to ~~study~~ ∧talk[∧] the
language. She found a summer in Berlin not quite paradise &
they brought her here. ~~Sh~~ We see her tolerably often as she
often comes to the Kursaal of an evening with Aunt Mary, to
hear the music. She is very pretty & charming & has come "out"
greatly—being almost as loquacious as Lily—but much less
boresomely. She ◇ told me to give you a great deal of love & beg
you to write to her. She has bad eyes—it's for that she came
here—& can't write at all herself. She talks by the hour about the
east & says they are to winter in Rome. All her folks, including
the Van H.'s have been spending the summer at Thun.—I
haven't seen another creature I know. I got a letter lately from
~~Miss~~ Mrs. Lombard, who seemed to be ◇ getting on with
Switzerland quite à la Mr. Boott, & waiting for Sept 1ˢᵗ to go ~~th~~
to the Lakes. I fancy by this time she has gone.—So much for
my own news. When I next write, I shall be better able to say
whither I shall next turn. I think I spoke in my last of the
possibility of ~~ho◇~~ having to go to Paris to have my teeth looked
∧to.[∧]. But this I am now hoping will not be necessary. I broke a
precious back tooth, it gave me much pain & all its fellows began

to ache in a rather alarming way. Since then they have become quiet, the back tooth slumbers, ⅋ I hope to end by convincing myself that I may wait six weeks ⅋ then trust for repairs to the American dentist in Florence. — The main news in mother's ⅋ father's letters was Wilkie's matrimonial intentions. I hope they will be crowned with happiness ⅋ Carrie turn out a solid woman. One trembles somewhat; it seems as if one mortal family couldn't reasonably expect to turn out more than one such a peculiarly blissful marriage as Bob's. — A propos of such things, A. K. related your f Fanny Perry episode. This seemed <u>peculiarly</u> blissful enough. — Youv'e seen the Bootts I suppose, if you are in Cambridge; ⅋ will find them, probably, good winter neighbors, without hotel relations   Give much love to them ⅋ tell Lizzie I lately wrote to her. Has my poor little Mary <u>cross</u> yet turned up? I hope my note was carefully kept, ⅋ that you have by this time been able to send them. Its' going on a year, now, that I announced to Bob that I meant speedily to send Mary something. — I hope you have found Willy as much better as he ₍ₐ₎must have₍ₐ₎ found you. I am expecting in a week or two to hear from him. Tell him I got his letter from C., with the enclosed note ⅋ scraps. Father must, in spite of St. John mitigations, be glad to get home again. Thank him for his letter, the magazines ⅋ everything. Is my <u>Albano</u> printed in the Sept. <u>Atlantic</u>? If so it will, I suppose, have been sent. Farewell. Your loving H.

No previous publication

∾

40.17 received · re= | ceived

40.18 ɵ ⅋ · [⅋ *overwrites* o]

40.28 reiterate · reit= | erate

41.8–9 ⋄ days · [d *overwrites illegible letter*]

41.9 picturesque · pic= | turesque

41.14 sweetend · sweet= | end; [*misspelled*]

41.15 s͟o and • [a *overwrites* so]

41.16 N̶ any • [a *overwrites* N]

41.19 walzing • [*misspelled*]

41.22 F̶ for • [f *overwrites* F]

42.10 b̶e̶ to • [to *overwrites* be]

42.17 S̶h̶ We • [W *overwrites* Sh]

42.21 ◇ told • [to *overwrites* illegible letter]

42.27 M̶i̶s̶s̶ Mrs • [rs *overwrites* blotted iss]

42.27 ◇ getting • [g *overwrites* illegible letter]

42.28-29 t̶h̶ to • [t *overwrites* th]

42.32 h̶◇◇ having • [a *overwrites* illegible letters]

43.9 peculiarly • pe= | culiarly

43.10 f̶ Fanny • [F *overwrites* f]

&

40.16-17 two letters, from F. & M. • Sr. to HJ, 8 August [1873]; and MWJ to HJ, 4 August [1873].

40.25 an art. on Turgenieff for the N. A. R. • *"Frülingsfluthen."*

40.26 my last • HJ to parents, 14 August [1873], pp. 31-34.

41.7 m'y soustraire • take myself away.

41.12 clairière • clearing.

41.31-32 I wrote to her about a month since • HJ to AK, 1 August 1873 (pp. 17-23).

42.2 Dr. Franklin • Arctic explorer Sir John Franklin (1786-1847). The disappearance of his 1845-47 Northwest Passage expedition was part of mid-nineteenth-century lore. Franklin was a fellow of the Royal Geographic Society and had received an honorary doctorate from Oxford.

42.8 "whirled round in earth's diurnal course" • "Rolled round in earth's diurnal course," from Wordsworth, "A slumber did my spirit seal," in *Lyrical Ballads*, line 7.

42.13 Miss Bessie Ward • Daughter of Samuel Gray Ward and Anna Barker Ward.

42.25 the Van H.'s • Baron Richard von Hoffmann and his wife, Lydia "Lily" Ward von Hoffmann, daughter of Sam and Anna Ward.

43.10 Fanny Perry • Thomas Sergeant Perry's younger sister.

43.14 tell Lizzie I lately wrote to her • HJ to Elizabeth Boott, 15
August 1873 (pp. 36–38).

43.14 my poor little Mary cross • See HJ to Mary Lucinda Holton
James, 8 July 1873 (*CLHJ, 1872–1876* 1: 334–35). A photograph of Mary
Holton James with a cross appears on page 90.

43.20 his letter from C. • WJ to HJ, 25 August [1873] (*CWJ* 1: 218–19).

43.23 my Albano • "Roman Neighborhoods."

WILLIAM DEAN HOWELLS   10
9 September [1873]
ALS Houghton
bMS Am 1784 (253), folder 1, letter 3

Homburg. Sept. 9ᵗʰ   15
    5 Kisseleff. Strasse.
Dear Howells—
        I have been meaning for many days to write & tell you
that your book came safely & very speedily to hand; but have put
it off for reasons doubtless not good enough to bear telling. The   20
work is at any rate by this time the better digested. I had great
pleasure in reading it over, & I have great pleasure now in
recurring to it. It gains largely on being read all at once and
certain places which at first I thought amenable to restriction (or
rather certain features—as zum beispiel a want of interfusion   25
between the "scenery" element in the book & the dramatic)
cease, quite, to seem so in the volume. But your people are better
than this background; you have done your best for the latter but
your story is intrinsically more interesting. This of course,
however. Vivid figures will always kill the finest background in   30
the world.—Kitty is ⊕ certainly extremely happy—more so even
than I feel perfectly easy in telling you; for she belongs to that
class of eminent felicities which an artist doesn't indefinitely
repeat. Don't be disappointed, then, if people don't like her later-

born sisters just as relishingly. If they do, however, you will have taken out an unassailable patent as story-teller & shown—what is the great thing—that you conceive the particular as part of the general. The ⬦ successful thing in Kitty is her <u>completeness</u>: she

5 is singularly palpable and rounded and you couldn't, to this end, have imagined anything p̶ better than the particlar antecedents you have given her. So! in the House of Fable she stands firm on her little pedestal. I congratulate you!—Arbuton I think, now that I n̶ know the end, decidedly a shade too scurvy. The charm

10 of Kitty, as one thinks of her, is that she b̶e̶l̶o̶n̶g̶s̶ ̶t̶o̶ ∧suggests[∧] a type—a blessed one, and the interest of the tale as one gets into it is the foreshadowing of a conflict between her type and another. But at the last, the man's peculiar shabbiness undermines this interest by making you think that she had simply

15 happened to get hold of a particularly mean individual—one, indeed, that she wouldn't have ∧even[∧] temporarily felt any serious emotion about. I know that a ∧great[∧] part of the idea of the story is that she shall be impressed by ∧his[∧] unessential qualities; but as it stands, you rather resent her drama—her own

20 part in it being so very perfectly analysed—having a hero who was coming to <u>that</u>! I was hoping that it was she ∧who[∧] was to affront him. She does, indeed, by her shabby clothes; but this ∧is[∧] an accident; that she should have done something, I mean, which even had she been dressed to perfection, would have left

25 him puzzled, at loss, feeling that she wasn't for him. This wouldn't, indeed, have, necessarily implied his being snubbed, but was that inherent in your plan? Your drama, as you saw it, I suppose was the irreconcilability of the two results of such opposed antecedents & not a verdict on one or the other.—But

30 you'll be amused at my "something", and ask me to dream it up for m̶e̶ you. Heaven deliver me! Your own at least is very neatly executed.—But I didn't mean to dig so deep. How i̶s̶ are the Venetian Priest and his fair one coming on? I suppose theyre' to begin in January & that your'e giving them touch upon touch &

line upon line. I wish you quiet days and propitious moods. The
wish for the former sounds sarcastic: for I suppose Cambridge is
still Cambridge, in your new house as well as your old. that ~~yours~~
your new roof covers you is almost all Iv'e heard about you in a
long time. The ~~art~~ arctic explorations of my own family have   5
made their letters rare and slow to arrive. I wrote you from
Berne, in June & you got the letter, because you sent me the
book: but don't let that be the only answer. I sent you also a
paper ("A Chain of cities") which I trust you received & can
sooner or later use. ~~I'l~~ I've not ◇ had a very productive summer—   10
directly at least; but indirectly, yes; ~~I~~ as I came here unwell &
shall be leaving permanently better as I trust, & apt for teeming
production, evermore. There isn't much to say about ~~b~~ my
summer. It has been ten quiet weeks of Germany.—Even while I
wrote, half an hour ago, came your letter of Aug. 26. Your 40   15
letters ~~from~~ ₍ₐ₎about₍ₐ₎ your story make me blush over all the
foregoing stuff. But with them & Miss Lane's reports, you
needn't heed late-coming praise or blame. I'm sorry your
Venetian priest is still so far off.—So my Chain of Cities did
arrive. I'm sorry it seems "meagre"—an idea that makes ~~m~~ one   20
weep salt tears. This, however, I fondly hope, was less ◇◇ owing to
my own poverty than to a constant fear to amplify and make it
too long.—I'm very glad to get news of you, but your letter was
cruelly brief. But I suppose such things must be with editors and
~~fathers~~. ₍ₐ₎householders₍ₐ₎. I'm glad your house is so good, and   25
should like vastly this horrible afternoon (a foretaste of
November) to spend an hour before that wonderful fire-place.
Farewell. I shall send you more things in these coming months,
~~but~~ ₍ₐ₎and₍ₐ₎ I shall heed your advice about unlaboriousness. I
know I'm too ponderous. But the art of making substance light is   30
hard. Love to your wife & kids. Your's always   H. James jr.
P.S. I start again very soon for Italy: but oh, blasé human soul!
with hardly more palpitation than if I were going to take the
horse-car at the corner!

Previous publication: *HJL* 1: 400–03; Anesko 86–88

∾

45.23 recurring • recur= | ring

45.31 e⊖ certainly • [e *overwrites illegible letter*]

45.31 extremely • ex= | tremely

45.34 disappointed • disap= | pointed

46.4 ⊖ successful • [s *overwrites illegible letter*]

46.6 p̶ better • [b *overwrites blotted* p]

46.9 n̶ know • [k *overwrites* n]

46.31 m̶e̶ you • [you *overwrites* me]

46.32 i̶s̶ are • [a *overwrites* is]

47.3–4 y̶o̶u̶r̶s̶ your • [r *overwrites blotted* rs]

47.5 a̶r̶t̶ arctic • [c *overwrites* t]

47.5 explorations • explora= | tions

47.10 I̶'l̶ I've • [v *overwrites* l]

47.10 ⊖ had • [h *overwrites blotted illegible letter*]

47.11 I̶ as • [a *overwrites* I]

47.12 permanently • per= | manently

47.13 b̶ my • [m *overwrites* b]

47.20 m̶ one • [on *overwrites* m]

47.21 ⊖⊖ owing • [o *overwrites illegible letters*]

47.29 unlaboriousness • un= | laboriousness

47.32–34 P.S. I start [. . .] at the corner! • [*written across the letter's first page*]

∾

45.19 your book • *A Chance Acquaintance* (1873).

45.25 zum beispiel • for example.

45.31 Kitty • Kitty Ellison, a character in several Howells novels, including *A Chance Acquaintance*.

46.8 Arbuton • Miles Arbuton, another character in *A Chance Acquaintance*.

46.32–33 the Venetian Priest and his fair one • Don Ippolito and Florence Vervain in Howells's *A Foregone Conclusion* (1874; novel published in 1875).

47.6-7 I wrote you from Berne, in June • 22 June [1873] (*CLHJ, 1872–1876* 1: 326–30).

47.9 "A Chain of cities" • "A Chain of Italian Cities."

47.15 your letter of Aug. 26 • William Dean Howells to HJ, 26 August 1873 (Anesko 85–86).

47.17 Miss Lane's reports • AJ wrote Annie Ashburner that "the Misses Lane's boarding house" in Quebec was "made famous by" *A Chance Acquaintance* (Moore, "The Letters of Alice James," pt. 1, 32).

WILLIAM JAMES
15 September [1873]
ALS Houghton
bMS Am 1094 (1956)

Homburg: Monday Sept 15.
Dear W^m. I have been some three or four days in recipt of your letter of Aug. 28th, but I have been waiting to answer it till I had made up my mind about my movements. I am very glad to hear you have determined to come abroad & sincerely hope you may make the arrangements which will enable you to do so. It will seem an immense pity that you should be kept, against your will, by Eliots' not finding a successor for you. I thought your successor stood ready in <u>Dwight</u>. I suppose he has backed out. Your decision seems to me a wise one; I should think the results of your summer would convince you that it is the thing for you to do ✧ and I shall be surprised if, having got under way with it, you don't get great help from it. If you can't come I shall be much disappointed, as your letter has greatly quickened my desire to see you. I wait impatiently for your next. My first impulse was to write to you that I would go and meet you & wait for you in Paris, but I have decided that I had better go down to Florence & wait for you there. You will probably not wish to remain in Paris longer than to rest from your journey from

England & will be able to make the journey to Florence alone.
Arrange it as I would, the journey & the stay in Paris would
consume more money than it is now convenient to get rid of and
one doesn't want to begin a Roman winter with diminished

5   funds. My present intention, therefore, is to go to Florence by
October 1ˢᵗ. May you promptly and safely join me! If you should
n't hear from me before sailing (after this) you will of course ask
for a letter at Brown & Shipley's. I had thought of going to Paris
to see a dentist, but I learn of there being a good one in Rome,

10 beside the one in Florence. — You see I'm still at Homburg,
lingering on after almost every other soul has departed. I have
been here nearly ten weeks. But my days too are numbered. I
shall start ∧in[∧] a day or two for Switzerland wait at Berne for
your letter, which I hope to receive by the 25ᵗʰ, and then proceed

15 to Italy. Homburg is very cold and wet just now & I am being
frozen out. The Tweedies lately departed for the Tyrol and
Vienna, in good health and spirits; but their place in my
affections has been taken by Mrs. Ward & Bessie who are
lodging in this house next door to me. M̶ Bessie is making a cure

20 & her mother has recently joined her. Sam, thank the Lord, is in
England; he gave us a taste of his presence for a day. I see them
rather much as I am their only friend here & as far as Bessie is
. concerned, I don't complain. She is very lovely. Mrs. W. is the
same old <u>discoureuse</u>, yet with the tatters & remnants of a charm

25 too. — There came to me no other home letters but yours.
Others I trust, from Canada, have arrived since & are awaiting
my orders in the Bankers hands; for my last (from father, St.
John's Aug. 8ᵗʰ) is now of very old date. You speak of your all
getting home "prematurely." I hope this implies nothing amiss

30 with you. I̶ Of your excursion to the Catskills I had heard
nothing. — Let me not forget to say apropos of your bringing
books &c. that you had better leave the Ferrari, as I can get a
cheap Italian edition of it, & I had rather fill the space in your

trunks with other things. If have undertaken to write for the
N. A. R. a series of French articles ȸ I mean to put them
through. I should therefore like such volumes as you can stuff in
of Ste. Beuve, A. de Musset ȸ Stendhal. Also if you can manage
it, with the Valery ȸ with my ƚ <u>Letters</u>, if possible of the P. de   5
Brosses, my <u>bound</u> volumes of Balzac. If to these you will add a
supply of Harrison's lozenges ȸ of Davis's tooth-soap, I will ȹ be
greatly thankful.—I continue to be much better in health and
each day confirms my belief that it is a progressive ȸ permanent
gain. I hope so.—I trust you found the family well and happy   10
after their absence. I have never heard so little of them ȸ felt so
detatched, as this summer.—I read with great pleasure your
<u>Vacations</u>. It was all very well worth saying ȸ was very well said.
It must have been much noticed, ȸ I hope they paid you decently
for it. Of Bob ȸ Wilk I hear little, ȸ expect soon to learn more   15
about Wilky's marriage. Have you seen the Boott's? They will
miss you.—Address your next to Brown and Shipley. Indeed all
please continue for the present to write to them. Farewell.
Come, ȸ I promise to send you home a better man. I have been
thinking ȹ so so much of talks we might have that I shall <u>miss</u>   20
you if you don't. Yours, H.

Previous publication: *CWȷ* 1: 220-22

ȣ

49.17 recipt · [*misspelled*]

49.20 determined · de= | termined

49.21 arrangements · arrange= | ments

49.27 ȹ and · [a *overwrites illegible letter*]

49.29 disappointed · dis= | appointed

50.10 Homburg · Hom= | burg

50.19 M̶ Bessie · [B *overwrites* M]

50.23 concerned · con= | cerned

50.30 I̶ Of · [O *overwrites* I]

50.31 forget • for= | get

51.1 trunks • [*blotted out*]

51.4 Stendhal • Stend= | -hal

51.5 ⊦Letters • [L *overwrites* l]

51.5 possible • pos= | sible

51.7 ⬦ be • [b *overwrites illegible letter*]

51.12 detatched • [*misspelled*]

51.17–21 and Shipley [. . .] Yours, H. • [*written across the letter's first page*]

51.20 ⬦ so so • [s *overwrites illegible letter*]; so | so

∿

49.17–18 your letter of Aug. 28ᵗʰ • WJ to HJ, 25 August [1873] (*CWJ* 1: 218–19).

49.20 you have determined to come abroad • See WJ to HJ, 25 May 1873 (*CWJ* 1: 207–10, esp. 208–9); and HJ to WJ, 5 August [1873] (pp. 24–26).

49.23 Eliots' • Harvard president Charles W. Eliot.

49.24 Dwight • Thomas Dwight (1843–1911), Harvard anatomy instructor.

50.18 Mrs. Ward • Anna Barker Ward.

50.24 discoureuse • talker.

50.27–28 from father, St. John's Aug. 8ᵗʰ • Sr. to HJ, 8 August [1873].

51.2 N. A. R. • *North American Review*

51.5–6 my [. . .] Letters [. . .] P. de Brosses • *Lettres familières écrites d'Italie en 1739–1740* by Charles de Brosses.

MARY WALSH JAMES
22 September [1873]
ALS Houghton
bMS Am 1094 (1814)

5

Berne Switz: Sept. 22<u>d</u>

Dearest of Mammies—

We have not been having very intimate or frequent   10
communion during these past weeks—I don't know why. Your
letters (I mean all the family's) have been rare & most slow to
arrive. Some time before leaving Homburg, I got a letter from
you & father each of Aug. 4 & 8., (from St. J.) ~~whio◇~~ which took
a month to come. Then came one from Willy, of Aug 28<u>th</u>,   15
telling me you were just coming home & this is all in now nearly
two mos. You wrote at any rate, I hope, after reaching
Cambridge, and ~~the~~ ∧your[∧] letter must come, any day. I know
very little about your month in N Canada, as your letters were
written just after you had got there and all since is darkness.   20
Also of Willy's ∧doings[∧] I know little. He wrote that he was
just home from the Catskills—but that was the first and last I
heard of it. But he had more important matters to write about. I
am waiting anxiously for his tidings as to whether or no he can
come out. I devoutly hope that he can, & that having made his   25
hard decision, nothing will come down on it. I strongly believe a
winter of European idleness and the European climate would do
much for him. So I am counting the days and the mails, till his
letter comes as it will probably do before the 25<u>th</u>. I wrote to him
~~sho◇~~ shortly before leaving Homburg, & I had written to Alice   30
shortly before that, after a good deal of an interval. I lingered on
and on there very comfortably, & think I should ~~hav~~ ∧be[∧] there
now if the weather hadn't become very cold & in-door life
emba∧r[∧]rassing. So I rooted myself up on the 18<u>th</u> & came

directly hither <u>via</u> Basel: where I find warmer weather, and an
atmosphere which makes me renewedly appreciate that of
Homburg. H. is certainly a very brave little place and I have not
been there for the last time. Every one had gone before me,

5 including the Tweedies; but not including Bessie Ward, who was
joined by her mother ᵭ whom I ~~became~~ ‸grew₍ₐ₎ very <u>thick</u> with.
She is so charming girl ᵭ bade me repeat to Alice (I have already
told her once) that she would be very thankful for a letter,
having bad eyes and no chance to write herself. The Tweedies

10 started some days before me for the Tyrol and Vienna, and
mean to try Dresden for the winter. Their weeks at Homburg
were very happy. They seem (almost) as simple in their old age
as innocent children ᵭ drift on from day to day in thankfulness
for the smallest favors. The Wards rave about the East ᵭ tried to

15 persuade them to try the Nile next winter, but they are afraid,
naturally, of losing their contentment by vaulting ambition. —I
haven't much other news ~~from~~ ‸for₍ₐ₎ you. Mrs. Lombard I have
just heard, has just crossed the St. Gothard <u>en route</u> for
Florence, after a month at Lucerne, ᵭ a good deal of illness. The

20 Andrews are at Lucerne, ᵭ preparing to enliven Italy ⋄ with
their ~~p~~ advent. I saw Mrs. Von Hoffman (Lily Ward) at the
railway station this morning, en route for Mt. Cenis, with her
husband, babies ~~an~~ etc. She has lovely children, but a very sickly
physiognomy. —This is the amount of my news. I continue to be

25 better in health ᵭ my improvement, though not uninterrupted,
is steady and I think certain. I feel rather low at times that after
all I haven't got a better ⋄ head for work; but I can do enough, ᵭ
with time, obviously, I can do more and more. Berne isn't very
lively or inspiring, but I shall remain here some days longer,

30 waiting for Willy's letter ᵭ then start for Florence via Lucerne ᵭ
the St. Gothard. If he comes, I should like to meet him in Paris,
ᵭ he of course would prefer to find me there; but on the whole I
shall consult my necessities, financial and physical, better by
repairing to Italy and getting under way there for the winter. I

will await him, de pied ferme, at the Florence station and receive
him with open arms. It will be a blessing to have a "superior
mind" to converse with, after the general Roman rabble & I
depend on our helping each other through the winter greatly. I
shall be sadly disappointed if he doesn't come, & for himself it
will, I think, be a lost advantage. I hope indeed that he will have
no disappointment.—About all the things of home, I feel, as I
said, extremely in the dark, & hardly know ~~to~~ how to picture
your respective autumnal attitudes. I hope you found the
summer really over when you reached Quincy St. & have had no
battles to fight with heat or mosquitoes. What news do you get
from the boys, and is Wilky's wedding day fixed? Will any of
you go to the wedding? I suppose it's too long a journey, but he
will bring his Carrie home, of course. Don't fail to give me a
minute account of her. Is Aunt Kate in Cambridge? Give her my
tender love, thank her for letter from Quebec, tell her I wrote to
her subsequently, but shall do so again when I get settled in
Italy. The Bootts, by this time, I suppose, are your neighbors—I
hope to your mutual contentment & convenience. Give them my
love & tell Lizzie I immediately answered her letter from
Beverly. If W^m comes to Rome, I'm afraid he will ~~w~~ miss one of
its brightest (social) ornaments. Miss Crawford has become
engaged at the B. of Lucca to a Baron Rabbe, a Prussian officer,
with one leg & is to be married in January. She hadn't the
sweetness of the dove, but she was agreeable for evening uses, &
the Palazzo Odescalchi will be boresome without her; for her
remaining sister has <u>not</u> the wisdom of the serpent.—Are the
Nortons back from the country & do you see them? I got lately
from Grace a very depressed sort of letter. Is Child ~~as~~ also back?
Better I hope, & with talk laid up, I suppose, for twenty years.
How is Sara S.?—and tell me about Arthur? Also about T. S. P.'s
in the "marriage relation." Write me dear mother, a loving &
teeming letter. You'll miss Willy, if he comes, greatly, & Father &
Alice & you will have a quiet house. But you'll survive I hope &

have spirits occasionally to bless us.—Farewell, sweet mammy, with yearning love to all.

Ever your fondest H. Address still to B. & S., until I know my winter address.

No previous publication

∾

53.13 Homburg • Hom= | burg

53.14 ~~whie~~ which • [ch *overwrites illegible letters*]

53.19 N̶ Canada • [C *overwrites* N]

53.30 ~~shoe~~ shortly • [r *overwrites blotted illegible letter*]

54.5 including • in= | cluding

54.11 Homburg • Hom= | burg

54.13 thankfulness • thank- | -fulness

54.16 contentment • con= | tentment

54.20 ◇ with • [w *overwrites blotted illegible letter*]

54.21 p̶ advent • [a *overwrites blotted* p]

54.23 husband • hus= | band

54.23 ~~an~~ etc. • [et *overwrites* an]

54.23 children • chil= | dren

54.27 ◇ head • [h *overwrites illegible letter*]

54.32 prefer • pre= | fer

55.8 ~~to~~ how • [h *overwrites* to]

55.16 Quebec • Que= | bec

55.19 contentment • content= | ment

55.21 w̶ miss • [m *overwrites* w]

55.26 Odescalchi • Odes= | calchi

55.29 ~~as~~ also • [l *overwrites* s]

55.31–32 T. S. P.'s in • [i *overwrites* s]

56.3–4 my winter address. • [*written across the letter's last page*]

∾

53.13–14 a letter from you & father each of Aug. 4 & 8 • MWJ to HJ, 4 August [1873], and Sr. to HJ, 8 August [1873].

53.15 one from Willy, of Aug 28ᵗʰ • WJ to HJ, 25 August [1873] (*CWJ* 1: 218-19).

53.29 I wrote to him • HJ to WJ, 15 September [1873] (pp. 49-51).

53.30-31 I had written to Alice shortly before that • HJ to AJ, 3 September [1873] (pp. 40-43).

55.1 de pied ferme • for certain.

55.16-17 I wrote to her subsequently • Possibly HJ to AK, 1 August 1873 (pp. 17-20).

55.22-23 Miss Crawford has become engaged [. . .] to a Baron Rabbe • Annie Crawford met Baron Eric von Rabe (d. c. 1885), of Lesnian in western Prussia, in 1873 and married him the next year.

55.26 Palazzo Odescalchi • Rome residence of the family of Luther Terry, Annie Crawford's stepfather.

55.26-27 her remaining sister • Mary "Mimoli" Crawford.

55.29 Child • Francis James Child.

55.31 Sara S. • Sara Sedgwick.

55.31 Arthur • Arthur Sedgwick.

55.31 T. S. P. • Thomas Sergeant Perry.

56.3 B. & S. • Brown and Shipley.

WILLIAM JAMES
26 September [1873]
ALS Houghton
bMS Am 1094 (1957)   25

Berne, Friday, Sept. 26ᵗʰ

Dear Willy—

I yesterday received mother's letter of Sept. 12ᵗʰ, telling me   30
that you had taken passage for October 11ᵗʰ. She tells me also
that you had already written to me, announcing your decision,
but strange to say, I haven't received your letter nor one of
Alice's written about the same time. I can't bear to think they

are lost—& they are probably not, for they are the first I have
ever missed. They may, carelessly have been sent to Homburg &
forwarded thence amiss. I have written to have them looked for,
& hope when I next write to be able to tell you they have turned
5 up. Alice's letter I should intensely regret not getting, as I have
long looked for it. Give her my love & thank her for it & tell her
I ardently hope to recover it.—I am greatly relieved to hear that
you have not been prevented from coming & that your way is
smooth. I wrote you a week ago, telling you that I could meet
10 you ◇ only at Florence↓, & I send this ◇ further information
hoping it may catch you just before you sail. At the date of
mother's letter you still expected I would be in Paris, & I hope
you won't be too much disappointed not to find me there. Since
I'm not obliged to go there, it suits me better to make straight
15 for Florence, where I hope you will overtake me without trouble
or fatigue. I should greatly enjoy spending a few days there with
you, & making the journey ~~in~~ southward in your company; but
t'other thing can be done on half the money & ~~ths~~ this must
decide it. I shall of course have a letter for you at the Adelphi,
20 giving you full instructions for your journey. I hope your
voyage will be fair & not too trying; I am most happy to hear ~~th~~
from mother that your doings this summer give you faith in
your travelling-powers. ◇ May they increase with each
succeeding mile. This will only just catch you I'm afraid, & to
25 make it do so I must catch the now departing English mail. I
have no last requests—save not to forget the Davis's tooth soap,
& the Harrison's Lozenges. Also a package or so, if you have
room, of Star-mills paper.—I suppose, making your journey (via
Mt. Cenis) comfortably you can reach Florence by the first days
30 in November. Buy a ~~ti~~ through ticket to Rome (good for ten
days) ⟋(or at least to Florence) at the office Alta Italia railway
co, back side of the Grand Hotel. This makes it very
reasonable.—But all this I will set forth in the Adelphi Letter.
My address is Fenzi, Florence. Farewell, à bientôt. Buonissimo

viaggio. — I was delighted to hear of Wilky's good marrying
basis. Love to all.

Yours ever

H. James jr.

I leave tomorrow or next day for Milan, via St. Gotthard. It is   5
very cold & I pine for Italy.

Previous publication: *CWJ* 1: 222-23

∾

58.10 ◊ only • [o *overwrites illegible letter*]

58.10 ¦, • [, *overwrites* .]

58.10 ◊ further • [f *overwrites illegible letter*]

58.17 ~~in~~ southward • [so *overwrites* in]

58.18 ~~ths~~ this • [i *overwrites* s]

58.21-22 ~~th~~ from • [f *overwrites* th]

58.23 ◊ May • [M *overwrites illegible letter*]

58.30 ~~ti~~ through • [h *overwrites* i]

58.31 ⨯(• [(*overwrites* —]

∾

57.30 mother's letter of Sept. 12ᵗʰ • MWJ to HJ, 12 September [1873].

57.33 your letter • Possibly WJ to HJ, 2 September 1873 (*CWJ* 1: 219-
20).

58.9 I wrote you a week ago • HJ to WJ, 15 September [1873] (pp. 49-
51).

58.19 Adelphi • Liverpool hotel; see HJ to family, 27 February [1869]
(*CLHJ, 1855-1872* 1: 219-22), and HJ to MWJ, 23 May [1872] (*CLHJ, 1872-
1876* 1: 4-7).

58.34 à bientôt • see you soon.

58.34-59.1 Buonissimo viaggio • Excellent journey.

WILLIAM DEAN HOWELLS
18 October [1873]
ALS Houghton
bMS Am 1784 (253), folder 1, letter 4

5

Florence Oct. 18<u>th</u>

Dear Howells—
    I send you another bundle of hieroglyphics (apart from
10 this, in a second cover) with hopes that matters are not
immutably disposed ⬦ against its coming to the front early rather
than late. If it suits you to have me figure in your january
number, if my two last sketches are printed ɟ my story is too
long for the purpose—if all this is blessed fact—here's your
15 chance. Siena, you'll see is my theme ɟ I have tried to remain
brief. My only fear is you'll find me too brief. Bald, however, I
have tried not ~~too~~ to be, nor yet too artfully curled and
anointed. In short, consider me discreetly light and agreeably
grave and print me when you can!—I ⬦⬦ am distinctly in Italy
20 again, as you see, ɟ am spending three or four weeks in Florence
previous to settling in Rome for the winter. If I could have my
wish I think I should remain quietly by the Arno ɟ write
enchanting stories; but ~~its~~ my brother is at present crossing ~~to~~
the ocean to join me (as of course you know) and Rome is his
25 goal. I had last winter there a bad time for work; but I must, can
ɟ shall do better now.—I wrote you some five weeks ago from
Homburg, just at the moment your last letter reached me. Mine
I suppose you duly received.—I know nothing about you now
save that you are watching the autumn days drop like ~~mellow~~
30 [ʌ]bright-colored[ʌ] leaves. My memory is full of uneffaced
Cambridge Octobers, ɟ every now and ʌthen[ʌ] I drop a tear on
them ɟ I seem to hear a little leafy rustle deep down in my
spiritual parts and to see a dim haze before my eyes. Here yet, it
is frank summer, but I don't complain, for ~~a~~ I don't like cold

weather any better as I grow older. If I only overtake the warmth yet in Rome I shall have had almost ten month's of it at a stretch. Envy me, ma non troppo; for ~~their~~ there are uncountable drearinesses in exile. In some future remission of it I'll tell you them. — What are you to be doing this winter, before that   5 picturesque fire-place? Is your novel coming on in a manner to make life tolerable? And your wife, without the consolations of authorship, does she find the days pass lightly? Of course they do when they march with the patter of ∧one's[∧] children's feet. What I meant was, — is she well ɗ a happy housewife? My love ɗ   10 compliments. Whom shall you see this winter whom you've not seen before? — When you wrote you were going to Ohio; was it done ɗ done prosperously? Ohio! I make this vague purposeless exclamation, simply as a Florentine. — I hope you will ~~take~~ ∧extend[∧] ∧some[∧] social charity to my people this winter, who,   15 with my brother W͞m now also absent, will be very lonely. — Do you often see the Nortons — ɗ what of Charles? I hope this winter to find Lowell in Rome. Oh for a man to talk a bit with! — Farewell. With every good wish ɗ tender invocation upon your wife your children ɗ your genius — Yours H. J. jr   20

Previous publication: *HJL* 1: 403–04; Anesko 88–89

∾

60.11 disposed • dis= | posed

60.11 ⬧ against • [a *overwrites illegible letter*]

60.17 ~~too~~ to • [o *overwrites* oo]

60.19 ⬧⬧ am • [am *overwrites illegible letters*]

60.23 ~~its~~ my • [my *overwrites* its]

60.23–24 ~~to~~ the • [h *overwrites* o]

60.34 ~~a~~ I • [I *overwrites* a]

61.3 ~~their~~ there • [re *overwrites* ir]

61.4 remission • re= | mission

61.9 children's • chil= | dren's

∾

60.9 I send you another bundle of hieroglyphics • "Siena."

60.13 my two last sketches • "Roman Neighborhoods" and "A Chain of Italian Cities."

60.13 my story • "The Last of the Valerii."

60.26 I wrote you some five weeks ago • HJ to Howells, 9 September [1873] (pp. 45–47).

60.27 your last letter • Howells to HJ, 26 August 1873 (Anesko 85–86).

61.3 ma non troppo • but not too much.

61.6 your novel • *A Foregone Conclusion.*

HENRY JAMES SR.

15   26 October [1873]

ALS Houghton

bMS Am 1094 (1815)

Florence Oct. 26<u>th</u>

20

Dear Father—I have been waiting to write again until I hard
heard from Willy and could let you know that I was in
communication with him. This morning his letter from
Liverpool arrived, ⅋ I delay no longer. He speaks with pleasure

25   of his ⋄ voyage ⅋ says sea sickness was <u>nil</u>; but this he will have
written you. When he will reach Florence he is yet unable to
say; not, I suppose, within ten days. I wrote last upward of a
fortnight since, to Alice, who, I hope rec'd. my letter. It was
from Siena, to which on arriving at Florence I repaired to escape

30   the mosquitoes   I have now been back here some twelve days ⅋
have found the weather charming ⅋ the mosquitoes departed.
Meanwhile have come 3 letters—mothers of Sept. 22<u>d</u>, ⅋ her
note ⅋ yours of Oct. 3<u>d</u> ⅋ 4<u>th</u>   Many thanks for all. I am sorry

you should have had any worry of mind about sending me back the Turgenieff ~~m~~ M.S., & most glad you decided to do so. I shall not fail to do everything I can to amend it. I am not a little disappointed to know it leaves so much to be desired, for a wrote it with great care, zeal & pleasure & said to myself when it was finished that it was the best thing I had done & would help me to some reputation. In my elation I ◊ offered to do a series of other articles for T. S. P. It shows how poorly we judge our own performances. But I have no doubt that I can improve this, & I am a hundred times thankful to you for giving me a chance. I will send it back as promptly as possible. Apropos of such matters, I am sorry to hear such accounts from you of the dishonesty of Sheldon & Church. They have two M.S. of mine— one a piece on Rome & one a story in 3 parts of which I can obtain no tidings whatever. I will write to them immediately either to let me hear something about them or of their intentions ◊ concerning them or else to enclose them to you. You in that case will please send them to Lippincott. I ~~hav~~ lately sent a M.S. to Scribner & am on the point of sending them another—a story in two parts: so that they are for the moment choked with my wares. Poor Howells is chronically; besides, he would not publish the Galaxy story on acct. of the subject, I'm afraid. (Its needless to say that I think the subject all right—in fact very fine.) But please mention to H., when you see him, for safety's sake, that that I sent him ten days since a short article on Siena⌐.—I have it at heart to say more about this matter of my writings & their getting published & paid for.—I am better & better in health (as you will be glad to hear on other grounds than it's helping simply to write)—better, indeed, I may say, as I never have been before. I feel more & more apt for writing, ~~&~~— more active and ambitious. At the same rate of improvement for the next year I shall be able to do really a great deal. Meanwhile I am able to do amply enough to secure a comfortable—an easy—monthly income. I have been working smoothly &

prosperously for the last six weeks ⅋ have taken the measure of
~~my~~ [∧]what[∧] health ~~al~~ allows me to do. But I had got so much
behind during the preceding six mos. that I had been
degenerating in health—that I'm afraid I have been rather
heavily testing your power of letting me draw on you while
waiting for my own efforts to produce something. Their doing
so—I can answer for it—their producing enough to completely
cover all my expenses—is only a question of time. The point
∧is—[∧] is not the temporary inconvenience to you very great? I
bear it in mind ⅋ draw no more money than I absolutely need. I
don't spend a sou idly; what I spend goes simply to my living—
which <u>must</u> of course be fairly comfortable. My recent travels
have made me draw more rapidly than I could have wished—as
well ∧as[∧] the imminent need of winter clothes ⅋c. But as I say, I
can count upon soon ◇ overtaking all these drafts, ⅋ more, with
my <u>envois</u> of M. S. It is a matter of these coming to light, ⅋⅋ of
my getting thoroughly started. This start has been delayed
pitifully long by ~~be~~ my being in poor working order; but I really
feel now as if I had passed through my last tight place. I shall
never be able, I believe, to work <u>largely</u>; but I shall—I already
am—to work in the modest manner that will bring me, ◇ say
$3000 a year—a sum on which I can ∧~~live~~[∧] in Europe, live
handsomely. I can assure you, I think, that at the end of six mos.
I shall be even with my drafts, without at all hurting myself. I
wish, with all the uses_× that you have your money, that it ~~was~~
[∧]might[∧] not take so long; but I shall try ⅋ manage it.
Meanwhile, short of real inconvenience, bear with me.—If all
this bores you, give it to mother to read. I had to say it; I can't
go on using my letter of credit without giving you some sign
that I am conscious of the situation. I have sent home since last
June the worth of, at a moderate estimate, (or at least not an
exaggerated one) $600 (in gold.) It must ∧all[∧] come into you,
sooner or later; ⅋ in the coming winter I shall be able, with my
better health, to at least double the sum. I have drawn in that

period (since June 1ˢᵗ) 3̶0̶ ∧100₍∧₎ £. I am by no means living, as
you see, at the rate of $3000 a year—in spite of my expensive
summer travelling. But enough of this.—I have b̶e̶ been enjoying
Florence extremely; it has never seemed pleasanter.—I have seen
a few people. Mrs. Lombard, I wrote you, I see every day or
so—oftener than in Cambridge! She is ill much of the time, but
keeps wonderfully cheerful & says she is better at least than at
home. She has many friends—& seems to have made many since
coming abroad, & both she and Fanny delight in Florence—
especially the drives. The Andrews are here for the winter. I
called and kept awake—or at least woke up in time to h̶o̶o̶ hear
them send much love to you. Bessie is no thinner, but very
sweet, & Edith charming. The Henry Greenoughs are here for
the winter—after a summer in Innspruck.—But this is all my
news. I am hankering fearfully to see Willy & have all my
curiosities and questions answered. You must have already begun
to feel lonely, but keep up your spirits. Wilky's nuptials are at
hand & will give you something to think about.—Please tell
Lizzie B. that I received her charming letter & will answer it at
my earliest leisure. Farewell dear father, with all thanks &
blessings on your heads. Much love to Mother, Alice & A. Kate.
Don't let W.'s having joined me keep you from writing.—I
suppose you recognized the letter fr. Darmstadt in the N. as
mine. How much has the N. paid for that & the <u>Homburg</u>? Your
affectionate <u>H. James jr</u>
Address Rome: <u>Spada & Flamini</u>

Previous publication: *HJL* 1: 405–8

ↄ

62.25 ◇ voyage • [v *overwrites illegible letter*]

62.33 Meanwhile • Mean= | while

63.2 m̶ M.S. • [M *overwrites* m]

63.7 ◇ offered • [o *overwrites illegible letter*]

63.9 performances • perfor= | mances

63.11 possible • pos= | sible

63.13 Sheldon • Shel= | don

63.17 ⬦ concerning • [c *overwrites illegible letter*]

63.18 ~~hav~~ lately • [lat *overwrites* hav]

63.21 chronically • chron= | ically

63.22 publish • pub= | lish

63.25 that that • that | that

63.26 ¦. • [. *overwrites* ,]

63.30 ⸒— • [— *overwrites* ⸒]

63.33 comfortable • com= | fortable

64.2 ~~al⬦~~ allows • [l *overwrites illegible letter*]

64.4 degenerating • de= | generating

64.7 completely • com= | pletely

64.15 ⬦ overtaking • [o *overwrites illegible letter*]

64.16 ⸍⸒ • [⸒ *overwrites* —]

64.18 ~~be~~ my • [m *overwrites* be]

64.21 ⬦ say • [s *overwrites illegible letter*]

65.3 ~~b⬦~~ been • [e *overwrites illegible letter*]

65.11 ~~h⬦⬦~~ hear • [ea *overwrites illegible letters*]

65.22–25 joined [. . .] H. James jr • [*written across the letter's first page*]

65.26 Address [. . .] Flamini • [*written across the letter's eighth page*]

◑

62.33 mothers of Sept. 22ᵈ • MWJ to HJ, 22 September [1873].

63.2 Turgenieff [. . .] M.S. • "*Frülingsfluthen.*"

63.8 T. S. P. • Thomas Sergeant Perry.

63.13 Sheldon • Isaac E. Sheldon managed Sheldon & Company, which published the *Galaxy* from 1868 to 1878.

63.13 Church • Either Francis P. or William C. Church.

63.14 one a piece on Rome • "From a Roman Note-Book."

63.14 a story in 3 parts • "Mme. de Mauves."

63.18–19 I [. . .] lately sent a M.S. to Scribner • "An Autumn Journey," actually published first in the *Galaxy* and later reprinted as "The St. Gothard" in *Transatlantic Sketches* (1875) and as "The Old Saint-Gothard" in *Italian Hours* (1909). See HJ to Sr., 22 December 1873 (p. 81).

63.20 a story in two parts • "Adina."

63.25 a short article • "Siena."

64.11 sou • a 5-centime piece.

64.16 envois • shipments.

65.12–13 Bessie [. . .] & Edith • Bessie and Edith Andrew.

65.13 The Henry Greenoughs • The family of Francis Boott's brother-in-law; see HJ to WJ, 8 January [1873] (*CLHJ, 1872–1876* 1: 184n177.30).

65.23 the letter fr. Darmstadt in the N. • The unsigned "An Ex–Grand Ducal Capital."

65.24 the Homburg • "Homburg Reformed."

HENRY JAMES SR.
2 November [1873]
ALS Houghton
bMS Am 1094 (1816)

20

Florence Nov. 2ᵈ
Dear Father:

I wrote to you a week ago, telling you of Willy's being on his way to me — & I had hardly sent my letter when he arrived. He had travelled very fast, stopping only a day in Paris, in his impatience to reach me. A compliment to me! I have delayed writing, as I wished to be able to tell you how he seemed, after a few day's observation. He felt, he says, the fatigue of his long journey from London very little and is at least as well as he expected to be. In appearance he is even more robust than your accounts have led me to suppose; he looks indeed in exuberant heath, & I am immensely struck with ~~the~~ ∧his∧ change in this respect since I last saw him. He is very much charmed with Florence and spends a great deal of time in going about the

25

30

streets and to the Galleries. He takes it all as easily as possible, of course, but he already manages to do a good deal and has made ~~such~~ a beginning ~~as is a~~ [∧]which[∧] augurs well for the future. He has fallen upon indifferent weather, but the air is

5 happily still very mild. I find great pleasure in seeing him and have plied him with all imaginable questions about you all. I feel ~~as~~ almost as if I had been spending a week in Quincy St. Would to heaven I could! — Your letter of Oct. 17ᵗʰ has just come in, to our great satisfaction. I'm glad to hear of your breakfasts

10 ↄ dinners and of your meeting foreigners of distinction. May such alleviations of your solitude not be wanting. — We shall remain in Florence a week ◇ or two longer — as long as the weather remains at all mild and then shall proceed to ~~t~~ Rome. How or where we shall arrange ourselves I don't know. We shall

15 have to decide, taking all things into account, when we get there. Considering our experimental (especially as regards W.) relation to the Roman climate, we shall do nothing that will bind us for more than from week to week. W. finds the Italian climate very soft and "flat", but not disagreeably so. I have very

20 good hopes of the profit of his undertaking, now that I have seen the apparently strong basis of muscular heath that he enjoys. — His arrival is my only news. I live quietly devoting my mornings to work. — I was very sorry to see that the <u>Atlantic</u> had again played me false. This long initiatory waiting is quite <u>accablant</u>

25 and in sombre moods, I feel as if I had no business to be over here, compromising you in the delay. This very moment, I would give — I don't what — for an hour's talk with mother and you. But I wrote you last week on this matter, ↄ will add no more now. My only course, for the present, is to ~~to~~ keep as well

30 as possible and do my daily work. Give me your blessing! — Willy tells me that he is going to write, so that I will let these lines suffice. Florence, apparently, is filling up for the winter with Americans. A day or two since I met Mr. Bradford. The same old Mr. B. He is going to Rome. Florence still is charming,

but as the autumn advances, I, too, feel the attraction! Love—
love to all. Ever dear father

Your affectionate H.

From your not mentioning it, I suppose the <u>Galaxy</u> too is void
of my work.   5

Previous publication: *HJL* 1: 408–9

&

68.7 a̶o̶ almost • [l *overwrites illegible letter*]

68.12 ◌ or • [o *overwrites illegible letter*]

68.13 ɍ Rome • [R *overwrites* r]

68.16 experimental • experi= | mental

68.17 relation • re= | lation

68.26 compromising • compro= | mising

&

67.23 I wrote to you a week ago • HJ to Sr., 26 October [1873] (pp. 62–
65).

68.24 <u>accablant</u> • <u>overwhelming</u>.

68.33 Mr. Bradford • George Partridge Bradford (1807–90), educator
and reformer.

HENRY JAMES SR. AND MARY WALSH JAMES
16, [17] November [1873]
ALS Houghton   25
bMS Am 1094 (1817)

Florence Nov. 16$\underline{th}$

Dearest parents—

Willy wrote you less than a week ago, so that I have   30
allowed a longer time than usual to pass w̶i̶t̶h̶ ₍ₐ₎in₍ₐ₎ silence. He
acknowledged in last writing mother's good letter to me, of Oct.
21$\underline{st}$. When I wrote he had been with me but a few days; but now
his presence is quite an old story, and we have got pretty well

used to one another. — You are of course anxious to hear how he
seems now that I have had prolonged observation. — He varies a
good deal at different times but he seems on the whole in a very
promising condition. There have been times when he has had
5   the appearance, the manner, and almost the activity of perfect
health. — His activity is very considerable and much greater than
I expected to see it. Not having seen him for a year and a half I
am greatly struck with his improvement in almost all ways. He is
evidently in a much better vein of feeling about himself — more
10 optimistic and taking things easier, and it seems impossible that
with his immense gains (as they strike me) he should not, at no
distant time, be in good working order. He enjoys Florence very
heartily and explores the galleries and churches, day after day,
like a regular vigorous tourist. He is of course often tired, but as
15 ∧the[∧] strongest people are tired with the same work. He
admires the Florentine painters greatly and his talk on all that
he sees is most suggestive and edefying to me. He strongly
inclines to think that the Italian climate is what ◇◇ he wants; and
in short his adventure seems to me up to this point ∧quite[∧] as
20 successful and as promising for the future as was to be hoped.
He has been moreover, for the greater part of his stay here, at
the disadvantage of ◇◇ hot weather which has prevented his
~~being~~ [∧]sitting[∧] and loafing much out of doors. — ◇◇ We are
lingering on in Florence, as you see, and shall probably do so till
25 the 1st December. There has been some sharp weather which
makes me long for the Roman softness, but we shall probably
have ∧it soft[∧] here again, as it is too early for winter. I have a
very pleasant large room in which Willy chiefly dwells & our life
is very harmonious and comfortable. He is ∧now[∧] sitting by the
30 fire writing to Wilky; it is a beautiful bright Sunday; we are just
going to have some lunch & then are going up to San Miniato. I
wish we could make a family party of it.∧Monday a.m.[∧] — I had
to break off my letter yesterday to get my lunch. Our walk was
beautiful but cold. I have no especial news for you. I am getting

on myself very fairly & the great improvement in my health
continues. My liver is somewhat out of time it with it & I don't
<u>feel</u> quite as well as I ought: but this is, I am sure, but a
transitory phase of the long row I have had to hoe & will
gradually pass away. Cold weather causes me especial discomfort   5
and I s expect to be in a better way in Rome.—We have been
with you in spirit, these last days, over your expectation of
Wilky's advent with his wife. I suppose they are with you at this
present moment & that you are feasting your curiosity on Carry.
A blessing on all your impressions—& a full account of them to   10
us. I hope Wilky's marriage will be to him even a fraction of
what Bob's is.—I rec'd. the last <u>Atlantic</u> & Galaxy, with great
bitterness of spirit at the non-appearance of my <u>Albano</u>. The
notes in the G. were badly printed & I regretted their being
stuck into that obscure corner. But ~~ones musnt~~ [∧]I am   15
thankful[∧] to be printed on any terms. They are to send you
$75.00 for the piece.—The <u>Nation</u> as you say is appreciative & I
shall cling to it devoutly. I have just sent it a letter from
Florence. I could easily review a book a week for it, if I could
only get the books. (I suppose you recognized the <u>Dumas</u> &   20
<u>Goethe</u> as mine.) If you see a couple of short notices (<u>Sandeau</u> &
<u>Mérimée</u> they are also mine.) You might mention (for safety's
sake) to T. S. P. if you see him that I lately sent him two
reviews—Howells's ~~p~~ <u>Poems</u> & Pater's <u>Studies</u>.) I am not at work
on the Turgeniew which I bless you for sending back.—We   25
dined two days since with the H. Greenoughs, who are most
~~lovel~~ loveing. I see Mrs. Lombard every few days—always
invalidical but serene, & with plenty of kind friends here. She is
socially much appreciated & moves in a higher circle than at
home. Her caps are the prettiest in Europe. Fanny seems very   30
hearty.—Farewell, dearest parents, sister & aunt, if she is still in
C. This is a thin letter, I know, but you shall have have a better
next time. Ever your loving H. Begin & address <u>Rome</u>: <u>Spada</u> &
<u>Flamini</u>.

Previous publication: *HJL* 1: 410–12

∿

70.6 activity • ac= | tivity

70.7 expected • ex= | pected

70.8 almost • al= | most

70.10 impossible • im= | possible

70.18 ⬦⬦ he • [he *overwrites illegible letters*]

70.22 ⬦⬦ hot • [ho *overwrites illegible letters*]

70.22 prevented • pre= | vented

70.23 ⬦⬦ We • [We *overwrites illegible letters*]

71.5 discomfort • dis= | comfort

71.6 s̶ expect • [e *overwrites* s]

71.20 recognized • recog= | nized

71.21 <u>Sandeau</u> • San= | <u>deau</u>

71.24 p̶ <u>Poems</u> • [P *overwrites* p]

71.27 ~~lovel~~ loveing • [i *overwrites blotted* l; *misspelled*]

71.32 have have • have | have

71.32–34 have a [. . .] *&* <u>Flamini</u>. • [*written across the letter's first page*]

∿

69.30 Willy wrote you • WJ to family, 9 November 1873 (*CWJ* 4: 453–54).

69.33 When I wrote • HJ to Sr., 2 November [1873] (pp. 67–68).

71.13 my <u>Albano</u> • "Roman Neighborhoods."

71.13–14 The notes in the G. • "From a Roman Note-Book."

71.18–19 a letter from Florence • "The Autumn in Florence."

71.20–21 the <u>Dumas</u> *&* <u>Goethe</u> • "Dumas and Goethe" (unsigned review of Goethe's *Faust* in translation by H. Bacharach with a preface by Alexandre Dumas *fils*).

71.21 <u>Sandeau</u> • Unsigned review of Jules Sandeau's *Jean de Thommeray; Le colonel Evrard*.

71.22 <u>Mérimée</u> • Unsigned review of Prosper Mérimée's *Dernières nouvelles*.

71.23 T. S. P. • Thomas Sergeant Perry.

71.23–24 two reviews—Howells's [. . .] <u>Poems</u> *&* Pater's <u>Studies</u> •

"Howells' Poems"; a review of Walter Pater's *Studies in the History of the Renaissance* (1873) was never published. However, some of the fruits of that unpublished review might have found their way into or have been published as "Old Italian Art" and reprinted as part four of "Florentine Notes" in *Transatlantic Sketches* (296–301).

HENRY JAMES SR.
3 December [1873]
ALS Houghton   10
bMS Am 1094 (1818)

Rome 101 Corso Dec 3$^{\underline{d}}$

Dearest father: We found yesterday at the bankers your   15
blessedly welcome letter of Nov. 14$^{\underline{th}}$, which was soothing balm
to our spirits in the midst of the inevitable puzzlements *&* small
drearinesses of a first installation in Rome. Willy wrote to ◇ you
a couple of days since—a letter teeming, I imagine with his first
impressions of the place; but you'll not be sorry to have a sketch   20
of the situation from me as well—*&*, for my own satisfaction, I
must write a word. We have been here now some four days *&* are
"settled"—at any rate for a month or two. We left Florence with
regret, for we had both grown very fond of it. If I had been
alone, I should have subsided for the whole winter there, I think.   25
It had begun to be very cold, however, *&* it was time for Willy to
address himself to the superior resources of Rome. We had a
lovely day for our journey *&* a lovely first day here ~~here~~—a great
felicity for W. He appreciated it fully—especially a moonlight
walk to the Forum *&* Colisoeum, of which he gave you an   30
account. I value greatly <u>his</u> impressions; they are always so lively
and original *&* sagacious that it is a real profit to ~~him~~ ₍ₐ₎me₍ₐ₎ to
<u>receuillir</u> ~~to recu~~ ₍ₐ₎them.₍ₐ₎ His society in this way, as well as
lighter ways, is altogether advantageous to me. We spent a

73

couple of mornings looking about for rooms—discouragingly as regards finding any thing at a reasonable price that would do for both of us, ◊ ʒ that could be obtained for a month at ‸a₍ʌ₎ time. People are all bent on letting their rooms for the season—till the

5 first of May, at least. We collapsed ~~on~~ as ~~room~~ ‸the₍ʌ₎ only solution, on a common basis, into a couple of sun=bathed chambers at the hotel de Russie. But yesterday the landlord of my old ~~quarteer~~ quarters of last winter came out with a reasonable offer for a single month ʒ we decided to separate. W.

10 remains at the hotel, which is his wisest ʒ most comfortable course ʒ I have just unpacked my things here, where I sit ʀ writing this in my warm and pleasant little parlor. It will amount to the same as our really dwelling together by day, as he will have the perpetual resource of my fireside and my balcony, ⟋ ʒ we

15 shall always lunch and dine together.—He has just gone off to the capitol, ʒ I am to rejoin him shortly over our two o'clock colazione. You want of course to know promptly how he seems and progresses. I don't know what report he has given of himself; but it seems to me that I am justified in giving a very

20 encouraging one. He does more and more, all the while, with little serious fatigue, ʒ in power of general locomotion ʒ exertion I see little difference between him and a usually well person. His last days in Florence his journey, and his first days here have been a constant call for activity—~~all of~~ which he is

25 apparently quite able to supply. His walking power has most materially increased, and this, it seems to me, cannot possibly fail to bring total improvement with it. His spirits, on the whole, are very good, ʒ his appearance excellent. He longs acutely and constantly, I think, to be at work; ʒ is doing all this à contre-

30 coeur, but is nevertheless well satisfied with the sensible effects of it, ʒ the promise that two or three months more of the same sort of thing, even at the same rate, will leave him with a really solid gain. I fully understand his impatience of his idleness ʒ the spirit in which he often exclaims—"Oh, if this were only a real

vacation after a long stretch of work—not a simple prolongation
of the effort to get well—how much more I should enjoy it!"
Nevertheless, I think that mentally as well as physically, he is
laying up substance which he will feel himself much the stronger
for. To walk much & sleep well this is the result for him to arrive   5
at—the result which will mean real health again; and I weigh my
words when I say that it seems to me ~~when I so~~ ^to be steadily[∧]
arriving. He has slept well, ~~from~~ ^with[∧] insignificant
interruptions, and it was only this morning that he expressed a
sense of the large & incontestable increase of his power of   10
locomotion. He <u>did</u>, Florence, at any rate as unstintedly as any
traveller need.—Rome is still the same old Rome, <u>minus</u>
Tweedies, Bootts, Wisters &c. I wish for W.'s sake the Tweedies
were here, with their fireside, their carriage & their dinners. But
we shall do well enough. We have already lunched at the Von   15
Hoffmanns!—owing to Sam Ward's inexplicable alacrity in
calling on us. He met us in the train coming from Florence told
us that his wife & Miss Bessie were lying ill with measles at the
hotel, that he was staying at the villa, that he would come & see
us &c. He did the next day & invited us to lunch, of which   20
yesterday we partook.—I have seen no one else. Rome is as yet
very empty & apartments abundant. The weather for two or
three days has been very dusky, but we hope for better things.—
Your letter was redolent of Wilky's hymeneal atmosphere—
which I hope seemed thoroughly salubrious on a near   25
acquaintance. We count the days till your report of Carrie
arrives. W's letter, which you enclosed, was strange &
characteristic, but I trust of purely good omen. All your
mention of household things (& persons) was pleasing to us.
May they long remain as pleasant! I shall be glad to get at last   30
the poor old <u>Villegiatura</u>. The letter from Albany was from ~~an~~ a
silly man wanting me to write him a <u>letter</u> to put in his
collection of autographs! Such is fame—& such is idiocy. But I
must join W. at lunch, & have only time to add my kisses for all &

my thanks, dear dad, for all your repeated benefits. Think of us
most contentedly, & often of your
  affectionate, H. J jr.

5   Of course we wonder about <u>Spain</u> &c: & think that bloody as
was the deed it would be most shabby in us to fight with that
distracted land.

Previous publication: *HJL* 1: 412–15

  ∾

  73.15 yesterday • yester= | day
  73.17 puzzlements • puzzle= | ments
  73.18 ⋄ you • [y *overwrites illegible letter*]
  73.29 especially • espe= | cially
  73.30 Colisoeum • [*misspelled*]
  73.33 <u>receuillir</u> • [*misspelled*]
  74.1 discouragingly • discoura= | gingly
  74.3 ⋄ & • [& *overwrites illegible letter*]
  74.5 ~~on~~ as • [as *overwrites* on]
  74.8 ~~quarteer~~ quarters • [rs *overwrites* er]
  74.11–12 ~~r~~ writing • [w *overwrites* r]
  74.14 ~~+~~ & • [& *overwrites* —]
  74.16 rejoin • re= | join
  74.26 possibly • possi= | bly; [b *inserted*]
  74.29 constantly • con= | stantly
  75.11 unstintedly • un= | stintedly
  75.29 household • house= | hold
  75.31 ~~an~~ a • [a *overwrites* an]
  ∾

  73.18–19 Willy wrote [. . .] since • WJ to Sr., 30 November 1873 (*CWJ*
4: 461–63).

  73.33 <u>receuillir</u> • <u>recueillir</u>; <u>collect</u>.

  74.7 hotel de Russie • Albergo di Russia, Via del Babuino 9.

  74.17 <u>colazione</u> • <u>lunch</u>.

74.29-30 à <u>contre-coeur</u> • <u>in spite of himself.</u>

76.5-7 Of course we wonder about <u>Spain</u> [. . .] to fight with that distracted land • The *Virginius,* a former Confederate blockade-runner, was
used by Cuban rebels during the first half of the Ten Years' War (1868-78),
Cuba's first attempt to gain independence from Spain. Loaded with men
and contraband, the vessel was intercepted by the Spanish *Tornado* on 30
October 1873. Swift trials ensued for the rebels, and fifty-three men were
executed, including American and British citizens. Although U.S. public
sentiment favored war with Spain, Secretary of State Hamilton Fish and
Spanish minister don José Polo de Barnabé brokered peace (see Bradford).

ELIZABETH BOOTT
10 December [1873]
ALS Houghton   15
bMS Am 1094 (510)

Rome 101 Corso 4° po. 10 Dec.
Dear Lizzie—
    Your lovely letter reached me some six weeks ago and was   20
prized as it deserved: but I have delayed answering it because—
first, W͞ᵐ's almost simultaneous arrival gave me for some time a
good deal of out of door occupation ⅋ abbreviated my writing
hours; ⅋ second because I wanted to address you rather from
this old Rome ⅋ secure for my letter at least such value (in   25
default of a greater ⅋) as ~~it~~ the Roman postmark would give it in
your affections. Not that you are especially fond of the Roman
post-office: it is probably the thing in Rome that you like least:
but nevertheless you may feel kindly to even a poor letter of
Roman origin. We came hither about a fortnight since, ⅋ owing   30
to a good deal of troublesome delay ⅌ in getting domiciled it is
only lately that I am beginning to feel shaken down and settled.
This has been helped along by the usual vicious cold with which
I inaugurate the winter: which keeping me indoors for several

days ~~have~~ has enabled me to become desperately at home with
my carpet and wall-paper. These indeed, however, are an old
story as I am back in the rooms I occupied last spring. They are
excellent quarters & I am very comfortable. I had been some two
5   months in Florence when I left and W$^{\underline{m}}$ about a month & we had
both grown so very fond of it that it was not at all easy to depart.
If I had been alone, I am sure I should have staid, for there is
something about the whole constitution & nature of Florence
that suits me wonderfully well. I had drunk deep of Rome last
10   winter, & was quite willing to let it serve for the present. We
shall probably go back ~~there~~ early⌞ ‸to the Arno-side.⌟[‸] My
winter here however promises to be of a much tamer pattern
than ~~the~~ last, & indeed I feel already very low in mind & haunted
with the ghost of all our old revelry. Rome itself is unchanged of
15   course, & has been putting forth her characteristic charms
through the lovely weather of the past fortnight. But I feel here
always the importunate <u>muchness</u> of the place—all the
memories & materials and elements which one cant assimilate
and do justice to. But it has an indefinable loveliness surely. W$^{\underline{m}}$,
20   rather to my surprise, doesn't as yet take to it as kindly as he did
to Florence (for which we quite emulated my own <u>gusto</u>)—but
one is safe, in the long ⱯΛ run to let Rome take care of itself, & I
expect him to come in some day and tell me that, after all, he
rather likes it. He wrote you I think, from Florence, and
25   probably told you, how, as we wandered about, your name and
your papa's, were forever on our lips. You were the genius loci.
We peregrinated most tenderly twice, out to Bellosguardo,
which I found more adorable even than I remembered it. The
view (from your back windows) has a most extraordinarily
30   poetic & solemn sort of loveliness. It seems strange that you
should have been "raised" upon it, as it were: or rather, it seems
not at all strange in the sense of being surprising; but most
awfully enviable. We had in Florence a rather social time—
seeing a good deal of the Greenoughs, who were most kind &

friendly,) the Huntingtons, who were blooming in their ruddy beauty (Miss Laura handsomer than ever;) the Whitwells, the Lombards & Andrews,—and somewhat, Dr. G. & Karl Hillebrand. The Doctor ◇◇ endeared himself to both of us; he is a wonderfully likeable man, certainly, & a clever withal. He says nothing about anything that isn't worth hearing. We also became intimate with Mrs. G., who showed us her apartment, minutely¦ & separately, lamp in hand & "pride in her port." It is very handsome, certainly, but terrifically cold—The drawing-room is as big as Papanti's hall, & marble-paved; cosy on the December nights! To Hillebrand we took very kindly & have seen him since here. W͟m ~~says~~ saw more of him than I, however; ~~I having~~ ∧as[∧] I was <u>vocalizing</u> all the evening to Mme. Laussot & her mother. What a queer household: it reminds me of Doctor Johnson's.—I have seen no one here as yet, & am disappointed in not being able to report ~~abou~~ ∧from[∧] the Palazzo Odescalchi— I was going there last Sunday, but my cold prevented me. But I shall see Miss Annie in good time & you shall have my impressions. Rome is as yet very empty, & I hear of no one coming to chase away last winter's ghosts. So be it: I prefer the ghosts: I'm afraid even my rides will be ghostly. We have eaten the inevitable dinner at the V. Hoffmanns; but I haven't seen Miss Bessie Ward, who is laid up with the measles. Farewell. I'm glad to hear that Cambridge serves your turn & that you can get up a fond illusion in your studio. But I don't despair of some more Italian days with you, some time. Affectionate regards to your father to whom I intend to write. Ever dear Lizzie most faithfully yours—<u>H James jr</u>

Previous publication: *HJL* 1: 415-19

∿

77.23 occupation • occu= | pation
77.26 ⨍) • [) *overwrites* —]
77.26 ~~it~~ the • [th *overwrites* it]

78.1 ~~have~~ has • [s *overwrites* ve]

78.3 occupied • oc= | cupied

78.4 excellent • ex= | cellent

78.4 comfortable • com= | fortable

78.11 ⊦ ∧ • [∧ *overwrites* .]

78.18 assimilate • assim- | ilate

78.22 ~~A~~ run • [ru *overwrites blotted* A]

79.4 ◆◆ endeared • [en *overwrites illegible letters*]

79.4 himself • him= | self

79.8 ⊦ • [*blotted out*]

79.9-10 drawing- | room • drawing-room

79.12 ~~says~~ saw • [w *overwrites blotted* ys]

79.15 disappointed • dis= | appointed

79.16 report • re= | port

79.27-28 to whom [. . .] H James jr • [*written across the letter's first page*]

∽

79.1 the Huntingtons • Family of Charles Phelps Huntington (1802–68) and Ellen Greenough Huntington. See HJ to AJ, 26, 29 July [1869] (*CLHJ, 1855–1872* 2: 71 and 74n71.17). The Huntington family owned Villa Castellani at Bellosguardo.

79.2 Miss Laura • Laura Huntington (b. 1849), daughter of Charles Phelps Huntington and Ellen Greenough Huntington.

79.2 the Whitwells • See 25, 26 August [1872] to MWJ and Sr. (*CLHJ, 1872–1876* 1: 92–93n88.20).

79.3 Dr. G. • Dr. Ernst Georg Friedrich Gryzanovski.

79.3-4 Karl Hillebrand • German author; see 24 January 1872 to Elizabeth Boott (*CLHJ, 1855–1872* 2: 431 and 435n431.32).

79.7 Mrs. G. • Mrs. Gryzanovski.

79.8 "pride in her port." • Probably an allusion to Oliver Goldsmith's *The Traveller, or a Prospect of Society* (1764), "Pride in their port, defiance in their eye." See also Joseph Rodman Drake's "To a Friend," "Pride in his port, defiance in his eye."

79.10 Papanti's hall • Papanti Dance Academy on 23 Tremont Row, Boston, founded in 1827 by Lorenzo Papanti.

79.13-14 Mme. Laussot & her mother • Jessie Taylor Laussot (1829–

1905) and her mother, Mrs. Taylor. Laussot was a benefactor of Wagner (with whom she was briefly involved in 1850); she later married Karl Hillebrand.

79.18 Miss Annie • Annie Crawford.

HENRY JAMES SR.
22 December 1873
ALS Houghton
bMS Am 1094 (1819)

Rome Dec. 22$^{\underline{d}}$ 73.

Dear Father—

I received a few days since your letter enclosing Scribner's note, and was going to answer it immediately, but I found that Willy was just writing to Alice, & I waited, to let my letter gain more relief. I' am sorry Scribner could not print my notes; but I suppose they have, in fact, a great deal of that sort of thing on hand. I am much obliged to you for having the thing sent you. Since it is written, it seems a pity that it shouldn't be used and something or other got for it. As the <u>Galaxy</u> printed the other, I suppose it would print this, and I beg you therefore to forward it with the note that I enclosed. I don't like the <u>Galaxy's</u> manners & customs, but one can't afford to be too fastidious, and the best thing is to hang on and make the G. do what it will. Scribner in spite of its refusal, seems agreeably hospitable. I h lately sent it a tale in two parts & am just sending it another of the same dimensions. I hope the January <u>Atlantic</u> has managed to squeeze in something of mine. The December number came duly to hand. So much for such matters, for the present.—Willy will have written you about himself, & given you, I hope, as good accounts of his progress as he daily gives me, and as his whole appearance and daily exploits tesst testify to so eloquently. He seems greatly contented with his condition and is sensible of its growing constantly better. He has just been into my Rome,

flushed with health & strength, to see whether I had found any
letters at the bankers this morning & to ask where he should go
to day. ~~Th~~ Seeing me writing, he says—"Give ~~me~~ them my love
and tell them I am doing splendidly." He does in fact, a great

5   deal, ◆◆ ∧and∧ ~~walks~~ climbs Roman staircases & sees sights in a
way most satisfactory to behold. It has been a measurely blessing
that the weather, ever since our arrival in Rome, has been the
finest on the whole, I ever saw;—as brilliant & clear and still as
our finest ~~J~~ Octobers and yet even milder than our mildest

10   autumns. The last day or two has come grey skies & soft sirocco;
but it is still winter with all the edge melted off—still delicious
out of door weather. I am sorry to say that I found nothing at
the Bankers this a.m.—nothing save a very pleasant letter from
Lizzie Boott to Willy, with an enclosure to me, for which when

15   you see her, please thank her. ~~I◆◆~~ Tell her also, if you
remember, that I wrote to her ten days since. (Three or four
days since Willy wrote to Alice.) À propos of messages, here is
one from Mrs. Ward. (We dined there a week ago & are to dine
again on Xmas. day, besides dining to day at the oft-recurring

20   Hoffmann's.) "Give my love to your father & thank him for his
lovely note. But tell him I can't answer it, because my heart is so
full of <u>tendresse</u> for him that if I were to dictate to my <u>dame de
compagnie</u> such a letter as alone I could write, she would be so
shocked that she would leave me. She thinks me very religious &

25   my letter would cast discredit on ~~the~~ my professions." Mrs. W.
and Bessie are up, smiling, from measles, & Sam is unwontedly
genial & friendly.—I am having socially (thank the Lord!) a
much quieter time than last winter. I ◆◆ have paid my respects
to the Storeys and ~~te~~Terrys but don't expect to see them, as

30   formerly, to satiety. The S.'s moreover are to be "quiet" on
account of Mrs. Story's health: <u>i.e</u> receive not on fixed days
twice, a week, but <u>every</u> <u>evening</u>, regular! I have seen (Mother &
Alice will be glad to know) Miss Crawford's young man, who is
youthful & ordinary, but a gentleman, & backed by a very

vigorous old dowager of a mother, with a big jaw, a high forehead & enormous hands. Also by a very charming sister; the most attractive German she I ever met. I ha Miss Crawford told me everything, among others that she was ^to be[^] none too rich. She has received a certain unwonted grace of softness from her engagement. — At this moment, in comes Willy, with Alice's blessed letter of Nov. 30ᵗʰ, describing the party for Wilky & Carrie. I thank her for it much & will answer it soon. It is pleasant to get such accounts of the success of the fête; but we are sorry that Alice didn't touch upon C. personally. The most fearful thing in letters from home is to be told that some one else has told us all about such and such a matter. Father & mother had indeed sketched Carrie ₣ quite vividly but what we hoped was that Alice might have added a few lights to the picture — not shades. I am sorry Wilky's wife is not more interesting to those who are fond of him: but that matters little, so long as practically she prove a help and not a hindrance. I devoutly trust she may, in spite of her diamonds. I had dreamed of offering her the tribute of some modest Roman toy; but the diamonds put me out of countenance, & I think I shall let it slide. — Your news of Bob and his Baby is most exhilarating & father's extracts from B.'s letters most refreshing ^extremely beautiful.[^] I long to see the wondrous child & pull its cheeks and pinch its legs. (I mean the Baby's — not Bob's.) I await with anxiety its baptism. If it should be a Henry no 3., I shall feel queer, so sandwiched between infancy and maturity. You and mother must be in a terrible state to behold it. It's a pity it can't be sent on by express, to spend alternate weeks at Cambridge & at home. — Very sad certainly is poor Emily Atkinson's death — & sadder her poor husband's state of mind. — Alice's letter contained an adjuration to me, from Howells, to print a volume of stories. Good advice, doubtless, but I must wait, to apply it, till I get home, when I shall attempt also to put forth a volume of articles & letters about Europe. I have written enough to make a very good one. I have an increasing feeling that I ought to go home to start myself on a remunerative ๕ perfectly, practical literary basis. I wrote you a couple of mos. ago (I hope you got the letter,) about my remaining abroad for the present—<u>i.e.</u> for

5 six months more. This would ~~pitch~~ ∧bring[∧] me home toward the close of next summer, and I should get a better market for my wares and more definite work to do (especially in the way of reviewing books) than in this far away region. My view of the case is to make a short winter here, go back to Florence soon (in

10 a sanitary way it suits me much better) and remain there till I'm ready to go home. I could spend four or five months in F. at a cost moderate enough not to fore me to draw unendurably on you, while waiting, always, for the realization of my investments; and it would, moreover, break the back of the summer. I don't

15 feel as if I had by any means sucked the European orange dry: but I am content to defer the completion of the process. —
À propos of Howells, tantôt, do you remember hearing him mention receiving from me long since an ~~letter fr~~ ∧article[∧] on <u>Siena</u>? He may not be able to use it in some time; but it is as well

20 to know that it reached him. I don't know that I have any more news for you—or any to add ~~of~~ to what I said about Willy¡ — which on reading it over doesn't seem to me at all too ~~col~~ <u>couleur de rose</u>. Certainly, a man couldn't look better—and what he distinctly says of himself quite justifies his looks. He got

25 some days since a charming letter from John Fiske, whom we may meet later in Florence. Lowell ~~฿s~~ ∧is[∧] there, now I believe, but unlikely to come to Rome. Story, last evening, was in despair at not being able to produce him, in the world. —Willy, who at first, hung fire, over Rome, has now quite ignited and confesses

30 to its sovereign influence. But he enjoys all the mealancholy of antiquity under a constant protest, which pleases me as a symptom of growing optimism ๕ elasticity in his own disposition. His talk, as you may imagine, on all things, is most rich ๕ vivacious. My own more sluggish perceptions can barely ◆

keep pace with it. Ever dear father, with love to all, your loving
<u>H. J. jr.</u>
W encloses a scrap to Alice. Happy Xmas! —

Previous publication: *HJL* 1: 419-23

જ

81.14 immediately • imme= | diately

81.25 refusal • re= | fusal

81.25 ~~h~~ lately • [l *overwrites* h]

81.31 progress • pro= | gress

81.32 ~~tesst~~ testify • [tif *overwrites* s *and blotted* t]

81.33 condition • con= | dition

82.3 ~~Th~~ Seeing • [S *overwrites* Th]

82.3 ~~me~~ them • [them *overwrites* me]

82.6 satisfactory • satis= | factory

82.9 ~~J~~ Octobers • [O *overwrites blotted* J]

82.15 ~~I◊◊◊~~ Tell • [Tell *overwrites* I ◊◊◊]

82.25 ~~the~~ my • [my *overwrites* the]

82.28 ◊◊◊ have • [hav *overwrites illegible letters*]

82.29 ~~te~~Terrys • [T *overwrites* te ; e *inserted*]

82.30 formerly • for= | merly

83.3 ~~I ha~~ Miss • [M *overwrites* I ha]

83.4 <u>everything</u> • <u>every=</u> | <u>thing</u>

83.13 ~~r~~ quite • [q *overwrites* r]

83.22-23 ~~most refreshing~~ ₍ₐ₎extremely beautiful.₍ₐ₎ • ~~most re‡~~ ₍ₐ₎ex-
tremely₍ₐ₎ | ~~freshing~~ ₍ₐ₎beautiful.₍ₐ₎

84.7 especially • espe= | cially

84.21 ~~of~~ to • [to *overwrites blotted* of]

84.21 ¦ • [*blotted out*]

84.22-23 ~~col~~ <u>couleur</u> • [u *overwrites blotted* l]

84.28 produce • pro= | duce

84.30 mealancholy • [*misspelled*]

84.34-85.3 rich ⅌ vivacious [. . .] Happy Xmas! — • [*written across the
letter's first page*]

84.34–85.1 ◇ keep • [k *overwrites illegible letter*]

∾

81.15 Willy was just writing to Alice • WJ to AJ, 17 December 1873 (*CWJ* 4: 471–73).

81.16 my notes • "An Autumn Journey." See HJ to Sr., 26 October [1873] (p. 63).

81.20 the other • "From a Roman Note-Book."

81.25–26 a tale in two parts • "Adina."

81.26–27 another of the same dimensions • "Eugene Pickering," published in the *Atlantic Monthly*. See HJ to Howells, 9 January 1874 (p. 101).

82.16 I wrote to her ten days since • HJ to Lizzie Boott, 10 December [1873] (pp. 77–79).

82.22 tendresse • tenderness.

82.22–23 dame de compagnie • lady's companion.

82.29 the Storeys • The family of William Wetmore Story. In his letters from Rome during the winter and spring of 1873 HJ had explained how regular gatherings at the Storys' apartments in Palazzo Barberini and at the Terrys' home in Palazzo Odescalchi were the two focal points of the social acquaintants he saw there.

82.33 Miss Crawford's young man • Eric von Rabe.

83.21 his Baby • Edward "Ned" Holton James, born 18 November 1873.

83.29 Emily Atkinson's death • Emily Cabot Atkinson Holdredge died on 17 November 1873 after giving birth to Henry Atkinson Holdredge. In his 21 November [1873] letter to HJ and WJ, Sr. wrote that "Emily Atkinson died on Tuesday of scarlet fever having given birth to a child five days previously" (see *CWJ* 4: 457, 458n2).

84.17 tantôt • meanwhile.

84.18–19 ₄article₍ₐ₎ on Siena • "Siena."

84.23 couleur de rose • romanticized.

84.25 John Fiske • Historian and philosopher; see 4, 5 February 1872 to Charles Eliot Norton (*CLHJ, 1855–1872* 2: 441n438.5–6).

85.3 W encloses a scrap to Alice • WJ to AJ, [22 December 1873] (*CWJ* 4: 473–74).

1. William Dean Howells, from a carte de visite, mid-1870s. By permission of the Houghton Library, Harvard University. bMS Am 1784.3 pf [26].

2. Henry James Sr., mid-1870s. By permission of the Houghton Library, Harvard University. pfMS Am 1094 box 3 [75].

3. Garth Wilkinson James in Milwaukee, 1873. By permission of the Houghton Library, Harvard University. pfMS Am 1094 box 3 [73].

4. Mary Holton James, c. 1873. By permission of the Houghton Library, Harvard University. pfMS Am 1094 box 3 [79].

5. Edmund Tweedy, 1882. By permission of the Houghton Library, Harvard University. pfMS Am 1094 box 1 [44].

6. Mary Temple Tweedy, 1882. By permission of the Houghton Library, Harvard University. pfMS Am 1094 box 1 [44].

7. Robertson James, 1873. By permission of the Houghton Library, Harvard University. pfMS Am 1094 box 3 [70].

8. Kursaal, Bad Homburg, c. 1860–90. Library of
Congress, LC-USZ62-109088.

9. Piazza Santa Maria Novella, Florence, c. 1880.
Alinari Archives, Florence.

1874

SAMUEL GRAY WARD
4 January 1874
ALS Houghton
bMS Am 1465 (736)

5

Florence Jan. 4th 1874.

H. de la Ville

Dear Mr. Ward—

 I should have dropped you a word touching my brother's
condition before this if I had not, ever since my arrival, been 10
myself less of a nurse than a subject for nursing—& that, also, he
was already better when I arrived. He was in good medical
hands, his fever was diminishing & is now, says the doctor,
completely broken. He is not even confined to his bed. He has
only to take quinine vigorously for a few days more to be quite 15
himself again. He thanks you & Mrs. Ward warmly for your kind
interest in his situation & wishes to be especially remembered to
you. Leaving Rome unwell I caught, naturally, a violent cold on
the journey, but I have been actively thawing it out and feel
quite in running order again. I confess I should like to use the 20
advantage to run away from Florence, which seems terribly
small beer after Rome; but I shall probably remain here as long
as my brother lingers on, & if that is for some time, I am afraid
that for this winter, I shall not again take the sun on the Pincio.
In that case, ~~hower~~ however, you will be coming up to Florence, 25
with which the springtime will ~~have~~ [∧]be[∧] putting us all into
good humor. With every good wish for your own prosperity &
the friendliest regards to Mrs. Ward & Miss Bessie

 Yours very truly

 <u>Henry James</u> jr 30

May I beg you to give my kind farewells & regrets to the Von
Hoffmans?

No previous publication

99

∾

99.11 subject • sub= | ject

99.14 completely • com= | pletely

99.15 vigorously • vigorous= | ly

99.25 ~~hower~~| however • [ver *overwrites* r,]

∾

99.9 my brother's • WJ.

99.28 Mrs. Ward • Anna Barker Ward.

WILLIAM DEAN HOWELLS

9 January 1874

ALS Houghton

bMS Am 1784 (253), folder 1, letter 5

15

Florence Jan 9ͭͪ 74.

Dear Howells—Your good letter of a month ago reached me
some ten days since, just as I was leaving Rome, ⅋ I have just

20   been reading it over, under these less balmy skies. My brother
had a mild stroke of malaria, in consequence of which the
doctor ordered him away, under penalty of being probably
worse; so he retreated upon Florence as the next best thing, ⅋ I
have followed him to keep him company. From the Cambridge

25   point of view I suppose Florence ought to be a very tolerable <u>pis
aller</u>, even from Rome: but I confess to utter corruption from
that terrible Roman charm, Florence seems to me a vulgar little
village and ~~the~~ life not worth the living away from the Corso
and the Pincio. With time however I don't despair of settling

30   down, doggedly, to my hard ◊ fate. Meanwhile, to beguile the
heavy hours, I turn to conversation with you. Many thanks for
your letter, which was most agreeable. The news of the sale of
the <u>Atlantic</u> set me wondering about you ⅋ I needed ~~my~~ ^your[^]
own word for it that you are contented to soothe my startled

sympathies. All prosperity to the new dispensation and fame and
fortune to both of us. I'm sorry you have to go and watch your
flock across the sands of Dee, as it were, but I suppose there is a
daily excitement in it. I have just received the new Atlantic,
which makes a very handsome appearance. I don't like the new
type as well as the old, which was remarkably pretty; but the
cover and the paper make one feel as if one were ministering to
the highest culture of the ◊◊◊ age. Give Aldrich my compliments
on his novel, which is̶ opens out most agreeably. There is
something in all the regular New England scenes and subjects,
in fiction, which strikes in a chill upon ◊ my soul; but with A., I
imagine, we shall get a great deal of prettiness. But for heaven's
sake, do hurry up with your Venetian priest; he can't help, at the
worst, being prettier than Parson Wibird. Thank you for
speaking well of my ₍∧₎own₍∧₎ tale; it reads agreeably enough,
though I suppose that to many readers, it will seem rather idle.
Let me explain without further delay the nature of the package
which will go with this, in another cover. It is the 1st half of a tale
in two parts, for use at your convenience. I have been reading it
to my brother who pronounces it "quite brilliant." I was on the
point of sending it to Scribner, but your words in deprecation of
this course have made me face about. I am much obliged for the
esteem implied in them; but it remains true, in a general way,
that I can't really get on without extracting tribute from that
source. It's a mere money question. The <u>Atlantic</u> can't publish as
many stories for me as I ought ∂ expect to be writing. At home,
it would, for then I needed scantier revenues. But now, with t̶h̶
all the francs it takes to live in these lovely climes, I need more
strings to my bow and more irons always on the fire. But I
heartily promise you that the <u>Atlantic</u> shall have the best things I
do; ∂ it is because this <u>Eugene</u> <u>Pickering</u> (, being perhaps
unusually happy in subject) is probably better than its next
follower will be, that I now make it over to you. The second half
will follow by the next mail: heaven's blessings attend it. —I

should like to gossip to you about Rome, which in this last
month I have been spending there, laid hold of me again with a
really cruel fascination. But talking is vain, for the thing can't be
described; it must be <u>felt</u>, as a daily, daily blessing. I believe that

5 if I could live there for two or three years I should finally, by
ₐmy₍ₐ₎ doings—my thinkings & feelings & scribblings—
quadruple the circulation of the <u>Atlantic</u>. Don't you want to
pension me, for the purpose?—But you remember it ₐall,₍ₐ₎
more or less, of course. Nay, I thought I did, even from last

10 spring: but it all came rushing back, in a wondrous wave, and
melted me into daily stupefaction. It's either very ~~very~~ ₐgood₍ₐ₎
for one, or very bad: I don't know which. My sternly scientific
brother thinks the latter; & there is indeed much in that view.
Thank your stars at all events, that you are not living in a place

15 whereof the delight demoralizes; and when you are buffeting the
breezes on that Campagna which leads to Riverside, reflect with
complacency that you are not a cringing parasite of the
Beautiful! ~~& I'm sorry~~ ₐFlorence,₍ₐ₎ after Rome, seems tame and
flat and infernally cold. It's cruel after basking for a month on

20 the Pincio to wake up in the region of chapped lips and
chillblains. But happily, even the Florentine winter is short and
before long I hope to be sniffing the vernal breath of the Tuscan
poderes.—I'm very sorry the N. A. R. couldn't give a corner to
my notice of your poems. It was written ₐquite₍ₐ₎ from my

25 tenderer part, & I think would have found assenting readers. But
I trust it may still find them somewhere.—I think I have no news
~~from~~ ₐfor₍ₐ₎ you. In ~~f~~ Rome I saw few people, & here I bid fair to
see no one. No one, that is, save Lowell, who is lingering here
on his way to Rome & with whom I lately passed an evening. He

30 was very jolly, tho' homesick, & taking Europe with the sobriety
of maturity. He says he ₐpositively₍ₐ₎ can't work here—& like
Bryant & May's matches won't go off unless struck on his own
box. He goes home in July, & if that will start him up, let him
hurry.—I'm not surprised at your finding Charles Norton an

impracticable comrade. He seemed to me to be ripening for home discomfort, when I last saw him. But I suppose you are tired of the theme. Whom <u>do</u> you see, then?—You'll see me, I apprehend, before very long: that is I hope to manage to stay abroad another six months ʒ to turn up in Cambridge e toward the close of next summer. I don't know that I shall undertake the winter in Cambridge; but I shall spend the autumn there. We shall have plenty to talk about—the more that in that case, I shall remain in Italy till almost the last.—Farewell! My affectionate regards to your wife ʒ blessings on all your house. Yours, dear H., always

    H. James jr.

Previous publication: *HJL* 1: 423–26; Anesko 92–94

∾

100.23 retreated • re= | treated

100.30 ⬦ fate • [f *overwrites illegible letter*]

100.33 wondering • won= | dering

100.34 contented • con= | tented

101.1 sympathies • sym= | pathies

101.2 fortune • for= | -tune

101.8 ⬦⬦⬦ age • [age *overwrites illegible letters*]

101.8 compliments • com= | pliments

101.9 ̶i̶s̶ opens • [op *overwrites* is]

101.11 ⬦ my • [m *overwrites illegible letter*]

101.23 general • ge= | neral

101.27–28 t̶h̶ all • [a *overwrites* th]

102.8 remember • re= | member

102.15 demoralizes • de= | moralizes

102.15 buffeting • buf= | feting

102.16 reflect • re= | flect

102.20 region • re= | gion

102.21 chillblains • chill= | blains; [*misspelled*]

102.27 ̶r̶ Rome • [R *overwrites* r]

103

103.2 suppose • sup= | pose

103.3 Whom • [m *inserted*]

103.4 apprehend • appre= | hend

103.5 e toward • [t *overwrites* c]

103.10 affectionate • affec= | tionate

∾

100.18 Your good letter of a month ago • Howells to HJ, 5 December 1873 (Anesko 89–92).

100.25–26 pis aller • for lack of anything better.

100.32–33 the sale of the Atlantic • James R. Osgood sold the *Atlantic Monthly* to Hurd and Houghton.

101.3 the sands of Dee • Refers to "The Sands of Dee," the poem by Charles Kingsley (1819–75) in which a young woman is swept off a sandbar by the rising tide, a situation potentially corresponding to Howells's having to cross east Cambridge marshland to reach his new office location. Hurd and Houghton, upon purchasing the *Atlantic Monthly*, moved the magazine's editorial offices to the location of Henry O. Houghton's Riverside Press in Cambridgeport, which lay close to the Charles River and to the east of Harvard Square.

101.8 Give Aldrich my compliments on his novel • Thomas Bailey Aldrich's *Prudence Palfrey* began serialization in the January 1874 issue of the *Atlantic* and ran through June.

101.13 your Venetian priest • Don Ippolito in *A Foregone Conclusion;* see HJ to Howells, 9 September [1873] (p. 46).

101.14 Parson Wibird • Wibird Hawkins, a character in Aldrich's *Prudence Palfrey.*

101.15 my ₐown₍ₐ₎ tale • "The Last of the Valerii."

101.18–19 a tale in two parts • "Eugene Pickering."

101.21–22 your words in deprecation of this course • Howells wrote to HJ on 5 December 1873: "By the way, I hope you wont send any of your stories to Scribner's. We have of course no claim upon you, but we have hitherto been able to print all the stories you have sent, and so it shall be hereafter. Scribner is trying to lure away all our contributors, with the syren song of Doctor Holland, and my professional pride is touched" (Anesko 90).

102.16 Riverside · The Riverside Press in Cambridgeport, east Cambridge.

102.23 poderes · farms.

102.23 N. A. R. · *North American Review.*

102.32 Bryant & May's matches · British safety matches.

ALICE JAMES
13 January 1874
ALS Houghton
bMS Am 1094 (1569)

Florence Jan. 13<u>th</u> 6 74.

Dearest Sister. —I begin this letter with a conscience overloaded with the sense of unrepaid obligations. We have received some four or five blessed letters from home since I last wrote & I can no longer delay thanking you ~~fro~~ ∧for∧ my share of all these. To Rome came duly your lovely letter, to me, of Nov. 30<u>th</u>; & then mothers ∧as lovely∧ of Dec. 8<u>th</u>, also to me; & then Fathers 2 of Dec. 18<u>th</u> & 26<u>th</u> & then yours again to Willy of Dec. 15<u>th</u> So we have had a feast home tidings & domestic affection. Willy has written a "vivacious" acknowledgement of all this, which I am to enclose h[ere]with. [ ] will know already of our being in Florence, and why: but I am afraid that since Willy wrote you, a week ago, we have left you too long without news: but it has been simply because Willy is now so completely restored to exuberant health that there seemed no reason for sending bulletins. But I was forgetting that you don't see him & his <u>belles couleurs</u> as I am doing. His touch of the fever was very mild, & not only didn't keep him in bed, but hardly, during the day kept him in the house. It consisted s of several night=chills which were kept under by quinine & effectually dispelled within half a dozen days after his arriving here. He is now riding on the crest

of the wave as before, & indeed the small ~~dispo~~ disadvantage he
has suffered from his indisposition has served mainly to show
me how strong he has become. I know it was the wise & right
thing in him as a precautionary measure to leave Rome, and the
doctor distinctly prescribed it: but I cant repress a world of
regrets that he should have been uprooted there in the hey-dey
of all the profit he was gathering. If he had staid the fever might
have ~~staid~~ [∧]fizzled[∧] out in a few days; & it might have
developed into a dangerous illness. Of course, having come to R.
for his health he had no business to run the latter risk, &
departure was the only course. But it was hard! He thought 1$^{\underline{st}}$ of
going to Sorrento; but this the doctor vetoed, at this season; ~~I~~
and after a day at Pisa, which didn't seem propitious, he came on
here. I followed him in two or three days, being rather seedy
myself at the moment of his departure. The Roman clime,
however, had nothing to do with my ailment; & I have satisfied
myself fully that the <u>malaria</u> has absolutely no message for my
organism. I had a disagreeable combination of indigestion &
rheumatism, which was a very proper thing to take, in Rome, a
feverish turn: but not the shadow of such a turn did it presume
to take. I was not especially well¦ at R.: but this was owing to my
undertaking to live in lodgings & feed about at trattorias; a
method¦ which, the latter being very poor, is hostile to my
welfare. I am afloat again now, & have good hopes of enjoying a
reasonable share of comfort. But for this I wait for the waning:
of the winter: cold is my cruel enemy. I make no apology for all
this apothecary's gossip; I know your sisterly soul will revel in
it. —I wish I could portray also to your sisterly soul the emotions
of one who is called upon, suddenly, in midwinter, to substitute
Florence the meagre, for Rome the magnificent. I was very
willing to abide quietly in Florence ~~for~~ [∧]in[∧] the autumn &
attempt ~~to~~ [∧]no[∧] higher flight: ~~to~~ [∧]but[∧] to go to Rome and take
root there, and ~~hav◊◊~~ have all the old satisfactions come crowding
back on one & call one's self a drivelling fool to have pretended

to exist without them—ᵭ then to brush away the magic vision
and wake up and see the dirty ice floating down the prosy Arno
and find ~~liif~~ life resolved into a sullen struggle to catch half an
hour's sunshine a day on a little modern quay, half a mile long—
this is a trial to test the most angelic philosophy! Willy, happily,   5
has no regrets to speak of, at finding himself back here and
Florence seems, in one way and another, to offer him as many
aids to improvement as he can make use of. Poor Florence itself,
is as good as it ever was, (bating the cold) and a month hence I
shall be in perfect good humor with it. But Rome changes one's   10
standard ᵭ blows out one's mind to a pitch of presumptuous
desire which its' own magic alone can gratify.—Never, too, had
it seemed so delightful. No too importunate friends—plenty of
time to ~~m~~ one's self—yet, with Wards, Hoffmanns, Storys ᵭc
enough society, the divinest weather that ever adorned the   15
planet, the lovely afternoon walks and drives, ᵭ for me, the
~~especiall~~ especial charm of seeing Willy thriving under it all as if
he were being secretly plied with ~~Dr~~ the ~~exilir~~ ₐex elixir₍ₐ₎ of life.
But I draw the veil, for fear of making you hate me more than
you pity. Florence is very decent ᵭ after two or three ~~mo~~   20
ₐweeks₍ₐ₎ more, when the winter cold begins to depart, will
become all that one needs. We are having really beautiful days,
sharp tho' the air is, and Willy is able to be out ◇ the greater
part of the time. We are living at a very tolerable little hotel—
the Corona d'Italia—where we each get a sunny room ᵭ no end   25
of food and general comfort for ten francs a day. The company
ₐwhich₍ₐ₎ is ~~n~~ scanty and American, is rather dingy and
grotesque, but one can't expect everything for ten francs. Of
outside company we shall enjoy no great store. We see
Gryzanowski frequently, who settles down on acquaintance as   30
less of an intellectual marvel than reported, but ~~into~~ ₐmore ᵭ
more as₍ₐ₎ a gentle ᵭ friendly creature who wears well. Lowell ◇
also I have seen two or three times, very pleasant and friendly ᵭ
lingering here on his way to Rome, where he is afraid of the

Storys introducing him to people   I went last night to a
reception at Mrs. Huntington's, where there were three
people—one of them happily your friend Miss Whitwell, who is
very handsome and a sweet creature. Mrs. Lombard & Fanny are
5   still here, & probably going in a F̶ fortnight to Rome. I shall
s̶o̶r̶r̶y̶ ∧not[∧] be sorry, as I have to call on them from time to
time & conversation languishes terribly. Poor Mrs. L. has been
condemned to lead here for the past two mos. an almost wholly
in=door existence, & though she may not be qualified
10   ∧financially[∧] to dwell in Rome, I don't wonder she wants to get
to a place where she can be out of doors.—It has been on my
conscience, t̶h̶a̶t̶ [∧]by[∧] the way, that mother interpreted in u̶ an
unfavorable sense some remark of mine about the Lombard
toilet. I never dreamed of accusing them of being extravagant;
15   indeed I think they have worn the same gowns ever since I saw
them first. What I meant was that they were also so crisp & clean
& neatly fluted and frilled & <u>coiffées</u> &c. They seem to be
practicing various economical arts in their living & are lodged at
a very cheap place.—But enough of the chapter of Florentine
20   Society. It has a terribly 3ᵈ rate aroma, every way; as if Rome
sifted ∧it[∧] out & skimmed off the cream. Mrs. Huntington's
soirées make Mrs. Storys seem like feasts of Olympus. Apropos
of such matters you will condole with me on my having been
unable before I left Rome to go to Miss Crawford's wedding. I
25   was too unwell b̶e̶f̶o̶r̶e̶ [∧]the[∧] ⬦ morning it came off, & had to
refuse just as I was departing an invitation from Mrs. Ward to a
dinner offered to the Bridesmaids, of whom Bessie W. was one. I
haven't heard a word about the affair since. A day or two before
it, however, I called at the Terrys & found Miss C. and her lover
30   more or less e̶ intertwined in a dusky corner & the trousseau—
very gorgeous dresses &c—tumbled over the drawing room.
(The Wards by the way—especially ⤴ Sam who altogether
redeemed himself, were very kind to Willy & me. Sam hearing I
was unwell before leaving F̶ Rome & unable to see him, wrote me

two notes in <u>one</u> evening!)—T̶ All this seems very frivolous, though, when I reflect upon the sterner stuff with which your ∧late[∧] letters have been filled: poor Wilky's matrimonial lights and shadows (the latter especially) Bob's noble <u>bambino</u>, the death of that poor nice Mrs. Agassiz, the Washburns tribulations, the Norton lamentations &c.—We a̶r̶e̶ take great pleasure in Bob's baby & if we had it here would pull it & pinch it to death between us. The name chosen was certainly a very proper tribute to the Holton acres. Thank father & mother greatly for their letters, & tell father that I ∧have[∧] received gratefully, the ∧January[∧] Atlantic and the late <u>Nations</u>. The <u>Independent</u> critic is an adorable creature & it will be well to cultivate him. I wrote a fortnight since, to keep up your spirits, that if nothing fetches me home sooner, I shall return in August. I am still of the same mind, & desire meantime¦ but to stick here in Florence without budging and work. Rereading my letter, I want to repeat explicitly that Willy is quite as well as I say. There is no exaggeration—not a bit. A. K. I suppose is still in N. Y. Send her my letters occasionally. Farewell sweet child & write again in the same delightful way as soon as you can. With many embraces to each parent & a little <u>tiss</u> to Sister—your loving <u>H James</u> jr

5

10

15

20

No previous publication

&

105.13 6̶ 74 · [7 *overwrites* 6]

105.16 obligations · obliga= | tions

105.23 acknowledgement · acknowledge | ment

105.24 h[ere]with. [   ] · [*ms. damaged*]

105.30 as · [*inserted*]

105.32 s̶ of · [o *overwrites* s]

106.1 d̶i̶s̶p̶o̶ disadvantage · [ad *overwrites* po]

106.5 distinctly · dis= | tinctly

106.6 hey-dey · [*misspelled*]

106.12–13 I̶ and • [nd *overwrites* I]

106.13 propitious • pro= | =pitious

106.18 indigestion • in= | digestion

106.21 ¦ • [*blotted out*]

106.22 trattorias • trat= | torias

106.23 ¦ • [*blotted out*]

106.30 magnificent • magnifi= | cent

106.33 ha̶o̶o̶ have • [v *overwrites blotted illegible letters*]

106.33 satisfactions • satisfac= | tions

107.3 li̶i̶f life • [f *overwrites* if]

107.3 struggle • strug= | gle

107.4 sunshine • sun= | shine

107.8 improvement • im= | provement

107.10 perfect • per= | fect

107.13 delightful • de= | lightful

107.14 m̶ one's • [o *overwrites* m]

107.17 e̶s̶p̶e̶c̶i̶a̶l̶l̶ especial • [l *overwrites* ll]

107.18 D̶r̶ the • [th *overwrites* Dr]

107.18 e̶x̶ elixir • [l *overwrites* x]

107.23 ◌̶ the • [t *overwrites illegible letter*]

107.27 n̶ scanty • [s *overwrites* n]

107.27 American • Ameri= | can

107.32–33 ◌̶ also • [a *overwrites illegible letter*]

108.5 F̶ fortnight • [f *overwrites* F]

108.12 u̶ an • [a *overwrites* u]

108.19 Florentine • Floren= | tine

108.22 Olympus • Olym= | pus

108.25 ◌̶ morning • [m *overwrites illegible letter*]

108.30 e̶ intertwined • [i *overwrites* e]

108.34 r̶ Rome • [R *overwrites* r]

109.1 T̶ All • [A *overwrites* T]

109.6 a̶r̶e̶ take • [tak *overwrites* are]

109.15 ¦ • [*blotted out*]

109.19–22 my letters [. . .] H̲ ̲J̲a̲m̲e̲s̲ jr • [*written across the letter's last page*]

∾

105.19–20 then mothers ∧as lovely[∧] of Dec. 8ͭͪ • MWJ to HJ, 8 December 1873.

105.22–23 Willy has written a "vivacious" acknowledgement • See WJ to family, 11 January 1874 (*CWJ* 4: 476–77).

105.25–26 Willy wrote you, a week ago • See WJ to family, 4 January 1874 (*CWJ* 4: 475–76).

105.29–30 belles couleurs • good color.

107.25 Corona d'Italia • The hotel, which still stands, is located near the Santa Maria Novella train station and is a short walk from the Duomo.

108.2 Mrs. Huntington's • Ellen Greenough Huntington.

108.13–14 some remark of mine about the Lombard toilet • See, for example, 16, [17] November [1873] to parents: "She is socially much appreciated ⅊ moves in a higher circle than at home. Her caps are the prettiest in Europe" (p. 71).

108.17 coiffées • coiffed.

108.24 Miss Crawford's wedding • Annie Crawford married Eric von Rabe.

109.3–4 poor Wilky's matrimonial lights and shadows • The James family had taken a dislike to GWJ's new bride, Caroline Cary. In addition there were other problems: the newlyweds were financially strapped because of GWJ's poor-paying railroad job, and Caroline's father failed to provide the couple a house as promised.

109.4 Bob's noble bambino • Edward Holton James.

109.5 Mrs. Agassiz • Anna Russell Agassiz (1840–73), wife of Alexander Agassiz, a Harvard marine biologist who made his fortune in copper mining.

109.5–6 the Washburns tribulations • Frank Washburn died on 29 December 1873 after suffering from typhoid fever; see WJ to AJ, 23 November 1873 (*CWJ* 4: 460, 461n4). In addition, his wife had recently given birth; see MWJ to HJ, 8 December 1873.

109.6 the Norton lamentations • See 14 January 1874 to Grace Norton in which HJ discusses Charles Eliot Norton "taking America rather hard" (p. 114).

109.9 proper tribute to the Holton acres • RJ and Mary Holton James named their son Edward Holton James after his maternal grandfather (see Maher 121–22).

109.11 the ∧January[∧] Atlantic and the late <u>Nations</u> • "The Last of the Valerii" appeared in the January *Atlantic Monthly*, and "The Autumn in Florence" appeared in the 1 January 1874 *Nation*.

109.11–12 The <u>Independent</u> critic • HJ's "Howells' Poems" had just appeared in the 8 January 1874 *Independent*.

109.13 I wrote a fortnight since • HJ to Sr., 22 December 1873 (pp. 81–85).

GRACE NORTON
14 January 1874
15   ALS Houghton
bMS Am 1094 (898)

Florence Jan. 14<u>th</u> 74.
Dear Grace—You are almost cruelly kind *&* you understand to
20 perfection the art of making a man hang his head and scourge
himself with spiritual stripes. I have in hand both your letters—
the long ago Ashfield one and the one of the other day. I
certainly excercised no ingenuity to not answer the first, but
circumstances were somehow ingenious in my despite *&* I have
25 had these many weeks the daily grievance of seeing myself ɴ
prevented from doing the thing I most wanted to do. But here I
am stranded on a kind of sand bank in the surging sea of life and
labor *&* I am almost selfishly glad that, not having written to you
sooner, I have it as a consolation now. By a sandbank I don't so
30 much mean Florence as my present humor with it. I have been
jerked away from Rome, where I had ex̶ been expecting to spend
the winter just as I was warming to the feast, *&* Florence tho'
very well in itself, doesn't go so far as it might as a substitute for
Rome. It's like having a great plum-pudding set down on the

table before you, & then seeing it whisked away & finding yourself served with wholesome tapioca. My brother, after a month of great enjoyment & prosperity at R., had a stroke of malaria (w̶h̶ happily quite light) which made it necessary for him to depart & I am here charitably to keep him company. I o̶u̶g̶h̶n̶ oughtn't to speak light words of Florence to you, who know it so well & with reason, love it so well: & they are really words from my pen's end simply & not from my heart. I have an inextinguishable relish for Florence & now that I have ∧been[∧] back here a fortnight this early love is beginning to shake off timidly the ponderous shadow of Rome. But the truth is that when one has come to know Rome well & feel its vast & various charm, & depend upon it for one's daily impressions it is h̶a̶ impossible for any other human habitation not to seem pale & tame & meagre. I had never felt its charm more than during this past December. It was empty, the weather was f̶i̶n̶e̶ ̶t̶o̶ ∧divine[∧] & I was getting from my brother's enjoyment an e̶n̶c̶l̶ echo of all my own first impressions. One's wanderings in Rome, during the mild sunny afternoons of midwinter are a most prodigious intellectual dissipation. The whole place keeps playing such everlasting tunes on one's imagination, that it seems, at first, when such a music stops, that one's whole intellectual life h̶a̶d̶ has stopped. But Florence is as good as need be, & I am getting reconciled to it so fast that I already think as well of it again as a quarter of an hour since, when I began my letter. I shall probably be here for several months to come—after which, if present prospects hold, I shall be making you my bow at shady hill.—We are having here a very keen but most brilliant ◇◇ & beautiful winter. The sun is pouring into my little southward facing room as it has done for a fortnight & promises to do for a fortnight more. i̶ In this little room much of my life goes on. We see very few people & I hear of no one who especially inflames my curiosity. In fact I have seen no one but the Lowells who as I suppose you know are lingering here on their way to Rome—but lingering at a rate which makes me doubt of their ever arriving. Lowell is jovial, but as Charles says, most lustily homesick, & profoundly convinced, I think, that the Charles is <u>par excellence</u> the beautiful river of the world. If you haven't drawn this moral

5 from your own European experiences, I imagine you will have several bones to pick with him. — But all this while I am not telling you how much I valued and how much I thanked you for it, as I read it under the trees at Homburg, your truly interesting letter of last July. But I confess that immediately I was not

10 disposed to answer it for I̶ ̶o̶o̶x̶ [∧]the[∧] humor of it was rather sad than joyous & yet I couldn't bear to assume in writing that you were not elastic & serene. In fact I'm not answering it now. But do we, in talk or in writing, ever really answer each other? Each of us says his limited personal say out of the midst of his

15 own circumstances, & the other one clips what satisfaction he can from it. — Just as I was leaving Rome came to me Charles's letter of December fifth for which pray thank him warmly. I gather from it that he is, in vulgar parlance, taking America rather hard & I suppose your feelings & Jane's on the matter

20 resemble his own. But it's not for me to blame him, for I take it hard enough even here in Florence & though I have a vague theory that there is a way of being contented there, I am afraid that when [∧]I[∧] go back I shall need all my ingenuity to put it into practice. What Charles says about our civilization i̶s̶ seems

25 to me perfectly true, but practically I don't feel as if the facts were so melancholy. The great fact for us all there is that relish Europe as we may, we belong much more to that than to this and stand in a much less factitious & artificial relation to it. ̶o̶e̶ I feel forever how Europe keeps holding one at arms length &

30 condemning one to a meagre scraping of the surface. I have been nearly a year in Italy & have hardly spoken to an Italian creature save washerwomen & waiters. This you'll say is my own stupidity; but granting this gladly, it proves that even a creature addicted as much to sentimentalizing as I am over the whole

<u>mise en scène</u> of Italian life, doesn't find an easy initiation into what lies behind it. Some times I am overwhelmed with the pitifulness of this absurd ~~conjooootion~~ ₍ₐ₎want of reci₍ₐ₎procity between Italy ~~oto~~ itself and all my ~~ra~~ rhapsodies about it. There is certainly, however, terribly little doubt that, practically, for those who have been happy in Europe even Cambridge, the Brilliant, is not an easy place to live in. When I saw you in London, plunged up to your necks in that full, rich abundant various London life, I knew that a day of reckoning was coming & I heaved a secret prophetic sigh. I can well understand Charles's saying that the memory of these & kindred things is a perpetual private joy. But pity our poor, bare country & don't revile. England & Italy, with their countless helps to life; and pleasure, are the lands for happiness & self oblivion. It would seem that ₍ₐ₎in₍ₐ₎ our great unendowed, unfurnished, unentertained & unentertaining continent, where we all sit sniffing, as it were, the very earth of our foundations, we ought to have leisure to turn out something handsome from the very heart of simple human nature. — But after I have been at home a couple of months I will tell you what I think. — Meanwhile I aspire to linger on here in Italy & make the most of it — even in poor little overshadowed Florence & in a society limited to waiters & washerwomen. In your letter of last summer you amiably reproach me with not giving you personal tidings & warn me in my letters against mistaking you for the <u>Nation</u>. Heaven forbid! But I have no <u>nouvelles intimes</u> & in this solitary way of life I don't even feel especially like a person. I write more or less in the mornings, walk about in the afternoons & doze over a book in the evenings. You can do as well as that in Cambridge. — I was extremely glad to hear from Lowell that Charles ~~had~~ ₍ₐ₎is₍ₐ₎ to occupy his college chair — glad, I hardly know which most, for the chair & for Charles. Certainly the main condition of a contented life with us, is having some absorbing definite work. I hope Charles will find all kinds of

satisfaction in his. Àpropos of messages pray tell my dear tho' of
late so distant Jane that I did write her in England, last May
(about the 1ˢᵗ.) But I shan't count her the letter. Farewell dear
Grace   My most affectionate regards to your mother, my love to
5   Charles & Jane, my blessings on the children, & my thanks to you
for all your benefits & forbearances. Yours ever, H. James

Previous publication: Lubbock 1: 35–37; *HJL* 1: 426–29

ᴖ

112.25–26 n̶ prevented • [p *overwrites* n]

112.31 e̶x̶ been • [be *overwrites* ex]

113.4 w̶h̶ happily • [ha *overwrites* wh]

113.5 depart • de= | part

113.5–6 o̶u̶g̶h̶n̶ oughtn't • [t *overwrites* n]

113.13–14 h̶a̶ impossible • [im *overwrites* ha]

113.17 e̶n̶c̶l̶ echo • [ch *overwrites* ncl]

113.22–23 h̶a̶d̶ has • [s *overwrites blotted* d]

113.28 ◊◊ & • [& *overwrites illegible letters*]

113.31 i̶ In • [I *overwrites* i]

114.3 convinced • con= | vinced

114.24 i̶s̶ seems • [se *overwrites* is]

114.28–29 ◊e I feel • [I fe *overwrites* ◊e]

114.29 Europe • Eu= | rope

114.30 scraping • scra= | ping

114.32 washerwomen • washer= | women

115.2 overwhelmed • over= | whelmed

115.4 ◊t◊ itself • [i *and* s *overwrite illegible letters*]

115.4 r̶a̶ rhapsodies • [h *overwrites* a]

115.10 understand • under= | stand

115.12 perpetual • per= | petual

115.13 ¦ • [*blotted out*]

115.15 unendowed • un= | endowed

115.20 Meanwhile • Mean= | while

115.26 nouvelles • nou= | velles

115.31 occupy • oc= | cupy

115.34 absorbing • absorb= | ing

116.5 blessings • bles= | sings

∾

114.3 the Charles • Charles River, Boston.

114.16-17 Charles's letter of December fifth • See Charles Eliot Norton to HJ, 5 December 1873.

115.1 mise en scène • spectacle.

115.26 nouvelles intimes • private news.

115.31 Charles [. . .] [ʌ]is[ʌ] to occupy his college chair • Charles Eliot was negotiating with Norton and James Russell Lowell so that Norton could take over from Lowell as Smith Professor of Modern Languages and Belles Lettres. Norton eventually accepted a lectureship on the fine arts and in May 1875 became professor of the history of art (see Turner 254–66).

HENRY JAMES SR. AND MARY WALSH JAMES
5 February [1874]
ALS Houghton
bMS Am 1094 (1820)

Florence ɟ Feb. 5ᵗʰ
        Corona d'Italia

Dearest parents: I can't write much of a letter; but I must scrawl a line or two, to tell you that I am better of the stupid malady from which Willy will have let you know that I have been suffering. Not only better but quite myself again & beginning to eat & sleep & move about like sane mortals. Willy will have told you, in so far as it is was tellable, what was matter the matter with me: but in truth it was a strange & mysterious visitation & it would be hard to say just what it was. It was an affair chiefly of the head which caused me much pain for many days & nights & would not be comforted. Ult Ultimately, however, it was, & since

then I have been steadily mending. I was ten days in bed; on the
eleventh I rose, & after some graceful convalescence in my
room, went out to drive. Yesterday I walked & did wonders, & to
day feel as good as new. In a few days more I shall be leading the
normal life again. I have had every blessing from the 1ˢᵗ. Willy
has simply been a ministering angel, & nursed & tended me
throughout with inexpressible devotion. For 3 nights I had a ~~soft~~
ₐgood₍ₐ₎ Italian matron who hovered about me with the
softness—& the size—of mother, A. Kate, & Alice rolled into
one. I had also a very capable & sagacious little ■ ■ doctor
(Parisianized German) the sensible efficacity of many of whose
remedies was most gratifying. Lastly, this house has been a
paradise to be ill in—from the quiet, the good servants & the
ease of getting things done to suit one.—These little details will
interest your sympathic hearts which I hope have been agitated
by no superfluous anxiety. As I say, my illness was strange &
unnatural & I can't tell you the whence ⋄ or the wherefore of it.
It arose in great manner from my chronic indisposition, & was
complicated by local & temporary influences. But now that I am
better, I flatter myself that it ~~is~~ ₐhas been₍ₐ₎ a sort of crisis which
I shall emerge from into more brilliant heath than ever. Let me
interpose, lest ~~m~~ dear mother should crazily murmur something,
that it had absolutely nothing to do with any use, over use or
abuse of my head. My use of my head has never been such as
would make a baby wink.—But I must=not expatiate: I will write
again in 3 or 4 days. Two blessed letters have come ₍ₐ₎from you₍ₐ₎
these last days: m.'s of Jan 13ᵗʰ & father's yesterday, inclosing
Independant &c, of 18ᵗʰ.—Willy is most vigorous & brilliant. He
seems me <u>entirely</u> the Willy of our youngers ₐyears₍ₐ₎ again—in
looks, spirits, humor & general capacity.—I can't help adding
that I have ₐbeen₍ₐ₎ revising my plans in the watches of the
night, lately, & have pretty well made up my mind to return
home ~~in~~ ₐduring₍ₐ₎ the coming spring. I merely touch on this: I
must keep reasons (which you will guess at, however, &

appreciate) & a decisive statement till I next write, a few days hence. Whether with W. or not would depend on the date of his voyage. Much love dear parents, & regret that you should have ∧been₍∧₎ troubled in thinking of all this. It is over now, for good I trust. Much love to Alice. Pray enclose this letter to A. K.

    Ever your H. J. jr

Previous publication: *HJL* 1: 429–31

∽

117.23 J̶ Feb. • [F *overwrites* J]

117.30 i̶s̶ was • [w *overwrites* is]

117.34 U̶l̶i̶ Ultimately • [t *overwrites* i]

118.7 inexpressible • inexpress- | ible

118.16 superfluous • superflu= | ous

118.17 ◇ or • [o *overwrites illegible letter*]

118.19 complicated • complica= | ted

118.22 m̶ dear • [d *overwrites* m]

118.25 must=not • must= | not

∽

117.26–27 I am better of the stupid malady from which Willy [. . .] • See WJ to MWJ, 26 January 1874 and 28 January 1874 (*CWJ* 4: 480 and 481, respectively).

ANNA HALLOWELL

11 February 1874

ALS Yale, Frederick R. Koch Collection

Beinecke Rare Book and Manuscript Library

GEN MSS 601, Box 22, folder 447; FRKF 138b

    Florence Feb. 11th '74.

My dear Miss Hallowell—

    I heard for the first time last evening of the sorrow that has come to you in the death of our friend. I learned it from Miss

Bancroft, and not a rumor, not an echo of it had reached me
before. Strange to say, I had not even had an intimation of Miss
Loulie's illness, & I can[*not*] think without inexpressi[ ] regret
that she may have wondered that she never received from me
during those many weeks of suffering a line of sympathy or an
offer of assistance. I should s take great satisfaction now in her
having had some last word from me. Bad news travels fast
enough, ⟨⟩ generally, & it is a strange unkind accident that I
should have remained in ignorance of her sad condition.—As for
the event itself, I imagine I agree with most of her friends and
with you, who knew and felt most & could judge best, in feeling,
first and foremost, an irresistible sense of relief. That such a
troubled life should be at rest, that such a weary frame should
cease to suffer, that the end should come at last to so much
pain—all this seems almost to stifle regret, almost to brig[*hten*]
the essential sadne[   ]ath. In Miss Loulie's life there ~~almost~~
always seemed to me something oppressively sad. Fortune had
given her everything so abundantly—friends & freedom & all the
opportunities of injoyment—& yet these brilliante gifts were
darkened always by the shadow of her poor suffering mortality &
turned, as one felt at times, into a mockery.—You have said
something of this kind to yourself, & yet I can easily feel that
now, after you have drawn the first long breath of immediate
relief—you should begin to know how valued a friend you have
lost and what an absorbing companionship has passed out of your
life. You knew from daily observation Miss Loulie's quiet natural
virtues—her sweetness & patience and firmness, her generosity &
tranquil acceptance of better days or worse. I only had a glimpse
of them from time to time, but I often said to myself that it was a
character one might greatly admire if ~~one's might~~ [ʌ]health[ʌ] had
only suffered it to play a more active part & spread its wings a
little. But you knew it better than any one & saw how active it
<u>could</u> be, privately, in spite of illness and depression. All this is
but to offer you a word of cordial sympathy & to hope you are

having perfect rest, without present thoughts for the morrow. I
know, or rather I can't begin to know, I suppose, how weary *&*
exhausted you must be. Remember the most you take will be but
a hundredth part of what our friend would wish you.—It must be
part of it that you don't dream of answering these few lines. Yours   5
ever my dear Miss Hallowell most faithfully—Henry James jr
Should you need to send me a word my address is: Em. Fenzi *&*
Co Florence
I return (probably) to America in a couple of months.

                                                                    10

No previous publication

〜

120.1 rumor • ru= | mor

120.3 can[*not*] • [*ms. damaged;* the bracketed insertion is taken from an
examination of Leon Edel's transcription. It is possible that Edel used a
less damaged manuscript.]

120.3 inexpressi[ ] • [*ms. damaged*]

120.6 s take • [t *overwrites* s]

120.8 ◆◆ generally • [gen *overwrites illegible letters*]; gen= | erally

120.9 condition • con= | =dition

120.15 brig[*hten*] • [*ms. damaged;* the bracketed insertion is taken from
an examination of Leon Edel's transcription. It is possible that Edel used a
less damaged manuscript.]

120.16 sadne[   ]ath • sad= | ne[   ]; [*ms. damaged*]

120.16–17 ~~almost~~ always • [ways *overwrites* m *and blotted* ost]

120.18 everything • every- | thing

120.19 opportunities • opportuni= | ties

120.19 brilliante gifts • [g *overwrites blotted* c]

121.7–9 Should you [. . .] of months. • [*written across the letter's first page*]

121.9 probably • prob= | ably

〜

120.2–3 Miss Loulie's illness • Mary Louisa "Loulie" Shaw died on 31
January 1874 following a long illness. See also HJ to his parents, 15 February [1874] (pp. 123–24).

HENRY JAMES SR. AND MARY WALSH JAMES
15 February [1874]
ALS Houghton
bMS Am 1094 (1821)

5

Florence. Feb. 15$\underline{th}$
Corona d'Italia

Dearest people—I wrote to you a short letter more than a week
ago, & I grasp the pen at present to write a not much longer one,
10   ~~wishl~~ wishing chiefly to let you simply see that I am pursuing the
even tenor of my return to my usual vigor. We have received no
letters since I last wrote save a sweet effusion from Alice to W$\underline{m}$
on her return from N. Y. Otherwise nothing has happened, save,
1$\underline{st}$: (I didn't see this was a half-sheet)—that I have steadily &
15   rapidly getting better, & am now quite (or almost) myself again.
I am a little weak in the legs & the digestion, but in, essentials,
I both look & feel salubrious.—2$\underline{d}$ Willy left me nearly a week
since for Dresden & the North via Venice & Munich. (He wrote
you, I suppose, that the Tweedies had kindly "invited" him to
20   visit them.) I was extremely happy when I at last saw him
starting on this enterprise. I wrote you in my last that he seemed
as well as his old self: but he told me shortly afterwards that he
had not profited especially by these rather dismal 5 6 weeks in
Florence, & ∧what∧ I, who knew of their monotonous tenor had
25   been struck with was that he seemed well & lively in spite of
them. He had first been nursing himself & consoling himself as
he could for the stupid rupture with Rome; & then had to fall to
work to nurse me assiduously for two weeks, nearly. A dull mood
was falling upon him & to plunge again into movement & test his
30   powers & see his beloved Germany was the best thing for him.
Unfortunately after nearly a month of mildness, just now a final
spasm of cold has come on, but the weather is still & brilliant. I
have got two notes from him from Venice, seemingly in the best
spirits, saying he is as well as ever again & "in splendid walking

trim." He is enjoying Venice vastly: I only wish I were with him.
He says he wrote from V. to Alice.—I have little news about
myself. I lead a very quiet life, still somewhat convalescent in
form. I wrote you in my last that I was making up my mind to
return soon (if possible with W^m.) It is about made up, though   5
W.'s last note makes it improbable that I shall sail with him. He
is intensely impatient to get home & back to work; if you were to
see him & hear him, you would understand it, & feel that beyond
a certain point he ∧it[∧] should be impossible to gainsay him.
Now that he has got a great deal of physical benefit every hour   10
that he stays is a vexation to him. ⤳ He talked while here of
going in March (early) & was to decide on arriving at Dresden.
He writes me that he inclines more & more to adhere to this plan
& in that case I shall have to wait. I don't feel equal to getting up
steam & strength for so immediate a start, m nor do I incline to a   15
voyage in that ∧most[∧] sea-sick of months. I am reluctant too to
leaving Europe so abruptly, on all grounds; there is no knowing
when I make get here again & I should like to take a more
contemplative & ceremonious leave. It doesn't seem worthwhile,
on the other hand for W^m, with so strong an inclination   20
otherwise to be waiting on here for me. If therefore he writes
me that he has settled to sail before mid-March, I shall
determine to start a month or six weeks later & make my way
north at my leisure. I shall go to Paris & stop there till it's time
to sail.—You will see that I perfectly perceive the propriety of   25
getting home promptly to heat my literary irons & get myself
financially & reputationally on my legs. I have long tacitly felt it;
but the moment for action has come. But I confess, I shall leave
Europe without alacrity.—I shall write however, on this matter,
more definitely a week hence.—You have heard I suppose ∧of   30
course[∧] of poor Loulie Shaw's death. I have had few details. I
had great regret that strangely, I had no tidings of her painful
illness. We had exchanged letters every 2 or 3 mos. for the past
year & she must have wondered I never sent her a line. But when

she was most ill, I was ill myself. — Of Bessie Ward's
engagement, too, you will have heard. Mrs W. communicated it
in a gracious note. It's called "brilliant." I don't know M. de
Schönberg, but have seen him I think at the Von H.'s. If 'tis the
5   same, he's youthful & not imposing. But perhaps it isn't.
Mrs Lombd. has had also a fever, but is mending fast & looks
well. Farewell, sweet ones. I will write speedily again. — Ever
your H.
Thank Boott for his note & his advice. I will soon answer the 1ˢᵗ
10   but don't expect to act on the last — for many reasons

––––––––

No previous publication

෴

122.10 ~~wishl~~ wishing • [i *overwrites blotted* l]

122.23 especially • espe= | cially

122.23 ~~5~~ 6 • [6 *overwrites* 5]

123.11 ~~—~~ He • [He *overwrites* —]

123.15 ~~m~~ nor • [n *overwrites* m]

123.19 ceremonious • cere= | monious

123.23 determine • deter= | mine

123.26 getting • get= | ting

123.27 financially • fi= | nancially

123.29 ~~ļ~~ • [*blotted out*]

124.3 gracious • gra= | cious

124.9-11 Thank Boott [. . .] ––––––– • [*written across the letter's first*
page]

෴

122.8 I wrote to you a short letter • 5 February [1874] to Sr. and MWJ
(pp. 117-19).

122.19-20 the Tweedies had kindly "invited" him to visit them •
Edmund Tweedy sent WJ 500 francs to pay for his journey to Dresden;
see WJ to MWJ, 28 January 1874 (*CWJ* 4: 481).

123.2 He says he wrote from V. to Alice • WJ to AJ, 13 February 1874 (*CWJ* 4: 484–85).

124.1–2 Bessie Ward's engagement • Bessy Ward would marry Ernst Schönberg.

124.2 Mrs W. • Anna Barker Ward.

124.4 the Von H.'s • The von Hoffmanns.

124.6 Mrs Lombd. • Mrs. Lombard.

HENRY JAMES SR. AND MARY WALSH JAMES   10
27 February [1874]
ALS Houghton
bMS Am 1094 (1822)

Florence Feb. 27ᵗʰ   15
Dearest Parents: I have been waiting for several days for another
letter from you, ~~but no~~ ‸and tho'₍‸₎ none comes, I won't revenge
myself by keeping you waiting longer than this. s Some days
since it is true, arrived a long & charming one from mother
which I immediately despatched off to ~~mother~~ ‸Willy₍‸₎, but I   20
‸have₍‸₎ had a sort of feeling that another was due. In a day or
two, I suppose it will come. Meanwhile I trust you have not been
without k news of us, for Willy must have sent you more than
one characteristic commentary on his late adventures. You know
that he left me nearly three weeks since to join the Tweedies in   25
Dresden whither he journeyed by way of Venice Verona, the
Brenner & Munich. The enterprise has evidently been a great
success, & feeling rather languid when he left Italy he wrote me
that on touching German soil he began to feel "hunky."
Dresden, the Tweedies and Mme. Spangenberg have quite   30
wound him up. Just now, however, I am without news of him, &
am anxiously expecting it. He <u>probably</u> sails for N. Y. by the
Bremen Steamer (the finest of the line he wrote) on March 4ᵗʰ:
but I am yet to learn the certainty. He left here so ‸intensely₍‸₎

impatient to get home ᵭ return to work that I ⊕ shall not be
surprised at his decision, ᵭ I hope you won't be made
uncomfortable by it. He had had a surfeit of holiday ᵭ was
~~uncomfortably~~ uncomfortable at idling ᵭ spending money

5   longer. That he should decide on Bremen is also natural enough
when the alternative was the expensive journey to England. If he
<u>does</u> sail, I wish him every blessing ᵭ comfort. I think you'll find
he's a much better man. I can't imagine all that he has done here
<u>not</u> having infused a great deal of permanent strength. — For

10   myself, Florence still holds me, ᵭ if I can do as I dream, will
hold me for some little time yet. Now that Willy is on the point
of sailing ᵭ I am not hurried to meet him or overtake him, it
seems the best thing I can do to stay on here till the really mild
weather. I desire on no grounds to make for the present the long

15   ᵭ money=using journey to England, ᵭ by lingering awhile here I
think I shall feel strongly disposed to sail by the line of steamers
(extremely good ones) from Leghorn. A south Atlantic passage
in the fine season ought to have no horrors at all ᵭ would have
the advantage of costing at most half of the other enterprise. I

20   feel within the last three weeks so well ᵭ so competent to work
that I desire greatly to make the most of my ~~last~~ ∧being₍∧₎ here
under these improved circumstances, as heaven only knows
when I shall be here again. I am really quite my better self again
ᵭ proving the truth of what I suggested — that I thought my

25   illness was really a contribution to my health. I am active,
cheerful, sound ᵭ altogether on the right track. I have in mind
half a dozen things to write about which will complete the series
of my Italian sketches and make a very pretty book. I don't
know whether my two or three recent letters have led you to

30   expect that I would turn up hand in hand with Willy, but you
will appreciate the merits of the above exposition ᵭ defer for a
while with a good grace the realisation of your caresses — and
mine. ~~caresses~~ I don't think that for the time that I remain I shall
drain you inconveniently. My things seem to be getting better

started at home in publication & I shall be now regularly sending
more. I am just posting three chapters of <u>Florentine Notes</u> to
the <u>Independent</u>: they are too pretty for it, but the note father
enclosed me makes me think it a profitable organ. So here they
go, to be followed by a fourth. —I have no news, save that with   5
the deepening breath of Spring, Florence grows daily more
lovely. I have quite forgotten Rome. I see few people, but
enough. There are some tolerable ones in the house here, & I
make the most of others. Mrs. L. goes ~~to~~ soon to Leghorn, to
complete her convalescence, wh. is slow. I have lately been   10
taking Fanny about to galleries &c: a great charity & no bore,
from her amiability & good taste in the picturesque. I went (tell
A.) to some theatricals arranged by Miss Whitwell. They were
poor save for Edith Andrew, who was brilliant & might make an
actress. Greenoughs, Huntingtons, &c are hospitable.   15
Hillebrand offers me the <u>entrée</u> of <u>any</u> Italian society <u>au
choix</u>. —I trust you are all well & happy & sniffing the spring,
too, in your measure & that I shall soon get a letter to tell me
so. Farewell to all—love to all. Endure my absence yet awhile
longer & I will return to you primed for immortality! Your   20
all-loving H.

Previous publication: *HJL* 1: 431–33

∾

125.18 myself • my= | self

125.18 ~~s~~ Some • [S *overwrites* s]

125.23 ~~k~~ news • [n *overwrites* k]

125.32 expecting • ex= | pecting

126.1 ⬦ shall • [h *overwrites illegible letter*]

126.4 ~~uncomfortably~~ uncomfortable • [e *overwrites blotted* y]; uncom= |
fortable

126.6 alternative • alter= | native

126.33 remain • re= | main

127.12 amiability • amia= | bility

∾

125.30 Mme. Spangenberg • Johanna Spangenberg (d. 1876), ran the Dresden boardinghouse where WJ resided in 1867.

127.2 three chapters of <u>Florentine Notes</u> • Probably the first two articles in the series "Florentine Notes" in the *Independent* and also "A Florentine Garden."

127.5 a fourth • Probably "Florentine Notes," *Independent* 21 May 1874: 1–2.

127.9 Mrs. L. • Mrs. Lombard.

127.13 A. • AJ.

127.16 <u>entrée</u> • <u>entrance</u>.

127.16–17 <u>au choix</u> • <u>at my choice</u>.

15 WILLIAM JAMES
[28 February 1874]
ALS Houghton
bMS Am 1094 (1958)

20   Florence. Saturday.
Dear W<u>m</u>—I received last night your letter from Dresden, ⅋ thanked the Lord for all your comfortable ⅋ agreeable impressions—especially for the good bread ⅋ butter. I hasten to reply however to its ⊕ more practical portions. I am very sorry
25 you should feel bothered ⅋ trammeled in your decision as to sailing by any thoughts of me. I beg you to cast them off instantly ⅋ decide simply w[ ] view to your own com[ ] I hope ∧for your own sake[∧] you don't overwhelmingly incline ~~for your own sake~~ to hurry off by March 4<u>th</u>: ⅋ I should think that
30 to wait along a while ⅋ take a Bremener at your ease would be the ~~bes~~ better thing or best of all take the Russia, Apr. 4<u>th</u>. I should think that with the T.s, in your sympathetic Germany you might spend the interval with out being too much harried by impatience. Or in April couldn't you take a Bremener? I say

this because—(as I was going to hasten to write you even if your letter hadn't come)—even by April 4ᵗʰ I think I should be reluctant to sail fr. England. In fact, to tell the truth, there has been germinating in my mind within the last days ᵈ in proportion as I feel (as I do daily) better ᵈ stronger, a most overwhelming desire to hang on here for three or four months longer. A project ha[ ]w taken shape of remaining till July or August 1ˢᵗ ᵈ sailing from Leghorn for N. Y. The boats are said to be large ᵈ good ₐᵈ cheap₍ₐ₎ and a south Atlantic passage at midsummer oughtn't to be so very trying. The voyage is 18 days, but the first 5 or 6 are taken up with ◇ dawdling about the Mediterranean ᵈ stopping at Naples, Messina ᵈ other picturesque places. But leaving this question quite aside, I feel as I say, a daily-growing desire, now that I'm here to stick here a while longer. I don't know when I may come again; ᵈ when I do it will be in an older ᵈ colder mood, when I shan't relish it as I do now nor get what I can now out of it. Four or five years hence I shall feel like you, about Italy, probably ᵈ be sorry that I didn't squeeze the orange tighter before the sensibilities of youth were quite extinct. I have got back to writing again ᵈ feel as if I might in the next 3 or 4 months do some things (dependent on being here) which are worth doing ᵈ which if I leave I shall never do. In short its' a healthy ᵈ vigorous longing that I feel ᵈ I think I shall entertain it a week (or even a fortnight longer) ᵈ then decide. Now that I feel well enough to write very sufficiently again, I can from appearances keep very reasonably abreast of father's financial advances—the more as my life here won't be dear, ᵈ I shall be spared the expense of the northward journey ᵈc ᵈ the Cunard voyage. I have no desire whatever to "see" Paris or London again at present: on the ~~country~~ ₐcontrary₍ₐ₎ I have an aversion to it ᵈ a desire to concentrate myself on Italy similar to yours to keep yourself down to your own studies. In fine I incline to make up my mind to stay—especially as I shall be pledged to nothing ᵈ can leave ~~when~~ ₐif₍ₐ₎ it became advisable.

The moral of all this is that you are to drop me from your mind & decide upon your own course freely. I only hope you will not have lost a chance you wished to take by waiting to hear from me. But I hope Dresden will hold you a while. When I go up to

5 post this I shall telegraph to you, if the telegr. is not too dear. My intestines remain the same. A week's rain, but to day clear, tho' unsettled. Florence is getting a more vernal atmosphere & under the shadow of departure I am getting to adore it. The days pass easily—tho' a trifle lonelily. I sent you yesterday a letter

10 from M. & one fr. A. K. Thank A. M. much for her's & love to both.

Write as soon again as possible. Yours

<u>H James</u> jr

Previous publication: *CWJ* 1: 224–25

∾

128.23 impressions • impress= | ions

128.24 ⬦ more • [m *overwrites blotted illegible letter*]

128.27 w[ ] • [*ms. damaged;* CWJ *offers* w{ith a}]

128.27 com[ ] • [*ms. damaged;* CWJ *offers* comf{ort.}]

128.31 ~~bes~~ better • [t *overwrites* s]

128.34 impatience • im= | patience

129.6 overwhelming • over= | whelming

129.7 ha[ ]w • [*ms. damaged;* CWJ *offers* ha{s no}w]

129.9 passage • pas= | sage

129.11 ⬦ dawdling • [d *overwrites illegible letter*]

129.12 Messina • Mes= | sina

129.27 financial • finan= | cial

130.9 lonelily • lone= | =lily; [*misspelled*]

130.12–13 Write as soon [. . .] <u>H James</u> jr • [*written across the letter's last page*]

∾

128.16 [28 February 1874] • Anticipating WJ's impending departure on "March 4<u>th</u>," the "Saturday" previous to 4 March 1874 was 28 February.

128.25–26 your decision as to sailing • WJ departed Bremen on the
Mosel on 28 February 1874 (see *CWJ* 1: 223–24n1).

128.32 the T.s • the Tweedies.

130.10 M. • Mother (MWJ).

130.10 A. M. • Aunt Mary Tweedy.

EDITOR OF THE *INDEPENDENT*
1 March 1874
ALS Yale   10
Beinecke Rare Book and Manuscript Library
Za James 11

Florence, March 1ˢᵗ 1874.
Dear Sir: 15
 I enclose you herewith, (in another cover) three chapters of
"Florentine Notes," which I hope the <u>Independent</u> will find
available. I trust also that the <u>quantity</u> will not seem excessive
and the quality entertaining enough to carry it off. In-deed, a
few weeks hence, if these are found useful, I should like to add   20
another chapter or two. I have divided the MS. into what I hope
you will find suitable lengths for three numbers, but you will see
that, if necessary, the subdivisions will permit of a different
arrangement. You will probably agree with me in preferring the
notes to be signed. With the best wishes for the prosperity of   25
my package—
 Yours very truly
 <u>Henry James jr.</u>
To the Editor of the <u>Independent</u>.
 P. S. Please address any word you should need to send me: 30
Care H. James esq. 20 Quincy St. ‸Cambridge, Mass.₍ᴧ₎ A
cheque also should be made out to my father's name.

Previous publication: *HJL* 1: 433

∾

131.16 herewith, • [, *inserted*]

131.18 excessive • ex= | cessive

131.25 prosperity • pros | perity

131.32 father's name. • [*written across the letter's last page*]

∾

131.16–17 three chapters of "Florentine Notes," • "Florentine Notes" (23 April 1874), "Florentine Notes" (30 April 1874), and "A Florentine Garden." See 27 February [1874] to parents (p. 127).

131.21 another chapter or two • "Florentine Notes" (21 May 1874), "Old Italian Art," "Florentine Architecture," "An Italian Convent," and "The Churches of Florence."

HENRY JAMES SR. AND MARY WALSH JAMES
9 March 1874
ALS Houghton
bMS Am 1094 (1823)

20   Florence March 9th '74.
Dearest parents—I received three or four days since your two letters of Feb. 17th, enclosing one from Dr. Holland. Of this anon. Long since, now, you will have been set at rest about my illness and forgotten the solicitude which you so tenderly
25   express. I wrote to you about a week ₍ₐ₎ten days₍ₐ₎ ago—since when, nothing of moment—save the news of W.'s departure— has stirred the tranquil current of my days. I'm afraid <u>his</u> current has not been very tranquil: but by this time it is near floating him ashore. Tell him when he arrives that I rejoiced in his letter
30   from Southampton & am truly happy that his last impressions of this decaying continent were so pleasant. I live on here safely, soundly and contentedly, liking Florence, Italy and Europe better every day, though I suppose it is disagreeable to you to

hear it. I see few people, but I distribute my small social resources as economically as possible over the days and weeks and manage generally to have a chance for company at hand when I need it. Principally, I am extremely well, and contentissimo with my bodily state. I'm much better since my fever than before, and think—if Willy will excuse my saying so—that it was quite worth having. The spring is coming on bravely and the lights and shadows on the mountains and the river, the sunsets and the moonlights, the walks in the dim palace-bordered streets of which ∧whose[∧] shadows are is now losing its winter chill—are all quite worth enjoying. These are my principal dissipations & distractions. I have also, since a few days, the diversion of attempting colloquial Italian, evenings, with a very nice young fellow whom Hillebrand procured, a Roman, a gentleman, though needy, and a very pretty talker. I expect in a few weeks to rattle the divine tongue like an angel, if we don't exhaust our list of topics en attendant. This is the danger.—Tell Willy his beloved Corona d'Italia is odiously full of new-comers, & that I am sandwiched between Miss Heidekoper and Mrs. Mallet—la bella e la brutta. Miss H. is charming, on closer acquaintance & her mother is forever talking of him. I also ∧called[∧] lately on the Whitwells & Miss W. was lovely as usual. I went 'tother night to an entertainment at the Lorrimer Grahams—the American consulate—and saw some gorgeous but uninteresting tableaux. This is all the gossip I can think of (—except that I enclose a card which will amuse Alice.)—I was of course much gratified by Dr. Holland's letter, & have been revolving it these last days. I am well disposed to ace accept his offer, but there is an obstacle. I feel myself under a tacit pledge to offer first to the Atlantic any serial novel I should now write—& should feel ∧consider[∧] my self unfriendly to Howells if I made a bargain with Scribner without speaking first to him. I am pretty sure the Atlantic would like equally well with

Scribner to have my story & I should prefer its appearing there.
It must depend upon the money question, however, entirely.
Which ever will pay best shall have the story, & if the Atlantic
will pay as much as the other, I ought, properly, to take up with
5   it. I have a vague notion that Scribner would ⬦ be more liberal &
perhaps pay down the money or a good part of it on receipt of
the MS. As for the "honorarium", I don't know what to ask at all
and wish I had someone to consult. I don't know, either, what to
write immediately to Dr. H. I will enclose here with a note to
10 him, however, to f be forwarded by you or not, according to the
answer you receive to a note I mean also to write to Howells,
and in which I shall request him to communicate with you. — I
have decided to ask $1,200 for my story. I thought at first of
asking but a thousand; but Dr. H. evidently wants it and why not
15 profit by such reputation as one has laboriously acquired? 1200 $
makes a hundred for each part, which is what I could earn by
writing 12 short stories. — One thing I must say, though, that if I
begin it within a month, I shall, of course, while occupied upon
it, be not be sending home many short things, and you may have
20 to wait, for partial reimbursement, at least, till the autumn. But
I shall certainly turn out several sketches of places and things
here which my heart is set upon noticing before I go ₍∧₎away₍∧₎ to
complete my little bundle of Italian articles, and make a good
volume. Please look out at the Independent. I have sent them a
25 review of Mérimée's Letters — besides the 3 Florentine chapters
I mentioned in my last, part of a series of five. Let me say finally
that father of ₍∧₎when₍∧₎ he gets answers from Scribner & the
Atlantic had better accept 1000$ rather than let the thing fall.
The writing and publishing a novel is almost as desirable a thing
30 for me as the getting a large sum for it. The money=making can
come afterwards. As I say, if the Atlantic wants the thing & will
give an equal sum for it, it must properly have it. I leave my
letter unsealed. — No news since yesterday, save a letter this a.m
fr. Aunt Mary, speaking of Willy's getting off. She wants to

come to Italy for the spring but the ~~ha~~ expaserating Tweedy
don't see it. She also quotes from a letter from Bessie Ward, wh.
I inclose for Alice.—Farewell, dearest parents, sister, brother
and aunt, if she is in Cambridge. Think of me as very
prosperous. Tell W$^{\underline{m}}$ I saw Gryzski. last night, who sent him his   5
love and said he was delighted with his book. I am to dine to day
at Hillebrand between two ladies, one stone=deaf ♂ the other
wooden-deaf. Tell Mr. Boott I wrote to him 3 days since. Your
devoted—

 <u>H. James jr</u>   10
I send <u>2</u> notes to Dr. H., to be ~~send~~ sent; one or the other after
f F. has seen Howells. The letter from A. M. is not detatchable.
Please send a copy of <u>Scribner</u>.

Previous publication: *HJL* 1: 434–36

 ∾

 132.22 enclosing • en= | closing

 132.24 solicitude • soli= | citude

 133.9 moonlights • moon= | lights

 133.10 shadows • [*blotted out*]

 133.10 ~~are~~ is • [is *overwrites* are]

 133.11 enjoying • en= | =joying

 133.12 dissipations • dissipa= | tions

 133.13 colloquial • col= | loquial

 133.13 ¦ • [*blotted out*]

 133.14 procured • pro= | cured

 133.19 between • be= | tween

 133.23 entertainment • en= | tertainment

 133.27 Holland's • Hol= | land's

 133.28-29 ~~ace~~ accept • [c *overwrites* ce]

 133.31 my self • my | self

 134.5 ◇ be • [b *overwrites illegible letter*]

 134.10 f be • [b *overwrites blotted* f]

 134.19 ~~be~~ not • [no *overwrites* be]

134.20 reimbursement • reim= | bursement

135.1 ~~ha~~ expaserating • [ex *overwrites* ha]; expas= | erating; [*misspelled*]

135.7 Hillebrand • Hille= | brand

135.11 ~~send~~ sent • [t *overwrites blotted* d]

135.11–13 I send 2 [. . .] copy of Scribner. • [*written across the letter's first page*]

135.12 f F • [F *overwrites* f]

135.12 detatchable • [*misspelled*]

&

132.22 Dr. Holland • Dr. Josiah Gilbert Holland (1819–81), editor and one-third owner of *Scribner's Monthly* and author of such books as *Bittersweet* (1858) and *Sevenoaks: A Story of Today* (1875).

132.25 I wrote to you about [. . .] ₐten daysₐ ago • See 27 February [1874] to parents (pp. 125–27).

133.5 contentissimo • most happy.

133.17 en attendant • in the meanwhile.

133.20 la bella e la brutta • the beauty and the beast.

133.23–24 the Lorrimer Grahams • James Lorimer Graham Jr. (1835–76) and his wife, Josephine Garner Graham (1837–92); see HJ to AJ, 6, [8] October [1869] (*CLHJ, 1855–1872* 2: 133n130.5–6).

133.25 tableaux • Either paintings or tableaux vivants.

133.29–31 I feel myself under a tacit pledge to offer first to the Atlantic any serial novel I should now write • The *Atlantic* published *Roderick Hudson* in its January through December 1875 issues.

134.11 a note I mean also to write to Howells • See 10 March [1874] to Howells (p. 137).

134.24–25 a review of Mérimée's Letters • "The Letters of Prosper Mérimée," HJ's review of Mérimée's *Lettres à une inconnue* (1874).

134.25–26 the 3 Florentine chapters [. . .], part of a series of five • See 27 February [1874] to parents (p. 127).

134.34 Willy's getting off • See [28 February 1874] to WJ (pp. 128–30).

135.5 Gryzski. • Gryzanowski.

135.12 A. M. • Aunt Mary Tweedy.

WILLIAM DEAN HOWELLS
10 March [1874]
ALS Houghton
bMS Am 1784 (253), folder 1, letter 6

Florence March 10<u>th</u>

Dear Howells—

    This is grim business, and yet I must be brief. Your dear
friend Dr. Holland has just proposed to me to write a novel for   10
<u>Scribner</u>, beginning in November next. To write a novel I incline
& have been long inclining: but I feel as if there were a definite
understanding between us that if I do so, the <u>Atlantic</u> should
have the offer of it. I have therefore sent through my father a
refusal to Dr. H., to be retained or forwarded according to your   15
response. Will the <u>Atlantic</u> have my novel, when written?
Dr. H.'s offer is a comfortable one—the novel accepted at rate
(that is if terms agree,) and to begin, as I say, in November & last
till the November following He asks me to name terms, and I
should name $1200. If the Atlantic desires a story for the year   20
and will give as much I of course embrace in preference the
Atlantic. Sentimentally I should prefer the <u>A.</u>; but as things
stand [w]ith me, I have no right to let it be anything but a pure
money question. Will you, when you have weighed the matter,
send me a line through my father or better, perhaps,   25
communicate with him <u>viva</u> <u>voce</u>?—This is not a love=letter &
I won't gossip. I expect to be in Europe &, I hope, in Italy, till
midsummer. I sent you lately, at three or four weeks' interval,
the two parts of a tale. You have them, I hope? Farewell, with
all tender wishes to your person & household. Yours ever,   30
<u>H James jr</u>

Previous publication: *HJL* 1: 436–37; *SL* 2: 116; Anesko 94–95

∿

137.11 November • Novem= | ber

137.22 Sentimentally • Senti= | mentally

137.23 [w]ith • [*ms. damaged; the bracketed insertion is taken from an ex-amination of* HJL. *It is possible that Edel used the undamaged manuscript.*]

137.26 communicate • com= | municate

∿

137.26 <u>viva</u> <u>voce</u> • <u>in person</u>.

137.29 two parts of a tale • "Eugene Pickering."

WILLIAM JAMES

22 March [1874]

ALS Houghton

bMS Am 1094 (1959)

Florence, Corona d'Italia:

March 22<u>d</u>

Dearest W<u>m</u>: After looking vainly for many days I at last discovered in the <u>Times</u> a couple of days since the arrival of your ship on the 13<u>th</u> I shudder at the thought of your 14 day passage, which implies that you were terribly tossed and afflicted. You wrote me a line, I trust, as soon as you landed, for I am anxiously expecting one. Till ~~the~~ [∧]I[∧] receive it, <u>taceo</u> & don't indulge in vain conjectures as to what you have endured & survived. Your at home and lapped in familiar joys, that at least is secure. I suppose Florence & Rome are already beginning to seem dim & visionary. Solid & sensible I hope will prove, however, such increase of strength as you have gained from them! You must have found at home letters with news me later than you had got before sailing: for you missed at least <u>one</u> from me, sent at the last to M<u>me</u> Spangenberg. I got from A. & M. T. after you left Dresden a letter speaking of you as seeming to be below par while there: but as this was opposite to the impression

I received from your own letters, I try to explain it away by her
somewhat crooked way of seeing things. She spoke at any rate
as if they had greatly enjoyed your visit.—I wrote home some
ten days since, in a manner which I trust will give general
satisfaction. Father will take charge of my notes to Dr. Holland,
& send one or the other according to the news he gets from
Howells to whom he wrote by the same mail. If the thing falls
thro' on the question of payment, it little matters, as I can make
quite as much in the same time by short pieces.—You will infer
from this remark that I am doing well in health & work. I am in
truth better every day—decidedly better than before my illness
& ‸even₍ₐ₎ than I was while you were with me here, before my
visit to Rome. My fever has really done me a service & been ꜰ a
blessing in disguise.—I am here at the Corona still, in as you
see, in your old room, & sandwiched daily between the
Heidekopers & Mrs. Mallet. My relations with the former are
genial & active: but I shall soon change my residence probably,
somehow. I lead the same quiet life & have made no new
acquaintances save that of a young Roman who comes 3 or 4
times a week to ⬦ act as a crutch to my hobbling Italian. He's a
bravo giovane (recommended by a friend of Hillebrand's) & I
think I shall learn something. In another way there is a very
good fellow here with his sister, by name Bancroft of Boston,
with whom I often walk & talk. He is indeed quite a resource.
Lizzie Boott will tell you about him, tho' probably,
remembering Rome, she will think that if I he is my mainstay,
Florence has indeed brought me low. I see Hillebrand once in a
while, & dined there lately, very pleasantly: out one of those
polyglot dinners which excite the imagination. Gryzanowski
I don't often see. I'm afraid I offended him the other night
(from hs his manner) by offering him payment for those visits
he made me. I insisted on his taking it—perhaps infelicitously.
À propos—I attribute great benefit to my ‸Davison's₍ₐ₎ remedy
Calcaria carbonica which I have been taking regularly since you

left.—Florence is of course lovely & the Spring fairly on us. The
air is more relaxing than I strictly care for; but I think I shall
do very well. Mrs. Huntington gave 'tother night a large party
(I didn't get home till 3) at which I talked long with Miss
5   Whitwell—not about you. Farewell, dear Bro. I have ordered the
trunk to be sent from L. & by Boston Curnarder & you will
receive the Bill of Lading & the key—by my sending which latter
to L. the box will go much more cheaply. Love—love love to all
& all blessings on Yourself. Your's ever <u>H. J jr</u>

Previous publication: *CWJ* 1: 227–29

ॐ

138.32 ⋄ M. • [M *overwrites illegible letter*]

139.13 ꜰ a • [a *overwrites* r]

139.14 ɪɴ as • [a *overwrites* in]

139.20 ⋄ act • [a *overwrites illegible letter*]

139.21 Hillebrand's • Hille= | brand's

139.26 remembering • remem= | bering

139.30 offended • offend= | ed

139.31 ʜꜱ his • [is *overwrites* s]

139.31 payment • pay= | ment

140.3 Huntington • Hunting= | ton

140.4 didn't • did= | n't

140.6–9 Curnarder [. . .] ever <u>H. J jr</u> • [*written across the letter's first
page*]

ॐ

138.24 <u>taceo</u> • <u>I keep quiet.</u>

138.31–32 <u>one</u> from me • Probably HJ to WJ, [28 February 1874]
(pp. 128–30).

138.32 A. ⋄ M. T. • Aunt Mary Tweedy.

139.3–4 I wrote home some ten days since • See 9 March 1874 to parents (pp. 132–35).

139.16 Heidekopers & Mrs. Mallet • Also referred to in HJ to parents,
9 March 1874 (p. 133).

139.21 bravo giovane · nice young fellow.

139.22–23 a very good fellow here with his sister, by name Bancroft ·
Possibly John Chandler Bancroft; see HJ to Elizabeth Boott, 7, 8 April
[1874], pp. 146–47, and Elizabeth Boott to HJ, 13 June 1874.

139.34 Calcaria carbonica · carbonate of lime, a homeopathic remedy
frequently used to treat skin disorders and anxiety and to improve digestion.

MARY WALSH JAMES
4 April [1874]
ALS Houghton
bMS Am 1094 (1824)

Leghorn, Villa Franco   15
    April 4ᵗʰ
Dearest mother—Your letter of March 17ᵗʰ has just come,
together with Willy's from Sandy Hook. I had been impatiently
waiting for both, & am thankful for them, tho' they do represent
Wᵐ as more tired & seedy with his journey than I hoped he   20
would be. His voyage per se, however, seems ₍ₐ₎to have been₍ₐ₎
better than I feared, as owing to the bad things that took place at
sea while he was out, I was prepared for all sorts of horrors. But
I congratulate him on their being behind him, great or small, &
not in prospect as they are for me. You see⋄ I am being reminded 25
of the charms of the brine—having taken up my abode for a few
days on these Mediterranean shores. I left Florence 4 days since
for a change of air & a little tour of observation through Pisa,
Lucca & Pistoia, of which you shall have news in detail. I came
hither 1ˢᵗ, partly to inhale the sea=breeze, (which the vernal   30
atmosphere of Florence caused me rather to hanker after,) &
partly to do a friendly turn to the poor Lombards, who have
been here in convalescence for a month. I find a very

comfortable Scotch pension kept in ~~an~~ a roomy old Italian villa,
& as one dwells here for 7 frs. a day & the Mediterranean blasts
are most invigorating I shall probably linger a couple of days
longer & not return to F. for a week. I write this in a vast old
5   Italian parlor out of which, from under blue <u>portières</u>, our
apartments respectively open. Mrs L. & Fanny are sitting by
with embroidery & with Mrs. Carroll, (wife of the Boston
ex=schoolmaster,) a much more agreeable person than her
husband. Mrs. L. is much better, but feeble, fluctuating &
10 without stamina, & just now much depressed by news of the
probable death of her friend Augustus Greenwood. She sends
you a great deal of love. Leghorn, as I say, is bracing, & the
journey is worth making only to see the Mediterranean blue;
ₐbut₍ₐ₎ for an Italian town its' strangely blank, modern & stupid.
15 But I shall rummage among plenty of rubbish at Pisa & Lucca.
The L.'s go back shortly to Florence, & thence to Venice for a
month. — Of my existence at Florence ~~before~~ ₐsince₍ₐ₎ I last
wrote there is nothing especial to tell, except that the weather
was lovely (though a trifle over=soft,) & that my good health
20 continues & increases in the most satisfactory manner. On my
return I shall change my residence, but I don't know whither.
Write ~~all~~ always care of <u>Fenzi</u>. Shortly before I left the Florence
hotel appeared Miss <u>Kellogg</u>, with a group of ~~Pitmn~~ <u>Pitmans</u>. I
had various interviews with her, & she seemed well, much-
25 enjoying, & disposed to remain abroad indefinitely. Tell W. that
<u>Fiske</u> spent ten days in Florence at the Grahams, but I didn't
hear of it till he was gone. I have seen no new people. — I
received by the way ~~th~~ Father's note with the London
commissions; it somewhat bewildered me at first, & I hope the
30 non=execution of them won't too much disappoint you. Of
course I can do anything later, as the notion of sailing from
Leghorn has received a blow from being confronted with
various Mediterranean steamers in the harbor here. — I'm glad,
dearest mammy, you forgive me so sweetly for wanting to stay

out over the summer. It will be worth much to me every way *&* I
forsee that I shall return to you in robustious health; for there is
no weak optimism; in my saying I am much better since my
fever. — I was interested in your mention of Loulie Shaw's
funeral, but sorry ◊◊◊ she was not able to leave f ˄more[˄] money   5
to Anna H. Just before I left Florence came a letter to W. from
Wilky, which I was very glad to read. I would send it back, but
that I inadvertently left it with my Florence luggage. He tells of
his projected withdrawal from the R.R. *&* going into the
enterprise for working iron. I had no idea he intended this; but   10
you of course by this time know all about it, *&* about the wisdom
of it. May it prosper! — I suppose ~~you~~ ˄father[˄] some time since
rec'd. my answer to Dr. ~~Ho~~ Holland's proposal, *&* my offer to
Howells. I am impatient to hear the consequences, so that, if
they are favorable, I may begin my work. I hope the thing has   15
given Father small trouble. — Farewell, sweet mother I have no
further personal news. W. I hope will write me the 1ˢᵗ letter he
<u>can</u> write, *&* will ˄have[˄] ~~find~~ found himself speedily as well as
he seemed in Rome. Much love to him *&* to all. My next shall be
to sister. A. K. seems still away, but I hope you often enclose my   20
letters to her. Addio: Your loving <u>H.</u>

No previous publication

&

141.18 together • to= | gether
141.24 congratulate • con= | gratulate
141.25 prospect • pros= | pect
142.1   pension • pen= | sion
142.1   ~~an~~ a • [a *overwrites* an]
142.5   <u>portières</u> • <u>por</u>= | <u>tières</u>
142.9   fluctuating • fluc= | tuating
142.11 Greenwood • Green= | wood
142.15 rummage • rum | mage
142.22 ~~all~~ always • [l *overwrites* ll]

142.23 ~~Pitmn~~ <u>Pitmans</u> • [a *overwrites* n]

142.24–25 much- | enjoying • much-enjoying

142.25 disposed • dis= | posed

142.26 didn't • did= | n't

142.28 ~~th~~ Father's • [F *overwrites* th]

143.3 ⌐ • [*blotted out*]

143.5 ◆◆◆ she • [she *overwrites illegible letters*]

143.12 prosper • pros= | per

143.13 ~~Ho~~ Holland's • [o *overwrites illegible letter*]

143.18 ~~find~~ found • [oun *overwrites* in]

143.20–21 I hope [. . .] loving <u>H.</u> • [*written across the letter's first page*]

∾

141.17 Your letter of March 17<u>th</u> • MWJ to HJ.

142.5 <u>portières</u> • <u>door curtains</u>.

142.7 Mrs. Carroll, (wife of the Boston ex=schoolmaster,) • Mrs. Charles Carroll. Her husband (born c. 1832) worked at the Young Ladies School and the English High School.

142.11 Augustus Greenwood • Augustus Goodwin Greenwood (1832–74), Harvard graduate and Boston lawyer.

142.23 Miss <u>Kellogg</u> • Julia Antoinette Kellogg (1830–1914), disciple of Swedenborg and Sr. and author of *The Philosophy of Henry James* (1883). Kellogg crossed the Atlantic on the *Spain* with WJ in October 1873, when WJ traveled from Cambridge to meet HJ in Florence.

142.23 with a group of [. . .] <u>Pitmans</u> • Probably Newport newspaper owner and publisher Theophilus Topham Pitman (1842–1930), his wife, author Marie J. Pitman (1850–88), who wrote under the pseudonym Margery Deane, and T. T. Pitman's sister Harriet. See *CWJ* 4: 473n5.

142.26 <u>Fiske</u> • <u>John Fiske</u>.

142.26 the Grahams • James Lorimer Graham and Josephine A. Garner Graham.

143.6 Anna H. • Anna Hallowell.

143.13–14 my answer to Dr. [. . .] Holland's proposal, ᵭ my offer to Howells • See 9 March 1874 to parents and 10 March [1874] to Howells (pp. 132–35, 137, respectively).

ELIZABETH BOOTT
7, 8 April [1874]
ALS Houghton
bMS Am 1094 (512)

5

Leghorn April 7<u>th</u>
  <u>Villa Franco</u>
Dear Lizzie—Certainly, I am rarely in your debt. Your two
lovely letters have been received & treasured: the 1<u>st</u>, some two
months since, the second, three weeks. Thank you for your   10
generous friendliness. Here I am at Leghorn for a few days—a
place which, as you know, makes one turn instinctively to one's
most effective sources of consolation. I didn't suppose that Italy
could produce anything so bare & bald & ~~dooo~~ ^blank.[^] It's
more American than America. True, one has the Mediterranean,   15
& I have been strolling beside it daily since my arrival. But to day
I am off to Florence again <u>via</u> Pisa & Lucca. I have been here
with Mrs. Lombard & her daughter, convalescents from
Florence, also about to return in improved health.—You will
have heard about me to your fill and beyond, from my brother   20
W<u>m</u>, news of whose arrival I have just received. He will have
gratified you with such small scraps of information about my
modest personality as your friendliness may have craved & I
fancy him talking so much about Florence & Rome & telling you
so many things, that little seems left for me to gossip about.   25
After he left me at the end of February I felt rather lonely &
disconsolate: so to console myself, I took to caring for Florence
quite violently again (it having been sadly eclipsed in my
affections by Rome.) I cared more & more as the weeks went on
& the spring began to lavish its loveliness on mountains & rivers 30
& bridges & haling days & lovely Moonlit nights. Now I feel
extremely at home in Florence & immensely satisfied with it, & if
I were not going to America in August, should certainly come
back there early in the autumn for another winter. What shall I

say? I adore it. I have been having, however, a very tame & sterile
winter socially & have made no new or valuable acquaintances.
The other day your friend Mrs. Perkins gave an afternoon party
at Bellosguardo, which I attended, to my intense rapture. It was
an enchanting day, the views from the windows were lovely, the
rooms were perfumed with a wealth of spring flowers — & the
whole thing gave me a sense that it might yet be strangely
pleasant to live in that grave, picturesque old house. I have a
vague foreboding that I shall, some day. The P.'s loggia on the
court, (all buried for the occasion, in masses of violets &
anemones,) their trrace beyond &c, seemed wonderfully
charming things. — About the same time I went out to the Halls',
where I had a lovely visit, & lost my heart both to the villa & its
mistress. Mrs. Hall is the sweetest of women, & deserving all I
remember you & your father said of her. The villa is charming,
but I really think I should prefer to live at humbler Bellosguardo.
It's much the more beautiful side of Florence, for views &c. Your
friend Miss Constance was free, frank & handsome, as before.
The eldest sister, who, I am told is handsomer was absent. The
house itself I thought peculiarly delightful, in its simple,
picturesque spaciousness. — Your cousins of the ~~Villa~~ Villino
della Torre I have not infrequently seen and always with
pleasure. They began the winter, I believe with hating Florence
(after Rome) but now delight in it. Miss F. rides upon the wave
of pleasure with a charming irresponsibility. They too gave the
other day a charming afternoon party. — Do you x x x x x x x <u>Pisa,</u>
<u>8th</u> I forget what I was going to ask you: I was interrupted
yesterday at Leghorn, & resume this in the shadow of the leaning
tower. — I think I must have been going to say — Do you
remember the <u>Bancrofts</u>, of Roman fame? I ~~have~~ ∧saw[∧] a good
deal of them for 6 weeks, being in the same house. Your
ci=devant cavalier is really a capital little fellow; I had him often
for a companion in those long walks in which I have tried to
quench the haunting memory of Roman rides. I never told him

that he used only to be taken to ride with you when I couldn't
go. But he is such a truly amiable little fellow that he would have
forgiven me — & you. They have gone to Dresden, each to enter a
family & study German. — To finish with Florentine people, I
often saw the Huntingtons; Mrs. H. being very motherly &
friendly. Miss Laura continues beautiful & buxom, & the
handsome Henry is the biggest man about town in Florence.
With Dr. Gryzanowski my relations are most pleasant, though I
don't see him with the frequency of intimacy. He is the best of
men; — but this you know. I have seen a good deal of Hillebrand
& Mme Laussot, whose house is a rather pleasant one for evening
calls. I like Hillebrand very well personally, but I detest his
opinions; Bismarkism being his 1st article of faith. He knows
every one & has offered to introduce ∧me[∧] to all Florence —
from the Marquis Gino Capponi down. But as yet, I have made
little use of him. — I would fain tell you something about Rome,
this winter; but I know nothing & haven't heard a syllable of
Roman gossip. I know nothing of Mme v. Rabe's fate since her
marriage, nor of Miss Mimolis celibatarian adventures. Nor
have I heard anything especially to the point about Miss Bessie
Ward's innamorato, except that he has been dangerously ill & ⋄ is
now recovering. It is not, I believe, financially, an at all splendid
match. — Of ⋄ last winter's Romans you will have heard as much
as I. From Mrs. W. I have had scant tidings in many months; but
hear vaguely that, with characteristic energy, she has been
~~extracting~~ ∧compelling[∧] Philadelfia in some way or other to
amuse her. Have you seen poor Mrs. Sumner=Mason? To her, at
least, Sumner's death must have brought some relief of spirit. I
hear occasionally from Miss Bartlett who has been wintering at
Pau in a fury of disgust with the place, the climate the people &
everything. She goes home for the summer. — What shall I tell
you of Pisa? Here I sit in a huge old picturesque bedroom
overlooking the Arno — watching the drowsy old city through a
melancholy drizzle of rain. Even in the rain it looks pleasant &

peaceful & stately—as if it were a place to come & end one's days
in if one had lost one's money, one's health & one's friends, &
could simply crawl up~~on~~ [∧]&[∧] down in the deliciously soft air
& wander over sometimes & stroll in the Campo Santo.—Mrs. L.

5   & her daughter came over with me yesterday, and we spent a
charming afternoon in the Cathedral & that wonderful old
frescoed cloister. They went back to Livorno in the evening.—
How stupid_x of you, to speak frankly, to be in America.—I see
it's going to clear. I'm going to the Campo Santo again this p.m,

10 & if you were hereabouts, as you ought to be, I should insist on
your going with me. Do you know I rather hate you for finding
everything so satisfactory at home. And why did you write to
Mrs. Tweedy that I was returning because I was "satiated" with
Europe? You little know the treasures of stoicism which I am

15 laying up against my residence at home. I mustn't omit to tell
you what pleasure your artistic prosperity has given me. This,
I suppose, has thrown a glamor over things in general & covered
a multitude of Bostonian sins.—Where are going for the <u>mesi</u>
<u>caldi</u>? I can't answer the question for myself—save that I shall

20 ∧probably[∧] not stay in Italy later than the last of June, & shall
sail for home about Aug. 20<u>th</u>. I have a stubborn vision of
Switzerland for the interval.—But I am writing at a rate which
will ruin me in postage. I am sorry you don't enjoy your visits at
the Nortons more. I haven't made one in some time; but the last

25 ~~seemed~~ ∧was[∧] very pleasant. You ought to like the ladies, for
they are most likeable. With Charles everyone must deal
according to his own light.—Have you read Mérimées <u>Letters,</u>
if not, I strongly recommend them. All this without a word,
especially, to your father. But li voglio tutto il bene del mondo.

30 I wrote to him a month since. I trust he got my letter. I hope you
will detect real improvement in my brother. A fervent blessing,
dear Lizzie, on your labours, & your life in general. Much love to
your father. Yours ever   H. James jr

No previous publication

∽

145.9 received • re= | ceived

145.22 information • informa= | tion

145.27 console • con= | sole

146.10 occasion • oc= | casion

146.11 trrace • [*misspelled*]

146.14 mistress • mis= | tress

146.15 remember • re= | member

146.21 ~~Villa~~ Villino • [i *overwrites* a]

146.28 yesterday • yester | day

146.30 <u>Bancrofts</u> • <u>Ban=</u> | <u>crofts</u>

146.33 companion • com= | panion

147.8 Gryzanowski • Gryz= | anowski

147.9 intimacy • in= | timacy

147.21 except • ex= | cept

147.21 ⬦ is • [is *overwrites illegible letter*]

147.23 ⬦ last • [l *overwrites illegible letter*]

147.25 characteristic • characteris= | tic

147.34 melancholy • melan= | choly

148.6 wonderful • wonder= | ful

148.18 Bostonian • Bos= | tonian

148.19 myself • my= | self

∽

145.18 her daughter • Fanny Lombard.

146.3 Mrs. Perkins • Mrs. Stephen Perkins.

146.12 the Halls' • Taylor and Elisa Hall.

146.17–18 Your friend Miss Constance • Constance "Connie" Hall.

146.21–22 Villino della Torre • Villino della Torre is located near the Boboli Gardens on Via de' Serragli.

146.24 Miss F. • Florence or Frances Greenough.

146.30 the <u>Bancrofts</u> • Possibly John Chandler Bancroft and his sister; see 22 March [1874] to WJ, p. 139.

146.32 ci=devant • prior.

147.5 Mrs. H. • Ellen Greenough Huntington.

147.6 Miss Laura • Laura Huntington.

147.7 Henry • Henry Huntington (1848–1926), son of Ellen Greenough Huntington; he later became American vice-consul in Florence.

147.18 M<u>me</u> v. Rabe's • Annie Crawford von Rabe.

147.19 Miss Mimolis • Mary "Mimoli" Crawford.

147.20–21 Miss Bessie Ward's innamorato • Ernst Schönberg.

147.24 Mrs. W. • Sarah Butler Wister.

148.4 Campo Santo • The great cloister-shaped cemetery adjoining the cathedral and Campanile, or leaning tower; its Renaissance frescoes were badly damaged during World War II; see HJ to WJ, 30 October [1869] (*CLHJ, 1855–1872* 2: 169n165.22–23).

148.18–19 <u>mesi caldi</u> • hot months.

148.27 Mérimées <u>Letters</u> • *Lettres à une inconnue.*

148.29 li voglio tutto il bene del mondo • I wish him all the good in the world.

ALICE JAMES
18, [19] April [1874]
ALS Houghton
bMS Am 1094 (1570)

Florence, M April 18<u>th</u>
10 Piazza Sta. Maria Novella
1<u>o</u> po.

Dearest sister: It's a long time since I have addressed one of my punctual missives to you, & I long to renew our sweet intercourse. But in order to be punctual this time, my missive must not be long, as I have but a brief interval before post-time. I wrote about a week ago from Leghorn to mother, in answer to her letter of March 24<u>th</u>. Since then (yesterday) has come father's ~~from~~ ʌof the 31<u>st</u>[ʌ] enclosing Howells's acceptance of my story for the Atlantic. With this I am very content: especially as

it gives me a longer time to write. I shall immortalize myself:
vous allez voir. I have been back in Florence about a week—
having prolonged my tour, briefly, to Pisa & Lucca. It was very
pleasant though marred by bad weather—Pisa in especial being
delicious. But I won't dilate, as I have just sent off some rather
indifferent gossip about it to the Nation. On my return, I fixed
myself in my present quarters—a little appartment all to myself
on the piazza of all Florence in which it always seemed to me I
should chose choose to live. I am established à merveille: &
indeed have a "guest chamber," to which you would be welcome,
were you here. I have a vast & luxurious sitting room & balcony,
two bedrooms, a scullery & a china closet: which at 100 frs. a
month is moderate. Blessed Florence! I couldn't face the idea of
returning to live in one small room at an inn; & my literary
labors will certainly show the good effect of my having space to
pace about & do a little fine frenzy. Tell Wᵐ I find the ˄French˄
restaurant in Via Rondinelli, with the lobsters & truffles in the
window an exellent place to dine, ⨍ so that I am altogether most
comfortable. I am also most well, & better in my health, without
exaggeration than for many a day. Ecco!—What shall I tell you
of Florence? The weather lately has been grey & rainy: but I
have rather relished it & find the Florentine spring generally less
deleterious to my nervous organism than the Roman last year.
The Lombards are back in ⨍ town: Mrs. R L. very poorly again.
She has come to a the wise decision that she ought to leave Italy
& I quite ˄shall˄ draw a long breath when I see her starting
northward & facing homeward. I have been taking poor Fanny
about to see a few more sights—having been much moved by the
pathetic fact, which she casually mentioned, that in the 6 mos.
she had been in Florence, she had been but twice to the Uffizzi
gallery. It is gallantry very well bestowed; for ˄the˄ poor F girl
is very appreciative. Mrs. L. is able to go nowhere.—I was going
this p.m. up to Bellosguardo to Mrs. Stephen Perkins's saturday
reception: but the skies are so black that I have stopped at home:

& hence this letter.—I have seen no one new,—unless perhaps
Mr. Bradford, retour de Rome. He lives across the way, & though
his poor little frame seems more ashen grey, & his conversation
more desultory than ever, his nose is as big & his virtue as
5   unbounded. I have effected the conquest of a Mme. von
Limburg, the wife of an old Dutch diplomatist, living here (she
was a Miss Cass, daughter of the General.) She is considered a
very fine lady, & followed me up, on my being introduced to her,
with an immediate invitation to a large dinner party.
10   Unfortunately I was at Pisa, & I am informed that she made no
secret of the fact that she was <u>inconsolable</u>! I'am waiting till
Monday, her day, to call upon her again; & if she bids me to
another banquet I shall certainly go & report you every thing of
interest. <u>Sunday</u>. I was interrupted yesterday &, but don't regret
15   it as I have this morning mother's sweet letter of April 3<u>d</u>
(describing her dinner at Boott's with the C. Perkinses) to
acknowledge. Apropos of which I can't imagine how I failed
yesterday to mention the receipt of Willy's a week since,
containing the portraitts. They caused me a sweet emotion—
20   especially yours, which is the best & wonderfully good. It is
indeed most lovely and a capital likeness. I tremble for future
days when I learn from Willy that ∧even[∧] he ~~can have~~ ∧finds[∧]
(or at first found) Cambridge mean and flimsy—he who used to
hanker so for it here. I should think that his three months in
25   Italy would seem wonderfully charming to him now. To me too
they have faded into a sort of half-reality, & I have to look at
some visible proof the fact—as for instance—a pair of old
stockings he gave me—to ~~really~~ believe that he was veritably
here. I have long ere this relapsed into my solitary single life, &
30   save that I should like to know an agreeable man ∧or two,[∧] I
bear it very contentedly. Tell Willy I am delighted to hear that
he regrets having "badgered" me about my fondness for these
parts, & gives me license to go on liking Italy, irresponsibly.
After he had left me, I rebounded, in this direction: & haven't

had an hour of <u>défaillance</u> since. Mother speaks of Wilky's
prospects, which I am glad to hear are fair, of getting
Mr. Tweedy's photo. and of Bessie Ward. I heard a couple of
days since from Aunt Mary who doesn't disguise her extreme
resentment at being kept in Dresden for many weeks after she
has had enough of it. But the poor Tweedys drift with a kind of
melancholy aimlessness when they are set in motion, & I shall
pity her rather more when she has to begin to decide again
where to go & what to do. — The Wards I am told passed through
Florence rapidly a few days since <u>en route</u> for Paris, where B. is
to be married — her lover being still in Bonn, too unwell to
travel. Last summer at Homburg à propos of the conjugal
sufferings of the German lady with whom she was staying she
used to rail sharply at German husbands; now she has got one I
hope her railings won't have reason to multiply. — I don't think
of any one or anything here more that may interest you.
Mrs. Effie Lowell, I am told, is in Florence, & I will call on her.
Does Loulie Shaw's property all go to the Hoopers, Tappans,
&c? Tell Willy I called at the Gryzanowskis one warm morning,
the other day, & that he can't fancy how charming that dusky old
apartment looks by daylight with the backs windows all open to
the garden & the view of the Cathedral. — Farewell, sweet sister.
Prove to me, as I contemplate your photograph, that handsome
is that handsome does by writing me a long & sprightly letter. I
hope father's indisposition is over; m Much love to both my
<u>genitori</u> & to W<u>m</u> & a tender folding in the arms to yourself. Ever
your bro.

    <u>H. James</u> jr.

Previous publication: *HJL* 1: 437–40

◊

150.24 M April • [A *overwrites* M]
150.30 interval • inter= | val
151.1 immortalize • immor= | talize

151.2 v̲o̲u̲s̲ · [*blotted out*]

151.7 myself · my= | self

151.7 appartment · [*misspelled*]

151.9 ~~chose~~ choose · [os *overwrites* se]

151.9 established · es= | tablished

151.18 exellent · [*misspelled*]

151.18 ~~&~~ so · [so *overwrites* &]

151.24 ~~r~~ town · [t *overwrites* r]

151.24 ~~R~~ L. · [L *overwrites* R]

151.25 ~~a~~ the · [th *overwrites* a]

151.31 ~~F~~ girl · [gi *overwrites* F]

151.34 reception · re= | ception

152.5 conquest · con= | quest

152.5 ~~a~~ Mme. · [M *overwrites* a]

152.8 introduced · intro= | duced

152.13 certainly · cer= | tainly

152.14 ~~&~~, · [, *overwrites* &]

152.19 portraitts · [*misspelled*]

153.7 aimlessness · aimless= | ness

153.19 Gryzanowskis · Gryzan= | owskis

153.21 back~~s~~ · [s *blotted out*]

153.24–28 writing me [. . .] H̲.̲ J̲a̲m̲e̲s̲ jr. · [*written across the letter's first page*]

153.25 ~~m~~ Much · [M *overwrites* m]

∾

150.31 I wrote about a week ago from Leghorn to mother · 4 April [1874] to MWJ (pp. 141–43).

150.33–34 my story for the Atlantic · *Roderick Hudson.*

151.2 v̲o̲u̲s̲ allez voir · you shall see.

151.6 gossip about it to the N̲a̲t̲i̲o̲n̲ · "Tuscan Cities."

151.8 the piazza of all Florence · Piazza Santa Maria Novella, near Florence's train station and dominated by the Church of Santa Maria Novella, famous for its cloister and frescoes by Masaccio (see p. 95).

151.9 à̲ ̲m̲e̲r̲v̲e̲i̲l̲l̲e̲ · m̲a̲r̲v̲e̲l̲o̲u̲s̲l̲y̲ ̲w̲e̲l̲l̲.

151.16–17 the ₐFrench₍ₐ₎ restaurant in Via Rondinelli · Victor's; Via Rondinelli is a small street between the Piazza degli Antinori and the Piazza Santa Maria Maggiore. See 3 May [1874] to WJ (pp. 159–60).

151.20 Ecco! · There!

152.2 Mr. Bradford · George Bradford; see 2 November [1873] to Sr. (p. 68).

152.2 retour de Rome · back from Rome.

152.5–6 Mme. von Limburg · Isabella Cass von Limburg (1805–79), daughter of Lewis Cass (1782–1866), a brigadier general during the War of 1812, first governor of Michigan (1813–31), and minister to France (1836–42). She married Baron Theodore Marinus von Limburg (b. 1800).

152.15 mother's sweet letter of April 3ᵈ · MWJ to HJ, 3 April [1874].

152.18 receipt of Willy's a week since · WJ to HJ, 22 March 1874 (*CWJ* 1: 225–27).

153.1 défaillance · weakness.

153.11 her lover · Ernst Schönberg.

153.17 Mrs. Effie Lowell · Josephine "Effie" Shaw Lowell (1843–1905), widow of Civil War colonel Charles Russell Lowell and sister to Anna Shaw Curtis, wife of George W. Curtis. In 1876 she was appointed the first female commissioner of the New York State Board of Charities.

153.18–19 Hoopers, Tappans, &c · Caroline Sturgis Tappan (1819–88) was Loulie Shaw's aunt, and Ellen Sturgis Hooper Gurney and Marian "Clover" Hooper Adams were her first cousins.

153.22 the Cathedral · Santa Maria del Fiore, or the Duomo, in Piazza del Duomo, built between 1296 and 1436.

153.26 genitori · parents.

WILLIAM DEAN HOWELLS
3 May [1874]
ALS Houghton
bMS Am 1784 (253), folder 1, letter 7

5

Florence, Piazza Sta. Maria Novella
May 3ᵈ·
Dear Howells—
        I rec'd. some days ago from my father the little note you
10 had sent him, signifying your acceptance of my story for next
year's <u>Atlantic</u>, ᵭ have had it at heart ever since to drop you a
line in consequence.—I'm extremely glad that my thing is
destined to see the light in the Atlantic rather than in 'tother
place ᵭ am very well satisfied with the terms. My story is to be
15 on a theme I have had in my head a long time ᵭ once attempted
to write something about. The theme is interesting, ᵭ if I do as I
intend ᵭ hope, I think the tale must please. It shall, at any rate
have all my pains. The opening chapters take place in America ᵭ
the people are of our glorious race; but they are soon
20 transplanted to Rome, where things are to go on famously.
Ecco. Particulars, including name, (which however I incline to
have simply that of the hero)—on a future occasion. Suffice i̶s̶ it
that I promise you some tall writing. My only fear is that it may
turn out taller than broad. That is, I thank you especially for the
25 clause in the contract as to the numbers being less than twelve.
As I desire above all things to s̶o̶u̶n̶d̶ ₍ₐ₎write₍ₐ₎ close, ᵭ avoid
padding and prolixity, it may be that I shall have told my tale by
the 8ᵗʰ or 9ᵗʰ number. But there is time enough to take its
measure scientifically. I don't see how, in parts of the length of
30 Aldrich's <u>Prudence Palfrey</u> (my protagonist is <u>not</u> named
Publicius Parsons,) it can help stretching out a good piece.—Of
Aldrich's tale, I'm sorry to say I've lost the thread, through
missing a number of the magazine, ᵭ shall have, like Dennett, to
wait till it's finished.—M̶ Why do you continue to treat me as if

I didn't care to hear from you? I have a vague sense of
unnumbered notes, despatched to you as an editor, but in which
your human side was sufficiently recognized to have won from
you some faint response. If you knew how dismally & solio
solitudinously I sit here just now before my window, ignorant of
a friendly voice, & waiting for the rain=swept piazza to look at
last as if it would allow me to go forth to my lonely pranzo at a
mercenary trattoria—you would repent of your coldness. I
suppose I ought to write you a letter flamboyant with local
color; but the local color just now, as I say, is the blackest shade
of the pluvious, & my soul reflects its hue. My brother will have
talked to you about Florence and about me, sufficiently too, I
suppose, for the present. Florence has become by this time to
me an old story—though like all real masterpieces one reads &
re-reads it with pleasure. I am here now but for a few weeks
longer, & then I shall leave Italy—for a many a year, I imagine.
With ineffable regret for many reasons; contentedly enough for
others. But we shall have a chance before long to talk of all this.
I return home at the end of the summer (& hope to bring my
tale with me substantially completed). To many of the things of
home I shall return with pleasure—especially to the less isolated,
more freely working= & talking=life.—Don't wait for this,
however, to let me hear from you; but write me meanwhile, if
it's only to tell me your'e glad I'm coming. I have had no
personal news of you in an age, but I trust you are nestling in
prosperity. It's a hundred years since I heard of your wife's
health: but I trust it is good, even at the advanced age which this
makes her. What are you doing, planning, hoping? I suppose
your Venetian tale is almost off your hands—I long to have it on
mine. (I'm delighted by the way to hear you like "Eugene
Pickering:" do, oh do, if possible put him through in a single
number.) Lowell has just passed through on his way to Paris. I
got great pleasure from his poem, which he read me in bits. I'm
impatient to see it all together. Farewell, dear Howells; the

rivulets on the piazza run thin, & I must trudge across & quaff the straw-covered fiaschetto. I shall do it, be ~~your~~ [∧]sure,[∧] to your health, Your gentilissima sposa's & your childrens'! Yours always <u>H. J. jr</u>

Previous publication: *HJL* 1: 443–45; Anesko 95–96; Horne 57–59

∾

156.10 acceptance • accep= | tance

156.12 consequence • conse= | quence

156.21 including • in= | cluding

156.21 incline • in= | cline

156.22 ~~io~~ it • [t *overwrites illegible letter*]

156.34 ~~M~~ Why • [Wh *overwrites* M]

157.2 despatched • des= | patched

157.4–5 ~~solio~~ solitudinously • [t *overwrites illegible letter*]; solitudi= | nously

157.33–158.4 I'm impatient [. . .] always <u>H. J. jr</u> • [*written across the letter's first page*]

158.1 rivulets • rivu= | lets

∾

156.10 my story • *Roderick Hudson.*

156.13–14 'tother place • *Scribner's Monthly.*

156.21 Ecco • There.

156.30 Aldrich's <u>Prudence Palfrey</u> • See HJ to Howells, 9 January 1874 (p. 101).

156.31 Publicius Parsons • A joke based on the name of Aldrich's Parson Wibird Hawkins in *Prudence Palfrey.*

156.33 Dennett • John R. Dennett; see HJ to Sr., 19 March 1870 (*CLHJ, 1855–1872* 2: 327, 329n327.5–6).

157.7 pranzo • dinner.

157.26–27 your wife's health • Elinor Mead Howells suffered from chronically poor health.

157.29 your Venetian tale • *A Foregone Conclusion.*

157.33 his poem • James Russell Lowell, "Agassiz."

158.2 fiaschetto · small wine bottle.

158.3 gentilissima sposa's · sweetest wife's.

WILLIAM JAMES   5
3 May [1874]
ALS Houghton
bMS Am 1094 (1960)

Florence, May 3ᵈ   10
Dear Wᵐ. I wrote some ten days ago to Alice, ⅋ I am not sure
whether I then had received your letter of April 5ᵗʰ. Since then,
at all events, ~~I hav~~ ₍ₐ₎has₍ₐ₎ come to me father's note containing
my notice of Merimée ⅋ also the N. A. R. (2ᵈ number,) for
which I am greatly obliged. I have sent the Review to Turgeneff   15
through Hetzel the Paris publisher, as I could find no other
address. — I was glad to get from you any new expression of
impressions of home ⅋ was much entertained by your
thermometrical record. But I could send you one almost as
entertaining. After ~~a~~ ten days a short time since, of very hot — of   20
really July ⅋ August — weather, some ₍ₐ₎thing₍ₐ₎ very like winter
has set in again ⅋ cold ⅋ rain are the order of the day. To day is a
raw, rainy Sunday of anything but an exhilarating kind. The
piazza di Sta Maria Novella, before my windows is a wide
glittering flood, with here and there two legs picking their steps   25
beneath an umbrella. I have already written you of my being
established at housekeeping — or something very like it. It wears
very well ⅋ my rooms are delightful; if I came back to Florence
again, I should certainly take them for the winter. The way of
life is rather solitudinous — especially the lonely feeding: but I   30
have found a very good dining=place, where I can at least
converse with the flower-girl who comes every day to distribute
rosebuds for the button=hole. (The place is Victor's, ~~Ron~~ ₍ₐ₎Via₍ₐ₎
Rondinelli, whose window, like those in the palais Royal you

must remember.) The days ~~goes~~ go on with me monotonously enough ⅋ I make no new friends. I spend my time very much as when you were here, save that when the s warm weather fairly set in, I took to going out in the morning ⅋ working during the

5   hot hours from lunch to dinner. There is nothing especial to tell you of your acquaintances here, tho' I continue to see most of them occasionally. I pay frequent short visits to the Lombards, ⅋ though long since mortally tired of their nature ⅋ conversation am reduced to accepting their parlor ~~grea~~ gratefully for half an

10 hour as the nearest approach to a domestic <u>foyer</u>. In fact I shall miss them, uncomfortably, when they go. Mrs. L. is better ⅋ worse, ⅋ lately much pleased to hear that Essie was coming out to join her. But E. will not find her anywhere in Italy, as she is constantly on the point of leaving. But she can't imagine where

15 to go. —I have had great pleasure lately in seeing Mrs. Effie Lowell, who is a most lovely being surely. I have seen her only in the evening, however, ⅋ haven't undertaken to "go round" with her. She says she doesn't care for "art", ⅋ the other day was going to visit the poorhouse in company with a colored

20 doctoress established here! Gryzanowski came in just as I was reading your last letter ⅋ told me to tell you that he had received the books you lately sent him ⅋ prized them greatly, but that ~~hi~~ your generosity made him uncomfortable. He is "simpatico" as ever. Hillebrand becomes to me less ⅋ less so; he is an

25 unmistakeable snob. I went the other evening to a large ⅋ very wearisome party given by Mrs. Taylor (M<u>me</u> Laussot's mother,) filled with very ordinary folk, Italian, German ⅋ English. — James Lowell ⅋ his wife spent a few days here on their return from Rome ⅋ have left for Paris—without revealing any new

30 traits of mind or character. I feel as if I knew Lowell now very well; but don't feel as I should ever get anything very valuable out of him. They (the Lowells) were very frankly critical of the Storys with ⬦⬦⬦ whom they staid a while in Rome ⅋ seem to have been chiefly busy after the 1<u>st</u> day in inventing subterfuges for

getting away. The Andrews are here, back from Rome, Edith ill
(slightly⁚ I believe) with fever, as you were.—Let me say,
without more loss of time, that my letter of Credit expires (the
date, not the sum) on May 27th, & that I should like father to
please ask Uncle R. to have it renewed for June, July & August.
The last was for £500; this had better be (nominally) for £250. I
shall draw no such sum, probably; but I had better be able to
draw all that I need for my expenses in getting home & making
any purchases for you. If this can be done without delay, it will
be a convenience to me; as I have left too long speaking of it. I
keep your various lists of commissions; though they imply as a
certainty my sailing via England. I have given up all idea of
taking an Italian steamer: but if I leave Italy in the early part of
June, I may be reduced to going to Homburg as are the best
place to spend the interval of ₐthe₍ₐ₎ 6 7 weeks of July & August.
In that case I shall hesitate to think it worth while to go to
England, expensively, when I can make the journey from
Bremen; & I suppose you won't want me to go there on purpose
to buy your things. But there is time to decide on this. Father
sent me a rather puzzling request in his last: i.e to buy $75 worth
of virtù for the tops of the bookcases. I can't very well buy it
here, as to send it would be (I'm told) very expensive—costing
as much, almost, as the thing itself. Then to carry it about with
me would be equally so, & not very convenient. I think therefore
I had better leo let my getting it depend on my being in Paris;
where the choice of things is probably better also. I see no
reason here to suppose it remarkable. Thank father à propos of
his last, for his care of the proof's of my last story. I suppose it
has been sent me, though it has not yet arrived.—I have fairly
settled down to work upon my long story for the Atlantic & hope
to bring it home finished or nearly so. Except therefore for two
or three more Italian sketches (if opportunity offers) I shall send
home no short things before I leave, & shall have to draw more
money than, for the present, I cause to flow in. But if I am paid

down, even in part, for my MS. I shall ~~now~~ ₐbe able₍ₐ₎ to offer
full reimbursement. I lately sent a tale to the Galaxy *&* a couple
more reviews to the <u>Nation</u>: but I want henceforth to give all
my time *&* attention to my novel. I am determined it shall be a
5   very good piece of work. Farewell, dear brother. Would that you
were here for an hour, this dreary day, at my solitary side. I'm
sorry Waterman doesn't give you your place since you are
disposed to resume it. But such is life. Farewell. My being aches
with unsatisfied domestic affection, *&* just now I could howl with
10 homesickness

      Ever yours
       <u>H. J.</u> jr

Previous publication: *HJL* 1: 440–43; *CWJ* 1: 231–34

      ❧

    159.13 containing • con= | taining

    159.20 ~~a~~ ten • [te *overwrites* a]

    160.1 ~~goes~~ go • [o *overwrites* oes]

    160.3 ~~s~~ warm • [w *overwrites* s]

    160.9 reduced • re= | duced

    160.9 ~~grea~~ gratefully • [a *overwrites* ea]

    160.13 anywhere • any= | where

    160.17 undertaken • under= | taken

    160.19 poorhouse • poor= | house

    160.20 Gryzanowski • Gryzan= | owski

    160.21 received • re= | ceived

    160.22–23 ~~hi~~ your • [yo *overwrites* hi]

    160.23 uncomfortable • un= | comfortable

    160.25 unmistakeable • un= | mistakeable; [*misspelled*]

    160.33 ◆◆◆ whom • [wh *overwrites illegible letters*]

    161.9 purchases • pur= | chases

    161.10 convenience • con= | venience

    161.14 Homburg • Hom= | burg

    161.14 ~~are~~ the • [the *overwrites* are]

161.15 6̶ 7 • [*7 overwrites 6*]

161.17 expensively • ex= | pensively

161.18 suppose • sup= | pose

161.19 decide • de= | cide

161.24 convenient • con= | venient

161.25 l̶e̶o̶ let • [*t overwrites illegible letter*]

162.2 reimbursement • reimburse= | ment

162.7-12 since you are [. . .] <u>H. J.</u> jr • [*written across the letter's first page*]

∾

159.11 some ten days ago to Alice • 18, [19] April [1874] to AJ (pp. 150-53).

159.14 my notice of Merimée • HJ's review of Prosper Mérimée's *Dernières nouvelles.*

159.14 N. A. R. • *North American Review.*

159.15-16 I have sent the Review to Turgeneff through Hetzel the Paris publisher • *"Frühlingsfluthen."* Hetzel was Turgenev's publisher in France.

160.10 <u>foyer</u> • <u>hearth</u>.

160.23 simpatico • nice.

161.5 Uncle R. • Alexander Robertson Walsh (1809-84), brother of MWJ.

161.28 my last story • "Adina."

161.30 my long story for the <u>Atlantic</u> • *Roderick Hudson.*

162.2 a tale to the Galaxy • "Professor Fargo."

162.2-3 a couple more reviews to the <u>Nation</u> • The unsigned review of Flaubert's *La tentation de Saint Antoine;* the unsigned review of Émile Montégut's *Souvenirs de Bourgogne.*

162.7 Waterman • Thomas Waterman (1842-1901), the American physician, had been teaching anatomy and physiology in lieu of WJ at Harvard.

SARAH BUTLER WISTER

10 May [1874]

TLC Bryn Mawr College Library

5   Florence May 10th.
              Piazza Sta. M. Novella 10.
Dear Mrs Wister:
      This is not a letter—that must be for another day when I've
not just been writing one of 16 pages: (to my mother.)—This is
10   simply a thank you (or rather twenty) for your own letter, which
illuminated my existence day before yesterday. It was very good
to hear from you & I shall always value doing so, incalculably, for
I feel as if we had had a glimpse of the beauté parfaite (or
something very like it) together. I shall answer your letter as it
15   deserves on the first possible day:—meanwhile I want simply to
enclose this newspaper scrap: which you would never otherwise
see. Read the book, decidedly: it's thoroughly interesting.—
Here I am at the end of a Florentine winter, which tho' socially
most tame and arid has been much more remunerative than I
20   expected when I wrenched myself (about from Rome to face the
prospect. Florence has worked pretty thoroughly into my
consciousness & I have grown foolishly fond of it:—but there are
no especial details to enumerate. It has been a very unpersonal
winter,—save as regards that very tiresome person myself of
25   whose society I've had a surfeit. Doesn't some one else want to
try him?—I can imagine your having deserved to have Boston
made amusing to you, but (quite apart from deserts) your story
doesn't make it even easy to go thither—which nevertheless I
rather distinctly intend in the autumn.—I saw a couple of nights
30   since (or rather mornings & it was at a ball, the only one I've
been to all winter) Miss Edith Story, who inquired about you,
very prettily. Also Mme de Rabe, née Crawford, with whom
nowadays one has to converse in French, as her husband knows
no English. I never wanted to marry her, surely, but I don't care

for her so much now that another man has done so.—So Porter
is painting you? I congratulate him on his opportunities[.] He
will do your dress very well, but I am dissatisfied in advance with
the face.—Mrs. Lawrence, on Cherbuliez, was excellent; but not
having reviews to write, she has no business to take such good   5
things out of the critic's mouths—I enjoy greatly your having
enjoyed my Turgenief, but think you are wise, morally, not to
read his books.—But I am writing the letter I didn't mean to. I
hope that that <u>malappris</u> of an Adams will make reparation by
printing your article in letters of gold.—Yes, the flowers do stand   10
in <u>shame</u> against the dark base of the Strozzi, your word makes
the picture: but somehow, I don't see or feel & smell & know the
Spring here, even in May, as I did in Rome last March. With
kind regards to Dr Wister: yours most faithfully & gratefully.

    Henry James jr.   15

    Excuse the shabbiness of the scrap. I sent it to a friend who
returned it so.

Previous publication: *HJL* 1: 445–47

   ↄ

   164.29 distinctly · dis- | tinctly

   165.2 opportunities[.] · [*copy text reads* opportunities,]

   ↄ

   164.8–9 I've not just been writing one of 16 pages: (to my mother.) ·
This letter is not extant. HJ's last known letter to MWJ, 4 April [1874]
(pp. 141–43), is six manuscript pages. The next one to MWJ, 17 May 1874
(pp. 166–71), is fourteen.

   164.13 beauté parfaite · perfect beauty.

   164.32 Mme de Rabe, née Crawford · Annie Crawford von Rabe.

   165.1 Porter · Benjamin Curtis Porter (1843–1908), notable society
portrait painter who resided in Boston and New York.

   165.4 Mrs. Lawrence, on Cherbuliez · It is possible that HJ refers to
the unsigned review of Victor Cherbuliez's *Prosper Randoce* in the April
1874 *Atlantic Monthly*, which Helen McMahon and Harlow attribute to

T. S. Perry (148; 367), or to an unsigned review of Cherbuliez's novel in
the April 1874 *Galaxy*.

    165.7 my Turgenief • *"Frühlingsfluthen."*

    165.9 <u>malappris</u> • <u>uncouth</u>.

    165.9 Adams • Henry Adams, editor of the *North American Review*.

    165.11 Strozzi • The Strozzi Palace. According to Baedeker's 1874 *Italy*,
"Farther on in the Via Tornabuoni is situated the *Palazzo Strozzi [. . .],
erected in 1489 by *Benedetto da Majano* for the celebrated Filippo Strozzi,
and presenting an example of the Florentine palatial style in its most perfect development" (349).

MARY WALSH JAMES
17 May 1874
15   ALS Houghton
bMS Am 1094 (1824)

    Florence, May 17<u>th</u> 74.
Dearest mother—I have before me two unanswered letters from
20   home: one from Willy of April 18<u>th</u>, received some ten days
since: the other yours of May 1<u>st</u>, which arrived yesterday. Many
thanks for each; they have helped to console me for the want of
your personal society. Your principal news was the snow and
sleet of your dreary spring; & unless things have greatly
25   improved since I shill excite your animosity by telling you how
much better they have been with us here in Florence. A little
rain, but nothing to complain of & day after day of lovely,
healthy coolness. To those who above all things dread being
"relaxed," this postponement of the warm weather is very
30   agreeable. Even yet, though the sky is brilliant, it fails to arrive
and to day is a radiant blue=heavened Sunday with much such a
crispness in the air as ~~we~~ you might have in early October. But
evidently there must be a change and it will be sudden & intense;
though Gryzanowski, who is as ingenious an observer of the

weather as of everything else, ~~phr~~ prophecies that this is to be,
in Italy, a cool summer. — The days pass with here evenly and
rapidly in my comfortable little dwelling on this lively (& alas
dusty) old Piazza Sta Maria Novella. (The centre of the square
is not paved and the dust hovers over it in clouds which compel
one to live with closed windows. But I remove to my bedroom
which is on a side-street & very cool & clean.) Nothing particular
happens to me & my time is passed between sleeping &
scribbling (both of which I do very well) lunching & dining,
walking & conversing with my small circle of acquaintance.
Florence is supposed to be in a very festal state just now, owing
to a great flower show which has brought a crowd; but it is to me
personally neither better nor worse than usual. I haven't yet
been to the flower show, which I believe is handsome — for Italy,
where the flowers don't match our northern ones. I have seen no
new person nor new thing — or rather I have; for I went a couple
of nights since to a very brilliant ball given by the jockey=club at
their Casino in the Cascine. The omnipotent Hillebrand sent
me an invitation & though it required much cold=blooded
energy to go travelling off alone at midnight to an entertainment
where I should ~~no~~ know one, I went for information's sake. It
was very brilliant and elegant & I saw a concentration of the élite
of Florentine society, and more tiaras of diamonds & ropes of
pearls and acres of <u>point</u> de Venise than I had ever beheld
before. There were also a few people I knew — Miss Story among
others, with her hostess the Princess Corsini, with whom I also
had a little talk. I left at 3 a.m. when the cotillion was still an
hour off! — I came the other day at my restaurant across M<u>me</u> de
Rabe (née Crawford) & her husband who are here "<u>incogniti</u>," to
escape visiting & visits. She seems very happy & I ~~su~~ think has
quite tamed her Prussian. Lizzie Boott, I suppose, will have
heard of the ₍∧₎last₍∧₎ engagement of Miss Mimoli C.; to one
Fraser, namely, attaché of the English Embassy at Rome, a very
respectable & worthy youth, who is to take her to live in Pekin,

whither he has been appointed. They are to be married
immediately. The good Terry is going for the summer to
America & Mrs. T. is to spend it at Dantzig (or thereabouts) near
M<u>m</u> de R. (This will interest Lizzie.) It will also divert her to
5   hear that Mrs. Carson is reported to be engaged to the blind
Duke of Sermoneta & that Edith Story has just refused Peruzzi,
aide de camp of the King & nephew of the Sindaco here; but
nearly fifty & penniless.—Tell Willy I thank him greatly for
setting before me so vividly the question of my going home or
10   staying. I feel equally with him the importance of the decision. I
have been meaning, as you know, for some time past two return
in the autumn, & I see as yet no sufficient reason for changing
my plan. I shall go with the full prevision that I shall not find
life at home <u>simpatico</u>, but rather ◇ painfully &, as regards
15   literary work, obstructively the reverse, and not even with the
expectation that time will make it ~~more so~~ [∧]easier; but[∧]
simply on sternly practical grounds: <u>i.e</u> because I can find more
abudant literary occupation by being on the premises & relieve
you & father of your burdensome ∧financial[∧] interposition. But
20   I shrink from Willy's apparent assumption that going now is to
pledge myself to stay forever. I ◇ feel as if my three years in
Europe (with much of them so <u>maladif</u>) were a very moderate
allowance for one who gets so much out of it as I do; & I don't
think I could really hold up my head if I didn't hope to eat a
25   bigger slice of the pudding (with a few more social plums in it,
especially) at some future time. If at the end of a period at
home, I ∧don't[∧] feel an overwhelming desire to come back, it
will so much gained; but I should prepare myself for great
deceptions if I didn't take the probability of such desire into
30   account. One oughtn't I suppose to bother too much about the
future, but arrange as best one can with the present, and the
present bids me go home and try and get more things published.
What makes the question particularly difficult to decide is that
though I should make more money at home, American prices

would devour it twice as fast: but even allowing for this, I should keep ahead of my expenses better than here. I know that when the time comes ̶I̶ it will be unutterably hard to leave ∂ I shall ∧be∧ wondering whether if I were to stay another year I shouldn't ~~propitatiate~~ propitiate the Minotaur ∂ return more resignedly. But to this I shall answer that a year wouldn't be a tenth part enough and that besides, as things stand, I should be perplexed where to spend it. Florence, fond as I have grown of it, is worth far too little to me, socially, for me to think complacently of another winter here. Here have I been living (in these rooms) for five weeks ∂ not a creature, save once Gryzanowski, has crossed my threshold—counting out my little Italian, who comes twice ∧a week,∧ ∂ whom I have to <u>pay</u> for his conversation! If I knew any one in England I should be tempted to go there for a year, for there I could work to advantage—i..e. get hold of new books to review. But I can't face, as it is, a year of British solitude. What I desire now more than anything else, ∂ what would do me more good, is a <u>régal</u> of intelligent ∂ suggestive society, especially male. But I don't know how or where to find it. It exists, I suppose in Paris ∂ London, but I can't get at it. I chiefly desire it because it would, I am sure, ~~help~~ ∧increase∧ my powers of work. These are doing very well, however, as it is, and I have for the present an absorbing task in my novel.—Consider then that if nothing extremely unexpected turns up, I shall depart in the autumn. I have no present plans for the summer beyond ending my month in my rooms—on the 10<u>th</u> June.—I hope, beloved mammy, that you will be able to devise some agreeable plan ∧for∧ your own summer ∂ will spend it in repose and comfort. I took great satisfaction in what you say of Wilky's prospects ∂ your quotation from his letter, about his wife. His state of mind is certainly a blessed "providence." Your mention of Howard's situation ∂ requisitions was sufficiently sickening.—T. S. P., then is married! Is it true that his wife is to be constrained to "give

lessons"—as Mrs. Lowell told me she had heard? What a grey
prospect!—À propos, I believe I wrote that I had been seeing
Mrs. Effie Lowell—less than I would, now that she is gone. She
is a ravishing woman & I came within an ace of falling
wholesomely in love with her.—Mrs Lombard (with whom I am
not in love) is still lingering on here, amid ups and downs of
health. She is living so comfortably and cheaply (a charming
parlor two ~~setting~~ ∧bed[∧] rooms & all her meals which are very
succulent, for 7 frs. a day—& in the Palazzo Machiavelli, once
the home of the great Niccolò, too,) that she fears to break the
charm, though having old designs upon Venice. I have by this
time put Fanny thro' all the sights & conducted the two the
other night to the opera to hear Cimarosa's Matrimonio
Segreto. This was poor Mrs. L's one revelry, since she has been
in Italy, & even this outwearied her. I also drove with them the
other day to Fiesole & Vincigliata, & tell Willy I thought most
achingly of him. If that was pretty in January he may fancy what
it is in May. But I have missed nevertheless that entrancing sense
of the Italian spring that I had so fully last winter in Rome. Here
there are so many fewer places to catch it—no Villa Borghese,
no Coliseum, no long walls, overtumbled with cataracts of white
roses. But here, nevertheless, you should see against the rugged
brown walls of the Strozzi palace the flowers standing in sheaths
for sale & climbing and breaking in verdurous spray away up in
the neighborhood of the 2$^{\underline{d}}$ story windows. The Cascine too,
now, are enchanting: but you haven't that delicious invasion of
spring that arrives with March, in Rome.
I'm glad to hear Chas. Norton has found some active work to
divert him from his dusky opinions. I hope you enjoyed his
Turner drawings: as I remember them there were some lovely
ones.—I received the other day, a <u>Scribner</u> with my story: the
nature of wh. (I had never seen a copy before) made me cross
myself with gratitude that nothing had come of Dr. Holland's
invitation. You speak of some <u>notes</u> of mine having appeared in

the Independent. If they were sent me, they have not arrived; &
would father kindly send another copy?—Has the trunk reached
Quincy St? Pray guard jealously my few clothes—a summer suit
& a coat & 2 white waistcoats that I would give much for here,
now. But don't let father & Willy wear them out, as they will   5
serve me still. Farewell, sweet mother, I must close. I wrote last
asking you to have my credit renewed. I suppose it has been
done. Love abounding to all. I will write soon to W. I wrote
lately to A. Yours ever H.

Previous publication: Lubbock 1: 38-40; *HJL* 1: 448-52

∾

166.32 ~~we~~ you • [you *overwrites* we]

166.34 ingenious • ingen= | ious

167.1 ~~phr~~ prophecies • [r *overwrites* hr]

167.10 conversing • con= | versing

167.19 required • re= | quired

167.20 travelling • travel= | ling

167.20 entertainment • enter= | tainment

167.21 ~~no~~ know • [kn *overwrites* no]

167.23 Florentine • Floren= | tine

167.30 ~~su~~ think • [th *overwrites* su]

168.4 M^m • [*misspelled*]

168.6 Sermoneta • Ser= | moneta

168.14 ◇ • [*blotted out*]

168.18 abudant • [*misspelled*]

168.19 burdensome • burden= | =some

168.21 ◇ feel • [f *overwrites illegible letter*]

168.29 deceptions • de= | ceptions

168.30 account • [ac *inserted*]

169.3 ~~I~~ it • [it *overwrites* I]

169.5 ~~propitatiate~~ • pro= | ~~pitatiate~~

169.14 conversation • conversa= | tion

169.31 quotation • quo= | tation

170.12 conducted • conduc= | ted

170.30 remember • re= | member

171.6–9 Farewell [. . .] ever H. • [*written across the letter's first page*]

ᔦ

166.20 one from Willy of April 18ᵗʰ • WJ to HJ, 18 April 1874 (*CWJ* 1: 229–31).

167.25 Miss Story • Edith Story.

167.28–29 Mᵐᵉ de Rabe (née Crawford) & her husband • Annie Crawford and Baron Eric von Rabe.

167.32 Miss Mimoli C. • Mary Mimoli Crawford.

167.33 Fraser • Hugh Fraser (1837–94) and Mary Mimoli Crawford were married in Rome on 15 June 1874. Crawford chronicled their travels in *A Diplomatist's Wife in Japan: Letters from Home to Home* (1898) and *A Diplomatist's Wife in Many Lands* (1911).

168.2 Terry • Luther Terry.

168.3 Mrs. T. • Louisa Crawford Terry.

168.6 Duke of Sermoneta • Michelangelo Caetani (1804–82), politician and writer.

168.6 Edith Story has just refused Peruzzi • Edith Story married Simone Peruzzi in 1876 (see James, *William Wetmore Story* 2: 264).

168.7 Sindaco • mayor.

168.14 simpatico • pleasant.

168.22 maladif • sickly.

169.18 régal • feast.

169.32–33 Howard's situation • Howard James was committed to an inebriate asylum (see Habegger 472).

169.33 T. S. P. • Thomas Sergeant Perry.

169.34 his wife • Lilla Cabot Perry.

170.9 Palazzo Machiavelli • Located on Via Boccaccio.

170.13–14 Cimarosa's Matrimonia Segreto • The comic opera *Il matrimonio segreto* (1792) by Domenico Cimarosa (1749–1801).

170.23 the Strozzi palace • See HJ to Sarah Butler Wister, 10 May [1874] (p. 165).

170.31 my story • "Adina."

170.34–171.1 of some <u>notes</u> of mine [. . .] in the Independent • "Florentine Notes."

171.2–3 Has the trunk reached Quincy St? • See HJ to WJ, 22 March
[1874] (p. 140).

171.6–7 I wrote last asking you to have my credit renewed • See HJ to
WJ, 3 May [1874] (p. 161).

171.8–9 I wrote lately to A. • 18, [19] April [1874] to AJ (pp. 150–53).

MARY WALSH JAMES
3 June [1874]
ALS Houghton
bMS Am 1094 (1825)

15

Florence June 3ᵈ. 10 P. Sta M. N.
Dearest mother—I must write to day, though I have nothing
whatever to relate: Nothing at least beyond the fact that I have
just recd. your letter of May 19ᵗʰ; & that a few days since came
Alices of the 10ᵗʰ: both most cheering to my soul athirst for   20
domestic affection. To you I wrote some ten days since. (This
morning also came an Atlantic & a ~~Galaxy~~ [ʌ]Scribner.)[ʌ] You see
I am still lingering on here in Florence—one of the few
survivors of the winter colony. The summer has begun in good
earnest—you would think so if you could peep with me through   25
the closed ◇ lattice of my sitting-room out into the wide, glaring
Piazza. It shines so as to scorch the eyes—in the shade ~~in~~ on one
side is huddled a cabstand with the drivers all asleep on their
boxes, and a collection of loungers of low degrees & no costume
to speak of lying flat on their faces on the stones & courting the   30
siesta. I am staying on because it is convenient & not
uncomfortable. ~~I we~~ In fact I have so much comfort in being
able to expand & perambulate in my three darkened rooms that I
dread to begin to travel & live in hotels & one small chamber. My

life is profoundly tranquil. I go out in the morning, walk about a
bit ⅋ court the dusky coolness of a church. The Cathedral just
now is divinely cool ⅋ picturesque, with its portals flung wide to
let the white sunshine of the ~~sunsh~~ ∧streets[∧] pour in ~~to~~ and lose

5   itself vainly in the gorgeous dusk. I lunch early ~~a~~ in a
beer=garden, in the green shade of a trellis ⅋ then come home ⅋
dwell through the long hot hours of the afternoon till about 7½,
at which fashionable hour I dine. The evenings I spend abroad in
one way or another. On this basis I shall remain here (if nothing

10   expels me sooner) till about the 20$^{\underline{th}}$ ⅋ then probably make
straight for Homburg. I suppose it is not ∧at[∧] all enterprising to
revert thus mechanically to a place I know so well: but I have no
time nor money to waste in explorations ⅋ I know Homburg to
be cool, salubrious, cheerful ⅋ propitious to ~~d~~ six weeks

15   scribbling. My present design therefore is to arrive there about
July 5$^{\underline{th}}$. ~~N~~ Absolutely nothing has befallen me since I last wrote,
⅋ I hardly speak to more than three or four persons a week. The
Lombards (the consolers of my solitude—for to that had I
come!) went off ⋄ to Venice about a week ago, ⤴ with

20   Mrs. Dana—(Willy will tell you who she is.) They were in a
very feeble way, but I imagine the change of air ⅋ the Venice
breezes have helped them. The Gryzanowskis rose in their
might the other day ⅋ invited me to dinner—a great event for
both of us: for since Xmas. I have dined out but twice, by the

25   charity of Mme. Laussot. Tell W$^{\underline{m}}$. I continue from time to time
to see that household, but with effort. I have tried to make a
friend of Hillebrand, but I like him too little, ⅋ the ladies are
really too deaf. Gryz'ski. spoke of enjoying much his
correspondence with father. I ⋄ lately got a letter from Wendell

30   Holmes, telling me he was coming abroad, ⅋ proposing we
should "travel together. This of course is impossible ⅋ I am
afraid we shall not even meet, as with his short allowance of time
he ~~po~~ probably won't care to touch at Homburg. I regard it as
fixed, however, that I shall return home either Aug. ~~15~~ 20$^{\underline{th}}$ or

about October 5ᵗʰ· In the 1ˢᵗ case from Bremen; in the 2ᵈ from
Liverpool. Each has its advantages, but I won't decide till I get
North of the Alps. Both your letter ɟ Alice's are a mine of
advice: Alice's that I must not turn up my nose at home things, ɟ
yours that I take a wife. I will bore a hole in my nose ɟ keep it
down with a string, ɟ if you will provide the wife, the fortune, ɟ
the "inclination" I will take them all.—I am sorry the summer
question pesters you so ɟ devoutly hope it will find some happy
solution. I am almost shamed to have a German watering place
to turn to so easily.—I hear once in a a while from A. M.
Tweedy, who does not, as you say, write a ~~very~~ ₍ₐ₎letter₍ₐ₎ of
genius. I wrote about a month ago, asking you to please ask
~~A. K.~~ Uncle R. to have my letter of credit renewed for a
convenient sum. I hope the letter duly reached you ɟ the thing
was done, as my present credit is exhausted (that is, the time the
letter was to run) ɟ I shall be left high ɟ dry unless the other
arrives. I await it from week to week.—I ~~wrote you~~ ₍ₐ₎have said₍ₐ₎
before that I would send home but one or two things more to
print this summer as I am occupying myself exclusively with my
novel. It is proceeding to my satisfaction—not very rapidly, but
very regularly, which is the best way. The produce of it will
make up all my arrears.—I ought to have told you in my last that
you will have to begin addressing me for the summer Care of
Brown Shipley ɟ Co. It is the only possible course, in view of the
uncertainty of my movements; I had bother last summer in
trying to give you local addresses.—I ought to tell you that I am
in health continually better ɟ this in spite of the heavy Italian
air. But I must close, with multitudinous blessings on all.—
Won't you send me those <u>Notes</u> from the Independent?—But I
~~lose~~ ₍ₐ₎have₍ₐ₎ less ɟ less desire to see my printed things over here,
the errors are so ~~de~~ distressing, ɟ always, by some cruel fate,
such bad ones. Two very bad ones in the <u>Siena</u>, ɟ the <u>Adina</u> also
much spotted. I lately sent an excellent review of Feydau's
Gautier to the <u>Nation</u>, but I see Laugel has anticipated me. I

will write to have it sent to the N. A. R. ~~Faref~~ Farewell, sweet
mammy & all the rest of you. Alice shall have a due response to
her brilliant letter. Ever your   H. J jr

Previous publication: *HJL* 1: 452–54

∾

173.17   to day • to | day

173.26   ⋄ lattice • [l *overwrites illegible letter*]

173.27   ~~in~~ on • [o *overwrites* i]

173.29   degrees & • [& *overwrites blotted* s]

173.31   convenient • con= | venient

173.32   ~~I we~~ In • [n *overwrites* we]

174.4   sunshine • sun- | shine

174.4   ~~to~~ and • [an *overwrites* to]

174.5   ~~a~~ in • [i *overwrites* a]

174.6   beer=garden • beer= | garden

174.13   explorations • ex= | plorations

174.14   ~~d~~ six • [s *overwrites* d]

174.16   ~~N~~ Absolutely • [A *overwrites* N]

174.19   ⋄ to • [t *overwrites illegible letter*]

174.19   ⋆ with • [w *overwrites* —]

174.29   correspondence • correspon= | dence

174.29   ⋄ lately • [l *overwrites illegible letter*]

174.33   ~~po~~ probably • [r *overwrites* o]

174.34   ~~15~~ 20ᵗʰ • [20 *overwrites* 15]

175.6   fortune • for= | tune

175.10   a a • a | a

175.21   regularly • reg= | =ularly

175.31   ~~di~~ distressing • [i *overwrites illegible letter*]

175.34   anticipated • antici= | pated

176.1   ~~Faref~~ Farewell • [w *overwrites blotted* f]

∾

173.19   your letter of May 19ᵗʰ • Probably MWJ to HJ, 18 May [1874].

173.21 To you I wrote some ten days since · 17 May 1874 to MWJ (pp. 166–71).

174.20 Mrs. Dana · Probably Sarah "Sally" Watson Dana (1814–1907), wife of Richard Henry Dana. She lived in Europe during the late 1870s.

175.10–11 A. M. Tweedy · Aunt Mary Tweedy.

175.12 I wrote about a month ago · 3 May [1874] to WJ (p. 161).

175.13 Uncle R. · Alexander Robertson Walsh.

175.19–20 my novel · *Roderick Hudson*.

175.29 those <u>Notes</u> from the Independent? · The eight-part "Florentine Notes" series.

175.33–34 an excellent review of Feydau's Gautier to the <u>Nation</u> · HJ's review of Ernest Feydeau's *Théophile Gautier, Souvenirs Intimes*, actually published in the *North American Review*.

175.34 Laugel has anticipated me · Auguste Laugel (1830–1914) had published "Feydeau's Life of Gautier" in the *Nation*.

176.1 N. A. R. · *North American Review*.

WILLIAM JAMES

13 June [1874]   20

ALS Houghton

bMS Am 1094 (1961)

<u>Monte Generoso</u>

    Near Como. June 13<u>th</u>   25

Dear W<u>m</u>. I am sitting under a sort of little shed, on a sort of terrace, overlooking a sort of view—writing this at a rustic table, the rusty nails of which lacerate my wrists as I drive the pen. Opposite are established Mrs. Lombard & Fanny!! But of them anon.—I wrote home last from Florence—speaking then, if I   30 remember, as if I expected to remain there till the 20<u>th</u>. I absconded at a day's notice, just a week ago, under pressure of the terrific heat which suddenly descended upon all Italy a few days before & sent all travellers spinning northward. I was greatly contrarié to leave, but the atmosphere was intolerable & work had become impossible. I came on to Milan, grasping on the way—a most scorching but most delightful day at Ravenna. Of this I shall write to the <u>Nation</u>. I At Milan I met the Fl Lombards fleeing

5   from Venice & much distracted to know where to go. I being minded to come up here to await, if possible July 1ˢᵗ, they decided to come as well: so we ascended together last evening, in a thunder storm which caused them much discomfiture, But this morning we are rested & dried; & though I confess to a certain

10   sinking of the heart at finding myself fixed on a mountain top, with the old too, too familiar Swiss pension life going on about me, & a dozen English clergyman clergymen in "puggaries" kicking their enormous heels on the front steps—yet I confess ₍ₐ₎am inclined₍ₐ₎ to take a cheerful view of things. A small closet

15   5 feet square isn't favorable to literary labor, but I shall give myself a chance to get used to it, & doubtless succeed. The air is delicious—Alpine freshness tempered by Italian softness—the views enchanting, the food eatable & the company ₍ₐ₎apparently₍ₐ₎ estimable. There are ad agreeable strolls & shady hillsides & I shall

20   perch till I can perch no longer. (Your letters, meanwhile, must come to Brown & Shipley.) The heat in Italy for the past fortnight has been extraordinary & for a week in especial, intolerable. The journey in ₍ₐ₎from₍ₐ₎ Florence & the couple of days at Milan were spent in a mere demoralized <u>soak</u> of perspiration. The Lombards

25   say Venice was fatally uncomfortable & seem to have come away with an indifferent opinion of it. I am more than satiated with their society, but they are too feeble for criticism; & they make no exactions. They will probably depart in a few days for Geneva to join Essie.—I have not heard from home in some time, & am

30   expecting letters to be sent from Florence. Just before starting I got a <u>nation</u> with my letter from Pisa &c. What do you think of this for a misprint:—"idle vistas & melancholy nooks"="<u>idle sisters & melancholy monks</u>!!" In the article on <u>Siena</u> the sense of two or three good sentences was also ruined.—But this is not a

letter—but only a notification of my whereabouts & I must not embark on details. I am rather stiff & sore with my climb yesterday & must lie off, horizontally. I am afraid you are all ~~suffering from~~ [∧]struggling painfully[∧] with the summer question, & I wish I had a bosky-flanked Monte G. to offer you. The opal=tinted view, the drowsy breeze, the stillness & the tinkling cow=bells are gradually sinking ~~i~~ [∧]into[∧] my soul.—I had been wondrous well in Florence, until the great heat began, & that rather undid me: but on this higher plane I shall doubtless mend. Much love to all: I shall write again speedily. In spite of the temperature, I have been ~~charmed to~~ [∧]lacerated at[∧] leaving Italy. Ravenna is remarkable: I wish I had given a 2$^{\underline{d}}$ day to it. I trust you are prospering & that the summer will pass well with you. I have not yet answered directly your letter about my coming home; but I answered it through mother. I shall certainly come.

Yours ever <u>H. James jr</u>

Previous publication: *HJL* 1: 455–56; *CWJ* 1: 234–35

∾

178.1   atmosphere • at= | mosphere

178.4   ~~I~~ At • [A *overwrites* I]

178.4   ~~Fl~~ Lombards • [L *overwrites* Fl]

178.10 mountain • moun= | tain

178.12 ~~clergyman~~ clergymen • [e *overwrites* a]

178.19 ~~ad~~ agreeable • [g *overwrites* d]

178.24 demoralized • de= | moralized

178.26 indifferent • in= | different

178.32 misprint • mis= | print

179.14–15 coming home [. . .] <u>H. James jr</u> • [*written across the letter's first page*]

∾

177.30 I wrote home last from Florence • 3 June [1874] to MWJ (pp. 173–76).

178.1   contrarié • bothered.

178.3–4 Of this I shall write to the <u>Nation</u> • "Ravenna."

178.29 Essie • Essie Lombard.

178.31 a <u>nation</u> with my letter from Pisa • "Tuscan Cities."

178.32–33 <u>idle sisters</u> ~~&~~ melancholy <u>monks</u>!! • The penultimate sentence
was corrected in *Transatlantic Sketches* to read: "How grass-grown it
seemed, how drowsy, how full of idle vistas and melancholy nooks!" (326).

178.33 the article on <u>Siena</u> • "Siena."

179.14–15 your letter about my coming home • WJ to HJ, 18 April
1874, discusses HJ's presumed reaction on returning to Cambridge (*CWJ*
1: 229–31).

HENRY JAMES SR.
23 June 1874
ALS Houghton
bMS Am 1094 (1826)

> Hotel Royal, Baden-Baden
> June 23ᵈ '74.

Dearest father: I wrote home about ten days ago from Monte
Generoso, giving an account of my departure from Florence and
subsequent adventures; but I am sorry to say that I have not yet
had time to receive the letters which I fondly hope have been
accumulating for me at Florence. I am expecting them speedily,
but I am unwilling to delay writing until they come, lest you
should fancy that I had fallen into a precipice of the ~~g~~ Generous
~~m~~ Mountain or that ~~Miss~~ Mrs Lombard had poisoned me in a fit
of jealousy of my attentions to Fanny.—You behold me now in
fresh fields and pastures new—among which however for rest and
comfort's sake, I hope to remain long enough to permit them to
grow stale and old.—A week of Monte Generoso convinced me
that the conditions of life on an even divinely beautiful mountain
top were not favorable to my prosperity, mental or physical, so
that without losing more time I repaired immediately to this

place. By immediately I mean _via_ the Splügen pass, Chur ᵭ
Basel—at each of which latter places I spent a night. I came down
from Generoso on Saturday a.m last (this being Wednesday,)
crossed the mountain that night on the summit of the diligence
and arrived here yesterday (Tuesday) afternoon. My stopping
here, experimentally, was a happy thought, for twenty four hours
observation of this enchanted valley have determined me to abide
here for the present. I was deadly sick at the idea of going back to
that too too familiar Homburg, ᵭ yet I didn't know what else to
do. This cuts the knot, as far as I can foresee, effectually. Baden,
judged by one walk ᵭ one séance last evening on the t̶o̶ terrace of
the Conversation House, listening to the Band is an absurdly
pretty ᵭ coquettish little _ville_ _d'eaux_ embosomed in a l̶a̶y̶b̶
labyrinth of beautiful hills ᵭ forest walks. In all this it leaves
Homburg quite behind—as also in the facilities for frugal living.
(I have just concluded an arrangement to dwell awhile at this
extremely comfortable little hotel to the tune of 10 frs. a day). It
is inferior to Homburg, I believe, in climate; but after Italy I
don't believe I shall find the air oppression. Besides, Turgeniew
lives here, ᵭ I mean to call on him. Many of his tales were
probably written here—which proves that the place is favorable
to literary labor. Thus encouraged I shall settle down to my own
ᵭ hope to p̶r̶o̶ ₐachieve₍ₐ₎ a quiet summers attention to it. I shall
not lack quiet, I imagine, as the racketing days of Baden are said
to be well over. I have no further news. Monte Generoso was
lovely—but a place to lie all day on the grass, rather than to work
indoors or to walk. The Lombards came down with me to Como,
ᵭ started for Geneva, _via_ Mont Cenis—there to await Essie   I
can't write more till I have heard from you again. Heaven bless
you all, poor b̶ Beloved Baden=less creatures! I will write again
promptly when I have h̶e̶a̶r̶d̶ ₐgot my₍ₐ₎ letters. Meanwhile I bless
you all ᵭ remain dear dad your loving son H.

Previous publication: _HJL_ 1: 457–58

❧

180.21 departure • [*first* r *inserted*]

180.26 g̶ Generous • [G *overwrites* g]

180.27 m̶ Mountain • [M *overwrites* m]

180.27 M̶i̶s̶s̶ Mrs • [rs *overwrites blotted* iss]

181.5 Tuesday • Tues | day

181.7 determined • de= | termined

181.11 t̶o̶ terrace • [e *overwrites illegible letter*]

181.12 Conversation • Conversa= | tion

181.13–14 l̶a̶y̶b̶ labyrinth • [by *overwrites* y *and blotted* b]

181.30 b̶ Beloved • [B *overwrites* b]

181.30 Baden=less • Baden= | =less

❧

180.18 Hotel Royal • Murray's *Handbook for North Germany* lists the Hotel Royal among Baden-Baden's high-class hotels with the following typical charges: "rooms from 1 mk. 70 pf. upwards, breakfast from 1 mk. 25 pf., service 70 pf." (419).

180.20 I wrote home about ten days ago • 13 June [1874] to WJ (pp. 177–79).

181.1 the Splügen pass • Mountain pass (2,113 m) on the road from Chiavenna, north of Lake Como, Italy, to Chur, Switzerland.

181.12 the Conversation House • The Conversationhaus, built in 1824, described by Murray's *Handbook for North Germany* as

> a handsome building [. . .] with a Corinthian portico, surrounded by pleasure-grounds, forming the lounge and chief resort—in fact, the grand focus of attraction for the visitors at Baden. It is one of the most splendid establishments of the kind in Germany, and includes a very fine and large assembly-room, where there is dancing at times, to which people repair in their morning dress. There is a *Restaurant* in the rt. wing, where dinners may be had à la carte; and in the l. the *Circulating Library* and *Reading-room* of M. Marx, open to all, where The Times, Galignani's Messenger, and other English papers are taken in. (420)

When gambling was still authorized in Baden-Baden, the Conversationhaus was the principal gaming location.

181.13 ville d'eaux • spa town.

181.28 Essie • Essie Lombard.

WILLIAM JAMES
6 July [1874]
ALS Houghton
bMS Am 1094 (1954)

Baden Baden July 6th
        Hotel Royal
Beloved Brother:
        I wrote home some ten days ago, while I was still waiting
for your letters to be sent from Florence. They came a day or
two later—one from you of June 1st, one from father of the 11th,
& one, forwarded from Wilky. Also ⊕ a number of the
Independent. The time has come round again for a new arrival,
but I won't wait to k acknowledge it. Your letter was most
welcome & satisfactory, but I am afraid I can give you nothing of
equal value in return. I am sorry your eyes had been bothering
you, but I trust you have worked them up by this time to their
normal level. What chiefly preoccupies me is my wonderment as
to what your are going to do in ∧with[∧] the summer. I saw in one
of the papers an allusion to some late terrific heat in New-
Y[o]rk. I hope it was not as bad as reported or that if so, it
stopped mer[c]ifully short of Cambridge. Alice & A. K. are of
course by this time packed off to the white ∧green[∧] mountains
& I hope you have salubrious retreat in prospect, for at least a
part of the summer.—Writing from out of these shady blue
forests of Baden, I feel as if it shamed me even to allude to your
possibilities of discomfort. Heaven bless you (or rather fan you,
all!) My last letter will have told you of my coming here straight
from Italy, of my having lost my heart my heart to the e
loveliness of the place & fixed myself here for an indefinite

period. I shall probably remain undisturbedly till ~~Aug.~~ ∧Sept.[∧]
1st, unless induced to adjourn to Homburg about Aug. 1st by the
Tweedies, who are probably coming back from England to go
there. But I hope, for a little conversation's sake, to make them
5   c[ome] here.—I have been [ ] passing a very tranquil &
uneventful ten days. I scribble in the morning, walk in the
woods in the afternoon & sit ∦ listening to the music on the
promenade & eating an ice in the evening. Baden is a
wonderfully pretty place & exactly arranged by nature for its
10 rôle. It is embowered in Forests & ~~their~~ they are singularly
handsome; I never knew to the same extent the fascination of
trees. The walks & strolls are multitudinous & wherever you go
you want to lie down on the grass ∧in beechen shade[∧] and look
at the blue hills. Socially, the beaux jours of Baden are over & the
15 life of the place is very dull. I have seen no one I know, &
converse with nature more than with man. Turgenieff, alas, has
just sold his villa & departed; I am told that in former years he
was constantly "round."—You will have learned by this time by
my late lett[er] [ ] intentions as to coming home, promulgated
20 in reply to your letter received in Florence. You will have
observed that I don't consider my return e now equivalent to the
design of fixing myself there for ever, as you seemed to imply.
But we can talk of this when I arrive, which ~~we~~ will probably be
in October via England. I ~~do n~~ regret that I cannot echo your
25 satisfaction on leaving Italy for Germany. I don't think a
residence of years would modify materially my joyless
∧attitude[∧] ~~to~~ ∧toward[∧] this people, their physiognomy & and
their manners. I didn't ~~n~~ know, until coming back here now, how
wedded I was to my preference for a life in Italy to any other, &
30 indeed if I couldn't live ~~theer~~ there I think I would rather not
live in Europe at all. Either Italy or downright Yankeedom! The
hitch in the matter is that I'm wrong in not caring for the
horrible G.'s, as Mrs. Lombard [woul]d say, more: but when I
[ ] a justification, I find it in their atrocious passion for foul air.

Reserve your opinion ◇◇ ∧until₍∧₎ you have had to sit down with
fifteen persons to a 1 o'clock dinner in a low=ceiled dining room,
t̶o̶ on a July day, with the thermometer at 86° ⅋ every crack ⅋
cranny hermetically sealed. We have been having very great heat
⅋ I'm afraid Baden isn't particularly cool. The nights however,   5
have been delicious. I don't know what to tell you. I note your
injunction if I stay in Europe to "get married" ⅋ if I write you
that I have changed my mind ⅋ mean to pass the winter, you may
∧expect to₍∧₎ hear of my <u>matrimonio</u> by the next steamer.
Perhaps the chambermaid here, the large-waisted Anna, will   10
have me. I got, apropos, a letter from Wilky in which, speaking
of his marriage, he says <u>more</u> <u>suo</u>: "The former condition is as
happy a one as any I ever made for myself!" Father's letter
contained an extract from Bob, about his baby [which] made me
feel unmis[tak]ably the bowels of an a̶◇̶ ₍∧₎uncle₍∧₎. It was a   15
charming sketch and must make mother and Alice hanker
terribly after the babe. Tell Alice ⅋ A. K. that they must write
me about their inn. Do you see Lowell, if as, I suppose, he has
returned? I parted from him in Florence most affectionately ⅋
promised him to dine with him at home, every Sunday: but I   20
confess I don't look forward with absolute enthusiasm to a life in
which the chief recreation should be a weekly dinner with L.
I wish you had given me more gossip about certain people at
home. How is T. S. P. in matrimony? Do you see La Farge, ⅋
what was the history, and what the results of his time abroad?   25
The result, I see by the <u>Nation</u>, was his getting his pictures
refused at the academy. I have written to W. H. but hear nothing
from him: I trust he will come here. Are there any more facts
about the Nortons? I heard from A. M. Tweedy lately, from
England, that they thought of coming to Homburg for August ⅋   30
wanted me to meet them there: but this I have mentioned. I also
shortly since heard from Mrs. Lombard, very desperate for a
refuge in Switzerland ⅋ wanting to come here. I wrote her a
report of prices, ⅋ as they are not high, she may arrive. I received

one Independent with a notice of the Pitti P[alace] father speaks
as if two had been [ ] the Indpt. the other day a sketch of my
journey out of Italy: but of meagre value, as the subject was no[t]
rich. Farewell, dear Bill: excuse this insipid scrawl. It is the best I
5 have just now. Thank father for his letter Ꝓ blessings on him Ꝓ
mother. Peace Ꝓ comfort to you all—Yours ever   H. James jr

Previous publication: *CWJ* 1: 238–41; *WHSL:* 96–98

∾

[*The lower part of the ms. is damaged. Bracketed material represents probable
missing and/or illegible text.*]

    183.16 Ꝓ a • [a *overwrites illegible letter*]
    183.18 k̶ acknowledge • [a *overwrites* k]
    183.22 preoccupies • pre= | occupies
    183.24–25 New-Y[o]rk • New- | Y[o]rk
    183.26 mer[c]ifully • mer= | [c]ifully
    183.33–34 e loveliness • [l *overwrites* c]
    184.7 Ꝓ̶ listening • [l *overwrites* Ꝓ]
    184.10 t̶h̶e̶i̶r̶ they • [y *overwrites* ir]
    184.19 promulgated • pro= | mulgated
    184.20 received • re= | ceived
    184.21 e̶ now • [n *overwrites* e]
    184.23 w̶e̶ will • [i *overwrites* e]
    184.24 d̶o̶ n̶ regret • [reg *overwrites* do n]
    184.27 Ꝓ and • Ꝓ | and
    184.28 n̶ know • [k *overwrites* n]
    184.29 wedded • wed= | ded
    184.30 t̶h̶e̶e̶r̶ there • [er *overwrites* eer]
    184.31 downright • down= | right
    185.3 t̶o̶ on • [on *overwrites* to]
    185.7 married • mar= | ried
    185.15 unmis[tak]ably • unmis[tak] | ably
    185.21 confess • con= | fess
    185.31 mentioned • men= | tioned

185.32 desperate · des= | perate

186.2 [ ] the · [*possibly more than one word missing*]

186.2–6 the Indpt. [. . .] H. James jr · [*written across the letter's first page*]

◆

183.13 I wrote home some ten days ago · HJ to Sr., 23 June 1874 (pp. 180–81).

184.14 beaux jours · happy days.

184.14 the beaux jours of Baden are over · Gambling was banned in Baden-Baden in 1872.

184.20 your letter received in Florence · WJ to HJ, 18 April 1874 (*CWJ* 1: 229–31).

185.9 matrimonio · marriage.

185.12 more suo · in his own way.

185.14 Bob · RJ.

185.24 T. S. P. · Thomas Sergeant Perry

185.27 W. H. · Oliver Wendell Holmes, Jr.

185.29 A. M. Tweedy · Aunt Mary Tweedy.

186.1 one Independent with a notice of the Pitti P[alace] · The third part of "Florentine Notes."

186.2–3 the other day a sketch of my journey out of Italy · "A Northward Journey," reprinted in *Transatlantic Sketches* as "The Splügen."

MARY WALSH JAMES
28 July 1874   25
ALS Houghton
bMS Am 1094 (1827)

Baden Baden July 28ᵗʰ 74.
Dearest mother—   30
     This cannot possibly be a letter, for I have absolutely nothing to write about. I only wish, in the 1ˢᵗ place, to thank you for your letter of July 7ᵗʰ which, with a note from Willy, came to me some days since, & in the 2ᵈ, to let you know that I sail from

Liverpool, in the <u>Java</u>, August 25<u>th</u>. I hope therefore to arrive
about the 3<u>d</u> or 4<u>th</u> September, by which time you will have had
leisure to return comfortably from the country & settle ~~yourself~~
yourselves in Quincy St. The interval, I trust, will pass speedily
for both of us & nothing will mar the felicity of our reunion. —
Beyond this, I have nothing to relate, nor even to mention. The
days ∧as they,[∧] follow each other, look so much alike that I can
hardly tell them apart. The extreme heat has within a ~~weak~~
week, somewhat subsided, & existence has consequently more
charms. But this is the only thing that has happened. Nothing
not only befalls me, but I hear of nothing that befalls any one
else. For a moment there was a possibility of my seeing Wendell
Holmes & wife; but that ~~hi~~ has evaporated, & we shall probably
not meet, tho' we sail from Eng. within 2 days of each other. He
is to spend August (I suppose visiting) in England. The
Tweedies too are not to turn up, as A. M. writes me they have
taken for two months a cottage near her sister's place. She
invites me to visit them & I shall probably look at them before
sailing. I am here for upwards of another week & then to
England, probably <u>via</u> the Rhine & Rotterdam. Now that I am
booked for home I am intolerably impatient to start & to arrive.
I was happy to have you give a cool acct. of your Summer up to
the time you wrote. May you have kept cool & be now about to
repair as you designed, to Alice & A. K.'s resort. I hope this has
turned out satisfactory to them, & that Willy is lodged
somewhere where the breezes play about his brow. His last note
contained a request to buy some surgical instruments in
Dresden for him, wh. I shall now not be able to do. I asked
father in my last to let me know of anything he wished me to do
in London for him. Farewell sweet mammy. I hope this will find
you reposing on that "elevated plateau" which Aunt. K.
describes in a letter to me just received, for which I beg you to
thank her. I hear Alice has taken to riding & rejoice in the noble
circumstance. I wish I were bumping by her side. — Farewell. In

one little month—hardly more—I shall press you in my arms. Be sure, about Sept. 4ᵗʰ to have on hand a goodly store of tomatoes, ice-cream, corn, melons, cranberries & other indigenous victuals. With love to all—your H.

Previous publication: *HJL* 1: 458–59

ॐ

188.3 comfortably • com= | fortably

188.3–4 ~~yourself~~ yourselves • [v *overwrites struck-out* f]

188.8–9 ~~weak~~ week • [e *overwrites* a]

188.13 ~~hi~~ has • [a *overwrites* i]

188.13 probably • pro= | bably

188.18 probably • pro= | bably

188.20 Rotterdam • Rotter= | dam

188.21 arrive • ar= | rive

188.32 describes • des= | cribes

188.33 rejoice • re= | joice

188.34 circumstance • cir= | cumstance

ॐ

187.33 your letter of July 7ᵗʰ • MWJ to HJ, 6 July [1874].

187.33 a note from Willy • Possibly WJ to HJ, 25 June 1874 (*CWJ* 1: 236–38).

188.1 the Java • According to the 9 September 1874 *Boston Daily Advertiser* passenger list, HJ sailed from Liverpool on the *Atlas*.

188.16 A. M. • Aunt Mary Tweedy.

188.17 her sister's • Charlotte Temple, Lady Rose.

ELIZABETH BOOTT
29 July [1874]
ALS Houghton
bMS Am 1094 (513)

5

Baden Baden July 29$\underline{th}$
Dear Lizzie—
     This is not a letter; it is only a word of thanks for your
lovely long letter (& your father's, not so long, but still lovely,)
10   received a short time ago. I shall see you so soon face to face that
I haven't the heart to embark on this thin epistolary intercourse;
it seems like an affectation. Moreover, if I wished to write, I
couldn't, for the dullest five weeks of my life, at this place, have
not only furnished me with no communicable matter, but have
15   left me nothing of the meagre stock of ideas I brought with me:
I have been living like the bears in winter on my accumulated
<u>fat</u>. Your letter, under these circumstances, was a tenfold greater
blessing than ever & made me long to find myself again in your
amiable presence. I rather object to your incorrigible satisfaction
20   with your native land, as I don't return with any great gusto, but
simply from the ~~forces~~ force of circumstances. But if you are
really as contented as you say I should do you a poor service to
undermine your comfortable faith. Perhaps, if I were a paintist I
might feel more with you, as nature in America, though much
25   less paintable than here, ~~is~~ ∧may[∧] still, being nature, sufficiently
attitudenize for you in her brighter moods.—Were you ever in
Baden∕B?—àpropos of nature? It is extremely lovely here & has
greatly consoled me for the extinction of man. The glory of
Baden has passed away with the cessation of the gambling, & tho'
30   the paths are raked & the flowers are watered and the music plays
nightly at the Conversation house, the only entertainment is to
sit and look at a troop of 3$\underline{d}$ rate Germans parading up and down
on the hottest summer nights in mufflers & cotton gloves. But
this Black Forest scenery is lovely & if you & your dear papa were

here I should propose our combining to take a carriage & drive
for ten days through the whole region—through vast shady
forests & past vine=smothered cottages, populous with the
handsomest possible little tow-pated, blue eyed children. You
could put it all into paint, your father into divine melody & I   5
into the <u>Nation</u>. We can't make such plans as that together at
home— —ungrateful maid! I left Florence melancholy ages
ago—driven away prematurely by a violent spell of heat. I left
your cousins there, caressing Miss Huntington on the occasion
of her engagement. I couldn't caress, but I could reasonably   10
congratulate her. M. Wagnière is a genteel little Swiss Italian
banker with affable manners & a talent for the violin. Miss Laura
rather overtops him I think; at any rate he is too little to beat
her.—I am told you are at Rye—a place of which my ideas are
vague. I hope at any rate it is not as hot as the cakes from which   15
it derives its name are required to be by connoisseurs. <u>Also</u>—
about Sept. 5$\underline{th}$ I expect to pull your bell-handle & not to be kept
waiting! Love & thanks to your father & every blessing to
yourself. Yours ever faithfully, dear Lizzie—<u>H. James</u> jr.

No previous publication

ᘉ

190.10   received • re= | ceived
190.17   tenfold • ten= | fold
190.21   ~~forces~~ force • [ce *overwrites* ces]
190.22   contented • con= | tented
190.25   sufficiently • suffi= | ciently
190.27   ⤳B • [B *overwrites* —]
190.31   Conversation • Conver= | sation
190.31   entertainment • en= | tertainment
191.3   vine=smothered • vine= | smothered
191.7   — — • — | —
191.8   prematurely • pre= | maturely
191.18–19   & every [. . .] <u>H. James</u> jr. • [*written across the letter's first page*]

॰

190.8–9 your lovely long letter (& your father's, not so long • Elizabeth Boott to HJ, 13 June 1874, and Francis Boott to HJ, 14 June [1874].

191.9 Miss Huntington • Laura Huntington.

191.14 Rye • Rye, New Hampshire, a coastal resort next to Portsmouth.

SARAH BUTLER WISTER

10 29 July [1874]
TLC Bryn Mawr College Library

Baden-Baden July 29th

Dear Mrs. Wister—

15   I wrote you some weeks since from Florence a few lines simply as an advance on a letter more worthy of your own gracious liberality. I hope you safely received it & have not been supposing that I have remained irresponsive & dumb until this hour. The days meanwhile have gone by & I have torn myself
20 away from Florence & am making the best of existence in this degenerate and melancholy spot. In truth, I had better have written my letters out and out in Florence, for my spirits have been chilled & my imagination blighted by the dullest weeks of my life, which I am now bringing to their lagubrious term. Were
25 you ever at Baden Baden, in the good old time of the gaming? With the suppression of this its light has quite gone out & you, even if you are visiting those Quaker relations again about whom you wrote me last summer so charmingly, are not spending days of a greyer hue than those which have been
30 passing over my devoted head, in the shadow of the despoiled conversation House. Fortunately Baden is enchantingly pretty & I have taken to the woods, like the hunted negro of romance & amused myself with long solitary strolls in the Black Forest.

This is really quite fabulously picturesque & has helped to
console me for the universal flatness of mankind as represented
at Baden. Fortunately, too, I have had a rather absorbing piece
of scribbling to do, & the weeks have taken themselves off with a
better grace than at one time seemed likely. I scribble in the
morning, & walk, as aforesaid, in the verdurant gloom of the
Schwarzwald in the afternoon & I sit and listen to the band on
the terrace & consume <u>force</u> glaces in the evening. I converse
with the waiter & the chambermaid, the trees & the streams, a
Russian or two, & a compatriot or two, but with no one who has
suggested any ideas worthy of your attention. My literary labor,
however, has interested me & I hope, before long will interest
you. I am writing a novel for the Atlantic next year (beginning
January) &, as I go, have had frequent occasion to think of you.
It all goes on in Rome (or most of it) & I have been hugging my
Roman memories with extraordinary gusto. The fault of the
story, I am pretty sure, will be in its being too analytical &
psychological, & not sufficiently dramatic and eventful: but I
trust it will have some illusion for you, for all that. Vedremo.
This is the only fact with color in it that I can offer you, save
except one other which just now rather takes the lead. I sail for
America on the 25th of August (from England)—a rather sudden
decision. I had had thoughts otherwise of going back to Rome,
but various practical considerations have turned the scale and
now that the thing is settled, (though the settlement cost me a
grievous pang) I am extremely impatient to have it over, to start
& to arrive. It has at least the merit that it will make it possible
for me to see you within some calculable period. I have no plans
of liking or disliking, of being happy or the reverse; I shall take
what comes, make the best of it & dream inveterately, I foresee,
of going back for a term of years, as the lawyers say, to Italy. I
shall spend two or three months at Cambridge, but I expect to
dispose of the winter in New York. Either there or in Boston or
in Philadelphia—wherever it can be most gracefully contrived, I

count upon seeing you. — All this is a copiousness of egotism
which it will take a friendly soul to excuse. Meanwhile, where
are you & what manner of life do you lead? Whom do you see. —
What do you do, or think, or feel? I imagine that your house in
the country, is by this time "done up" as they say in England, & I
hope your days there are filés <u>d'or & de aise</u>. Is Porter's picture
finished & does it please those whom it should please?
Particularly, have you seen that brave Miss Bartlett, who, I hear,
with her woe-worn friend, is coming back to Rome for the
winter. A winter's riding on the Campagna I think, may do
much to mitigate even such infelicities as Mrs. Sumner's. I cut
out of the Galignani the other day, to send you, a paragraph on
Miss Lowe's marriage, at Venice, but have stupidly lost it. You
have of course heard of the event but this had some account of
the happy man's pedigree & affiliations. He is apparently a
reputable British gentleman — & so much for Bellay! I call him —
the husband (I forget his name) the happy man: ∧but is he, <u>con
rispetto</u>, so ideally happy?[∧] By which gross speech I mean is his
wife, after all, the intensely interesting personage she seemed &
generally passed for? Miss Lowe always reminded me somewhat
of that Chief Justice of England, of whom some one said that
"no man was ever as wise as Lord So and So looked!" Beautiful,
mysterious, melancholy, inscrutable and all that — was it simply
her way of seeming, or had she unfathomable depths within?
Her marrying a British consul seems a little of a prosy
performance. — But these are impertinent reflections, at this
time of day, & she is certainly handsome enough to have a right
to be as much more or less as she choses. Apropos of the ancient
Romans, do you continue to hear from Lefevre? I suppose he is
biding his time & clutching at the skirts of fame. If the world is
to hear from him, however, I hope it will not be as the composer
of another Fille de Mme Angot — the surest passport to glory,
apparently, now possible in France. (I speak with the echoes of
last night's dreary performance of that work in my ears.) But I

194

must pull up   I remain here a few days longer & then go down
the Rhine to Holland, to take a look at Dutch pictures, which I
adore, & thence cross to England for a fortnight before sailing. I
shall see no one, save the Tweedies who have taken a house in
the country for the summer. Think of me after that as in a not-   5
to-be-thought-of state for ten days, & then as doing battle with
first impressions at Cambridge. It would be a blessing if ten lines
from you were to arrive there (at 20 Quincy St.) to help the
good cause. Farewell! My friendliest regards to Dr. Wister &
kind remembrances to your mother if, as I suppose, she is still   10
near you. Yours, dear Mrs Wister, most faithfully
    Henry James jr.

Previous publication: *HJL* 1: 459–62

    ∾

   192.17 liberality • liber- | ality

   192.22 Florence • Flor- | ence

   192.24 lagubrious • [*misspelled; possibly transcriber's error*]

   193.8 <u>force</u> • [*copy text reads:* <u>forci</u>]

   193.12 interested • inter- | ested

   193.18 psychological • psychol- | ogical

   194.6 filés • [*copy text reads:* file's]

   194.6 aise • [*possibly transcriber's error*]

   194.12 paragraph • para- | graph

   194.13 Lowe's • [*copy text reads:* Lane's]

   194.16 Bellay! • [*copy text reads:* Bellaq'.]

   194.20 Lowe • [*copy text reads:* Lane]

   194.28 choses • [*misspelled; possibly transcriber's error*]

   194.33 apparently • app- | arently

    ∾

   192.15 I wrote you • HJ to Sarah Butler Wister, 10 May [1874]
(pp. 164–65).

   193.3 a rather absorbing piece • *Roderick Hudson*.

   193.7 Schwarzwald • Black Forest.

193.8 <u>force</u> glaces · Many ice creams.

193.19 Vedremo · We shall see.

194.6 filés <u>d'or & de aise</u> · threaded <u>with gold and with ease</u>.

194.9 her woe-worn friend · Alice Sumner (Mason).

194.11–13 I cut out of the Galignani [. . .] a paragraph on Miss Lowe's marriage · *Galignani's Messenger* reported on the 20 June 1874 marriage in Venice of Elena Lowe, "daughter of the late Francis Lowe, Esq., of Boston," and "Gerald Raoul Perry, Esq.," British consul to the Island of Reunion and son of Sir William Perry, "for many years H. B. M.'s Consul-General at Venice" (9 July 1874: 3). See also *HJL* 1: 462n2.

194.16 Bellay · Possibly Charles-Alphonse-Paul Bellay; see HJ to Sarah Butler Wister, 10 August [1873] (p. 29).

194.17–18 <u>con rispetto</u> · <u>with respect</u>.

194.29 Lefevre · Charles Edouard Lefebvre; see HJ to Sarah Butler Wister, 10 August [1873] (p. 30).

194.32 Fille de Mme Angot · *La fille de Madame Angot*, an operetta by Alexandre-Charles Lecocq (1832–1918).

195.10 your mother · Fanny Kemble.

ROBERTSON JAMES
13 October [1874]
ALS Houghton
bMS Am 1975 (34)

25

Cambridge Oct 13<u>th</u>
Dearest Bob—

I have not written to you for so long that I am afraid you will think that I have abjured correspondence, on principle. This
30 is not the case, & I may truly say that during the last half of my stay in Europe there was a certain intended letter to you which continued to get put off from day to day & from week to week. I had so much writing, epistolary & other, to attend to that it never came to the light. You know of course of my being at

home & have, I hope, received good accounts of me. My arrival
is now a month old, first impressions are losing their E̶ edge &
Europe is fading a̶w̶o̶ away into a pleasant dream.—But I confess
I have become very ∧much[∧] Europeanized in feeling, & I mean
to keep a firm hold of the old world in some way or other.—But
home sems very pleasant, after the lonely, shiftless migratory life
that I have been leading these two years. Cambridge has never
looked so pretty as during the last month & I have seen nothing
in Europe in the way of weather equal to the glory of an
American autumn. I have extracted from mother & Alice all the
gossip they could furnish about you & Mary & (conjecturally)
about your infant son, & of course I feel nearer to you than I did
on the other side of the Atlantic; but after the modest little
railway journeys of Europe, you seem still to be divided from
me by a formidable gulf of time & space. Gradually, however, I
shall get re-accustomed to the American scale of things & then, I
trust, I shall pick up energy (to say nothing of funds) to come
out and take a look at you.—I should like to share your daily life
for awhile & have a glimpse of Western civilization. I never
think without silent applause of your hard laborious career;
fortune & fame, I doubt not, will crown it in the end. Meanwhile
you are happy as a husband & a father, & with these blessings,
one can live one's life.—They have been coming lately to Wilky
too—we are all extremely glad he has got a boy. I should like
hugely to see you, dear Bob, & to make the acquaintance of
Mary & the Babe. Some day I will. Love & blessings to them
meanwhile & a line from you when you have time. Ever your
brother—<u>Henry James</u> jr.

Previous publication: *HJL* 1: 466-67

❧

197.2 E̶ edge • [e *overwrites* E]
197.3 a̶w̶o̶ away • [a *overwrites illegible letter*]
197.6 sems • [*misspelled*]

197.6 migratory • mi= | gratory

197.10 American • Ameri= | can

197.11 conjecturally • con= | jecturally

197.24 extremely • ex= | tremely

197.28 brother—<u>Henry James</u> jr. • [*written across the letter's first page*]

197.12 your infant son • Edward "Ned" Holton James.

197.24 a boy • Joseph Cary James (1874–1925), born on 4 October and named after Carrie's father.

H. O. HOUGHTON AND CO.

[18 or 25 November, or 2 or 9 December 1874]

AL Houghton

15   bMS Am 2048.1

Mr. Henry James jr. accepts with pleasure Messrs. H. O. Houghton & Co's. invitation for the 15th inst

20   Cambridge
     <u>Wednesday p.m.</u>

No previous publication

198.13 [18 or 25 November, or 2 or 9 December 1874] • Letter written on a Wednesday after 15 November 1874 but prior to 15 December.

198.18 invitation for the 15th inst • The invitation was to the *Atlantic Monthly* commemorative dinner on 15 December 1874.

WELCH AND BIGELOW
[late December 1874–January 1875]
ALS Houghton
bMS Am 1094.1 (243)

5

New York 111 east 25<u>th</u> st.
Messrs. Welch & Bigelow—
Dear Sirs:
Will you be so good as to insert in the copy of
<u>Transatlantic</u> <u>Sketches</u>, which you are now printing, the   10
enclosed fragment, originally omitted? I am unable to page it:
but it belongs in the series entitled <u>Florentine Notes</u>, and ~~may~~
ₐhad₍ₐ₎ best be numbered IV or V. If these numbers have been
◊◊◊ ₐset₍ₐ₎ up, it may go last—as VIII or IX.(?)
Yours very truly <u>Henry James</u> jr   15

Previous publication: *HJL* 1: 472

∾

199.10 <u>Transatlantic</u> • <u>Trans=</u> | <u>-Atlantic</u>

∾

199.1 Welch and Bigelow • Cambridge printers.

199.2 [late December 1874–January 1875] • Letter written after HJ
took up residence at 111 E. 25th Street and before page proofs were set up
by Welch and Bigelow. HJ's residence at 111 E. 25th Street began after his
attendance at the reception given by Houghton and Co. on 15 December
1874 (see p. 198), HJ's last known date of residence in Cambridge before
he moved to New York City. In this letter HJ, now writing from New
York, implies that he had not yet received proofs for *Transatlantic Sketches*.
Thus, this letter must have been written before his 29 January [1875] letter
to Welch and Bigelow from 111 E. 25th Street, in which HJ indicates he
has received the proofs for his forthcoming book (p. 210).

ELIZABETH BOOTT
[22, 29 December 1874, or 5, 12, 19, or 26 January, or 2 February 1875]
ALS Houghton
bMS Am 1094 (514)

5

111 east 25<u>th</u>. Tuesday

Dear Lizzie —

A hundred thanks for your letter, & for the charming news
that you are coming to this place. I will give you an ardent
10   welcome & spend the whole period of your visit at your feet,
even tho' they <u>be</u> clad in Arctics. You have very strange notions
of my gayeties here. Pray on what are they based? — I am leading
the quietest & most humdrum of lives seeing few people & those
very stupid. You will be indeed an enchanting apparition. I will
15   take you anywhere you want to go — even to J. L. F.'s studio,
though he is out of town & it is closed. But we will manage to get
in. I am curious to know what you think of N. Y. It's a rattling
big luxurious place, but I prefer F— Excuse me! I can't trust
myself on that chapter. I am enchanted that things are so well
20   with you in Cambridge & that your'e having such comfortable
dances. I wish I had been there that night to share your joy.
Methinks that in a walz with you I might have renewed for an
hour my lost youth & fancied I was again in R—! It will out, you
see. La nostalgia non è nè p melio ne peggio. Non puo ne
25   crescere ne guarire. C'è un solo rimedio! Ma il vedervi sarà
almeno per l'ora ~~uno~~ una consolazione. I suppose you see my
people often & I am glad you are coming to report of me to
them. I hope your father is well & happy & I wish he were
coming with you. My affectionate salutations to him. On you,
30   dear Lizzie, my blessing & a speedy meeting.

Yours ever — H <u>James</u> jr

Previous publication: *HJL* 1: 471–72

∞

200.19 enchanted • en= | chanted

200.22 walz • [*misspelled*]

200.24 p̶ melio • [m *overwrites blotted* p; *misspelled*]

200.25 rimedio • ri= | medio

200.26 u̶n̶o̶ una • [a *overwrites* o]

∞

200.2 [22, 29 December 1874, or 5, 12, 19, or 26 January, or 2 February 1875] • Letter written from New York on a "Tuesday" before Lizzie Boott's visit to New York, which was also a month prior to HJ's recollection of that visit (see "un mese fa") in his next letter to her, 8 March [1875] (p. 211). Assuming the visit took place during the second week of February 1875, this letter would have been written on one of the Tuesdays prior and yet subsequent to HJ's arrival in New York in late December 1874 or early January 1875.

200.15 J. L. F. • John La Farge.

200.24–26 La nostalgia [. . .] una consolazione. • My nostalgia is neither better nor worse. I can neither grow nor heal. There is only one remedy! But seeing you shall at least be a consolation for now.

1875

WILLIAM DEAN HOWELLS
13 January [1875]
ALS Houghton
bMS Am 1784 (253), folder 1, letter 8

5

111 east 25th st.
　　Jan. 13th

Dear Howells—

　　I have just received your telegram about the proof,　　10
which went this p̶ [∧]a[∧].m. I was in the country when they came,
& they had been lying two days on my table, but I ⬦⬦ despatched
them as soon as possible on my return. Don't lose courage about
sending me more; I have made probably my only absence for the
winter. I hope this has not seriously bothered you.—I found also　　15
your letter which gave me all the pleasure I had given you.✓My
notices of the F. C. were written most pleasurably to myself.—I
am glad you are dining out & liking Boston. I'm afraid the tender
grace of a day that is dead will not revisit <u>this</u> stagnant heart.
But I come back to N. Y. (from near Philadelphia ∧to be　　20
sure,)[∧]) with a real relish. I feel vastly at home here & really like
it. Pourvu que ça dure! I have been staying at Mrs. Owen
Wister's & having Fanny Kemble read Calderon for me in tête à
tête of a morning. How is that for high? She had on a cap &
spectacles, but ⬦ her voice is divine. I see a little of Sedgwick &　　25
dine with him at theatrical chop-houses. ꞑ Naughty Bohemian!
Would that I were either! Farewell.—I seem to have books
enough on my hands for the Nation just now, but if you would
like a notice of Emerson's <u>Parnassus</u>, I might try it. In a week or
two begins the annual exhibit of water-colors at the Academy.　　30
Would you like a couple of pages on it, if I can supply them?—It
may interest you to know that the N. has dropped noticing the
magazines, a competent hand not appearing. I have looked up
Lathrop, but hardly f̶ seen him̶. I'm afraid he finds his ~~career~~

$_{\wedge}$experiment$_{[\wedge]}$ here not a bed of roses. With love a casa—Yours
H. J. jr.

Previous publication: *HJL* 1: 468–69; Anesko 106–07

205.10 received • re= | ceived

205.12 ~~⊖⊖~~ despatched • [d *overwrites illegible letters*]

205.16 ~~—~~My • [My *overwrites* —]

205.20 Philadelphia • Phila= | delphia

205.25 ~~⊖~~ her • [h *overwrites illegible letter*]

205.26 ~~n~~ Naughty • [N *overwrites* n]

205.29 Parnassus • Par= | nassus

205.30 water-colors • water- | colors

205.34 ~~f~~ seen • [s *overwrites blotted* f]

205.34 ~~;~~. • [. *overwrites* ;]

205.10 the proof • Presumably page proofs for one of the early *Atlantic Monthly* installments of *Roderick Hudson*.

205.16–17 My notices of the F. C. • HJ's two unsigned reviews of Howells's *A Foregone Conclusion*.

205.22 Pourvu que ça dure! • May it last!

205.23 Calderon • Pedro Calderón de la Barca (1600–1681), Spanish dramatist.

205.29 a notice • The *Atlantic Monthly* did publish an unsigned review—apparently by neither HJ nor Howells—of Emerson's *Parnassus* in the Recent Literature section of the April 1875 issue.

205.29 Emerson's Parnassus • Emerson edited *Parnassus* (1874), an anthology of poetry by English and American authors.

205.30 the annual exhibit of water-colors at the Academy • See HJ's "On Some Pictures Lately Exhibited," which he published in the *Galaxy*.

205.34 Lathrop • George Parsons Lathrop (1851–98), American author and husband of Nathaniel Hawthorne's youngest daughter, Rose (married

1871). He would become associate editor of the *Atlantic Monthly* (1875–77) and write *A Study of Hawthorne* (1876).

206.1 a casa • at home.

SARAH BUTLER WISTER
23 January [1875]
TLC Bryn Mawr College Library

    111 East 25th St.
     Jan 23rd.   10
Dear Mrs Wister—
    Butler Place & my visit there have had time to become a part of the "dreadful past" as Tennyson says—but I want to keep them a bit longer in the present if writing to you will help me to   15
do so—It has been on my pen's end to write before this—any one of half a dozen recent evenings when I have come in from the outer world to my smouldering fireside, put myself into slippers & felt the need of spending a rational hour before going stupidly to bed. That my letter didn't get written was I think in a   20
great measure owing to the fact that, sitting down by my fireside as before mentioned, I fell a-musing about you & prolonged my vigil in a sweet inaction which I really felt loath to interrupt by the (to me now-a-days) very vulgar act of scribbling. I came nearer doing so the other evening, however, on coming back   25
from a dinner at Mrs Lockwood's. I have seen that lady twice, in her own tranquil home & have felt, after each occasion, burdened with emotions which it would have been a relief to transfer to a sympathetic ear. They were emotions of high admiration & they were commingled with a very [*lively*]   30
gratitude to you for having made me know her. Most truly, she is a remarkable woman & a very exquisite creature. I think I may say that she gives me an impression of a finer intelligence, a finer mental machinery than any woman I have known. She strikes

me as rather too tense—too tendue—too <u>intense</u>; but I find it
does not at all keep my relations with her from being easy, & the
stuff she is made of is so thoroughly [*superior*] & the person is so
singularly lovely that a tête-à-tête with her is a great bliss. I
5 hope to have many.—Except those I speak of I have had nothing
since my return to town that is worth your hearing of.—I have
seen a certain number of ordinary people & read some dullish
books, & walked in Broadway, & eaten some good dinners &
worried through the days in one way or another. Life, alas, isn't
10 all resting on one's oars and staying at Butler Places and
breathing the atmosphere of intelligent hospitality. Since I came
back I have liked New York decidedly less—so little in fact that
<u>tedious</u> is the most amiable word I can find to apply to it. If one
could only get over the trick of judging things aesthetically.
15 With you, pray, how have things gone? Are you alone—that is
<u>en famille</u>—or have you had any more guests, punctual or
otherwise? Especially, have you danced the tight-rope over the
snow again to Germantown—alone, or with a companion of a
dancing disposition? I have thought a good deal about that
20 <u>premier mouvement</u> of mine & on the whole I don't repudiate it.
Properly looked at it had its fine points. Your mother, I hope, is
well & serene. I should like to send her my most cordial
salutations. I hope Dr. Wister has worked off his patriotic wrath.
Since my return here I found people trampling on Grant very
25 comfortably indeed. Pray give my kind regards to your husband
& lay my blessings on the head of that charming boy if he is still
at home. I have been out tonight among some people who were
telling ghost stories, & heard for the first time a young woman
maintain that she had seen a ghost with her own eyes. It was a
30 very pretty story—only too pretty to be true.—But I see ghosts
all the while over here. I live among 'em: the ghosts of the old
world & the old things I left là bas. I hope nothing disagreeable
has yet crossed the threshold of that little grey room—or any of
your thresholds.—I wish I could tell you all the good wishes I

have for you. Find a few between the lines here ↵ believe me
always yours very faithfully

H. James jr.

Previous publication: *HJL* 1: 469–71

∾

207.25 however • how- | ever

207.30 [*lively*] • [*The TLC does not transcribe this word; it offers a caret and
a gap. The bracketed insertion is taken from the published version in* HJL. *It is
possible that Edel used the manuscript following his receipt of the typed letter
copy.*]

207.33 intelligence • intelli- | gence

208.3 [*superior*] • [*The TLC does not transcribe this word; it offers a gap.
The bracketed insertion is taken from the published version in* HJL. *It is possible
that Edel used the manuscript following his receipt of a typed transcription of the
letter, which is the copy text here.*]

208.20 mouvement • [*Copy text reads* movement ; *since there is no evidence that Edel compared our particular TLC with the letter itself or corrected the
copy text, our rendering is based on* HJL, *which gives the word as "mouvement."
It is possible that Edel used for his version the manuscript of the letter to correct
what is given in the copy text.*]

208.26 if • [*copy text reads* If]

208.32 là bas • [*misspelled*]

∾

207.26 Mrs Lockwood's • Florence Bayard Lockwood (1842–98),
daughter of a prominent Delaware political family and wife of Maj. Benoni
Lockwood (1834–1909).

208.1 tendue • tense.

208.16 en famille • amongst your family.

208.20 premier mouvement • first step.

208.26 that charming boy • Future novelist Owen Wister Jr. (1860–
1938).

208.32 là bas • back there.

WELCH AND BIGELOW
29 January [1875]
ALS Special Collections, Olin Library, Washington University
William K. Bixby Collection

New York—
111 east 25th St. Jan 29th

Dear Sir.

I return you, corrected, the proof, <u>Transatlantic</u> <u>Sketches</u>, received ~~the~~ this morning. I wish urgently to call your attention to the fact that <u>each chapter must</u> <u>follow on a fresh page</u>. Here they follow without spaces & I think it terribly ugly. I beg you therefore to make the change. I wish this to be the case throughout, <u>except</u> in "<u>Florentine Notes</u>", in a <u>Roman Notebook</u> & (I believe) one other case where there are Roman numerals. Pray attend to this, at whatever inconvenience, & greatly oblige Yours truly   <u>Henry James</u> jr.

No previous publication

∾

210.11 ~~the~~ this • [i *overwrites* e]

WENDELL PHILLIPS GARRISON
[February 1875]
ALS Library of Congress
J. L. M. Curry Papers, General Correspondence, Second Series, volume 3, item 505

Dear Mr. Garrison—
Here is the notice of Theodore Martin—very slight—& here also a couple of <u>notes</u>—very light. But may also serve. I have yet two or three more little things to send you.

Very truly yours
    H. James jr.

No previous publication

∾

210.32 the notice of Theodore Martin • "The Prince Consort," a review of Theodore Martin's *The Life of His Royal Highness the Prince Consort*.

210.33 also a couple of notes • Probably HJ's review of *The Last Journals of David Livingstone in Central Africa* (entitled "Livingstone's Last
Journals") and his "Notes on the Theatres."

ELIZABETH BOOTT
8 March [1875]
ALS Houghton   15
bMS Am 1094 (515)

New York March 8ᵗʰ
    111 east 25ᵗʰ St.

                                                                                20
Mille grazie, cara Lisa, di vostra graziosa lettera, scritta nella
vera lingua di Dante—Dio la benedica! Sapete che la vita di
N. Y. è nemica di tutta occupazione seria e simpatica, e potrete
dunque perdonar al mio silenzio fin'ora. Penso spesso a quelle
poche orette che abbiamo potuto passar insieme un mese fa,—   25
mi rammento specialmente qulla cara ~~colazon~~ colazione da
Delmonico. Dico cara senza pun—non ho mai avuto tanto
piacere a cosi basso ◊ prezzo! E per provarvi che non mi ha
rovinato vi dico che vi prendo ancora la colazione ogni ~~d~~
Domenica nello stesso posto! ~~donna famosa~~ I Giorni vengono e   30
vanno, sempre aspri e selvaggi, mutando dalla pioggia alla névica
e vice-versa, senza apportarmi nessun avvenimento di vero
interesse. Ora [∧]che[∧] non ~~tr~~ posseggo più un orecchio
amichevole, per ricevere le mie ~~confidenza~~ confidenze

nostalgiche, sono forzato di seppelirle in mio tristo cuore, e
temo molto che mio eh carattere non ne prendi un brutto piego
permanente. Scrivete mi dunque, vi congiuro, qualche ◆◆ parole
consolatrici il più spesso che potrete; farete veramente opera di
5   carità. Andai una sera cercar consolal consolazione dai Botta;
trovai invece un German, ballato da giovani New Yorkesi dei
due sessi—ma d'Italiani, mica! Cercar un Italiano e trovar un
"Tedesco" è veramente crudele! Ho passato le mie ultime sere
ʌrecente₍ʌ₎ a sentir la Ristori, che ci da delle rappresentazioni da
10 una settimana. Donna vecchia e faticata, ma grand' artista, gran
stilo, e atmosfera Italiana.—Cosa vi dirò? La Wister ha passato
un giorno a N. Y., poco tempo fa, ed io l= ʌne₍ʌ₎ ho passato la
maggior' parte con lei, rae rinchiuso in vettura sotto pretesto di
errands.—Questo è un racconto romantico! Il vero dell'affare fù
15 molto prosaico.—E voi, cosa fatte ed a che santo vi ◆ndiz
indirizzate per soccorso in questi giorni uggiosi? Lavorate senza
dubbio splendidemente e vi fatte una vita col aiuto dei vostri
talenti ed ʌartistici₍ʌ₎ e sociali. Vedete spesso, io spero, la ʌmia₍ʌ₎
famiglia e loro dite del bene di me. Il padre ʌ—il vostro—₍ʌ₎
20 beve il caffè, passegia e fa la musica.—piaceri sufficienti per un
filosofo. Io che non ho ne caffè ne musica—ho bisogno, delle
volte, di tutta la mia filosofia. Addio, cara L◆◆ Lisa. Spero coi
primi giorni di vera primavera di darvi un colpo d'occhio a
C. Tanti complimenti al onorato padre. Vi auguro tutto il bene
25 del mondo e rimango il vostro amico—H. James jr

Previous publication: *HJL* 1: 473-74

211.26 qulla • [*misspelled*]
211.26 eolazon colazione • [io *overwrites* on]
211.27 Delmonico • Del= | monico
211.28 ◆ prezzo • [pr *overwrites illegible letter*]
211.29-30 d Domenica • [D *overwrites* d]
211.32 avvenimento • avveni= | mento

211.33 t̶r̶ posseggo • [p *overwrites* tr]

211.34 c̶o̶n̶f̶i̶d̶e̶n̶z̶a̶ confidenze • [*second* e *overwrites* a]

212.2 c̶h̶ carattere • [c *overwrites* ch]

212.2 piego • [*misspelled*]

212.3 permanente • perma= | nente

212.3 congiuro • [*misspelled*]

212.3 ◆◆ parole • [pa *overwrites illegible letters*]

212.5 c̶o̶n̶s̶o̶l̶a̶l̶ consolazione • [z *overwrites* l]

212.13 r̶a̶e̶ rinchiuso • [in *overwrites* ac]

212.15 fatte • [*misspelled*]

212.15 ed • [d *inserted*]

212.15–16 ◆n̶d̶i̶z̶ indirizzate • [i *overwrites illegible letter and* r *overwrites blotted* z]

212.17 fatte • [*misspelled*]

212.21 ne caffè ne • [*misspelled*]

212.22 L̶◆◆ Lisa • [is *overwrites illegible letters*]

∾

211.21–212.25 Mille grazie [. . .] vostro amico • A thousand thanks, dear Lisa, for your gracious letter, written in the true language of Dante—God bless it! You know that New York life is inimical to all serious and pleasant occupations, and you can then forgive my silence until now. I think often of those few little hours that we were able to spend together a month ago,—I remember especially that dear dinner at Delmonico's. I say <u>dear</u> without <u>punning</u>—I have never had such pleasure at so low a price! And in order to prove to you that it didn't ruin me let me tell you that I still dine every Sunday at the same spot! w̶o̶n̶d̶e̶r̶f̶u̶l̶ l̶a̶d̶y̶ The Days come and go, always bitter and savage, changing from rain to snow and <u>vice-versa</u>, without bringing me anything of real interest. Now that I no longer possess a friendly ear to receive my <u>nostalgic</u> c̶o̶n̶f̶i̶d̶e̶n̶c̶e̶ confidences, I am forced to bury them in my sad heart, and I fear very much that my character will be permanently twisted. Write to me, therefore, as often as you can, I conjure you, some consoling words; it would be a real act of charity. I went one evening to look for consolation at the Bottas; I found instead a <u>German</u>, danced by young New Yorkers of both sexes—but nothing Italian, at all!

To look for an Italian and find a "German" is really cruel! I spent my ~~last~~
recent evenings listening to Ristori, who is here for a week giving shows.
An aging and tired lady, but a great artist of the grand <u>style</u>, and an Italian
atmosphere. — What shall I tell you? Mrs. Wister spent a day in N. Y.,
a little while ago, and I spent the major part of it with her, shut up in her
carriage under the pretext of <u>errands</u>. — This is a romantic tale! The truth
of the affair was most prosaic. — And you, what are you doing and which
saint do you address for help during these gloomy days? No doubt you
work splendidly and you make yourself a life with the aid of your artistic
and social talents. You see often, I hope, my family and you speak well of
me to them. Father — your father — drinks coffee, goes for walks and makes
music. — sufficient pleasures for a philosopher. I, who have neither coffee
nor music — I need, some times, all my philosophy. Good-bye, dear Lisa.
I hope with the first <u>true</u> spring days to be able to give you in C. a quick
glance. Many compliments to the honorable father. I wish you all the good
in the world and remain your friend

    212.5 Botta • Vicenzo and Anne Charlotte Lynch Botta; he was an
Italian scholar and she a painter and poet. Their home on West 39th Street
in New York was a literary and artistic salon (see Edel 2: 189).

    212.9 Ristori • Actress Adelaide Ristori. See HJ to AJ, 3 February
[1867] (*CLHJ, 1855–1872* 1: 159, 160n159.9), and HJ's "Madame Ristori."

WILLIAM DEAN HOWELLS

[19 or 26 March 1875]
ALS Rutherford B. Hayes Presidential Center

    111 east 25th st.
      Friday evening.

Dear Howells —

    I read this morning your notice of A P. P. &—Well, I
survive to tell the tale! If kindness could kill I should be safely out

of the way of ever challenging your e ingenuity again. Never was friendship so ingenious—never was ingenuity of so ample a flow! I am so new to criticism (as a subject,) that this rare sensation has suggested many thoughts, & I discern a virtue even in being overpraised. I lift up my hanging head little by little & try to earn the laurel for the future, even if it be so much too umbrageous now. Meanwhile I thank you most heartily. May your fancy never slumber when you again read anything of mine!—

I hope to be in Cambridge for two or three days about April 10ᵗʰ, if by that time there is any symptom whatever of sprouting grass or swelling buds. We will take a walk together & you will help my town=wearied eyes to discover them. I will bring with me the "balance" as they say here, of my novel or at least the greater part of it. I hear rumors that you are coming this way (i.e. to New Jersey:) I hope it won't be at just that time. Of course you won't be here, with whatever brevity, without looking me up. The wheel of life revolves, here, but it doesn't turn up any great prizes. I lead a very quiet life & dwell rather in memories & hopes than in present emotions. With love to your home   Yours ever—more than ever— H. James jr.

Previous publication: Anesko 114

215.1 e ingenuity • [i *overwrites* e]
215.3 sensation • sensa= | tion

214.25 [19 or 26 March 1875] • 19 and 26 March were the last two Fridays in March 1875 and therefore, presumably, the most likely Fridays when HJ would have read the April 1875 *Atlantic Monthly*, which would have appeared between the middle and end of March.
214.32 your notice of A P. P. • Howells's review of *A Passionate Pilgrim, and Other Tales*. See also HJ to MWJ, 24 March 1873 (*CLHJ, 1872–1876* 1: 243).
215.13 my novel • *Roderick Hudson*.

ANNA HAZARD BARKER WARD
[spring 1875]
ALS Houghton
bMS Am 1465 (735)

5

My dear Mrs. Ward—

   It was wondrous kind of you yesterday to send me those
charming flowers, & I assure you I appreciate the favor from my
10   heart. I don't know what I have done to deserve it, or how I can
worthily repay it, but I ventured to enjoy the flowers as much as
if they formed the crown of virtue or of wisdom. They reminded
me indeed of the Roman springtime & I howled, fairly, in spirit
when I looked at that enchanting cyclamen & thought of the
15   sheets of it one sees at this time in the villas & on the
Campagna—& then saw from my window the hideous driving
sleet. It was not the least part of your kindness that it was so
singularly well-timed. I imagine that, in spirit, you were
wandering through that delightful Roman world, & I esteem it
20   an honor that in casting about you for sympathy you thought of
me. Such sympathy I assure you I can always offer you.—To day
is better, but your flowers, glowing there on my mantel-shelf,
make it better still. With many thanks & good wishes,
      yours most truly
25   <u>Henry James</u> jr.

III east 25<u>th</u> st.
   <u>Thursday noon</u>.

No previous publication

☙

216.22 mantel-shelf · mantel- | shelf

CAROLINE DALL
16 April [1875]
ALS Massachusetts Historical Society
Caroline H. Dall Collection, box 6, folder 8

111 east 25<u>th</u> St.
<u>N. Y. C.</u>
My dear Mrs. Dall—
    I found on the arrival of your little book that a notice of
it, by a person with whom I am not acquainted, was already in   10
t̶y̶◊ type. You are mistaken in supposing that I <u>have charge</u> of
the literary department of the Nation: I am a mere contributor.
On learning, therefore, that the notice in question was of a
somewhat restrictive character, I was simply able to repeat the
purport of your letter, ꝑ leave it to whatever consequences may   15
be. I send you this line because I desire you should know, should
the notice appear, that I am not the author of it. This is someone
more deeply versed than I in New England genealogies.
    Yours very truly
        <u>Henry James</u> jr.   20
<u>April 16th</u>

No previous publication

∾

217.9 arrival • ar= | rival

217.11 t̶y̶◊ type • [p *overwrites illegible letter*]

217.18 genealogies • gene= | alogies

∾

217.1 CAROLINE DALL • Caroline Wells Healey Dall (1822–1912), Boston feminist and author of *Transcendentalism in New England: A Lecture* and
The Romance of the Association; she met Sr. around 1866 and wrote about
him in her private journal.

217.9 your little book • *The Romance of the Association.*

217.10 a person with whom I am not acquainted · An unsigned review by William Henry Whitmore (1836–1900) of Dall's book appeared in the 13 May 1875 issue of the *Nation* (Haskell 1: 47, 2: 516). Whitmore called *The Romance* "a needless amount of gush" that "attempts to falsify the histories of the families" involved (334). See also HJ to Dall, 7 June [1875] (pp. 222–23).

H. O. HOUGHTON AND CO.
27 April [1875]
ALS Houghton
bMS Am 1925 (942), folder 1, letter 2

New York.
111 east 25<u>th</u> St.
April 27<u>th</u>

Messrs. H. O. Houghton ~~esq~~ & Co.
Dear Sirs—
        I drop a line to request that you will kindly direct future cheques to my order not to my present address, but
    <u>20 Quincy</u> <u>St. Cambridge</u>.
        Yours very truly
        <u>H. James</u> jr.

No previous publication

❧

218.18 ~~esq~~ & Co. · [& C *overwrites* esq]

MARY LUCINDA HOLTON JAMES
27 May [1875]
ALS Houghton
bMS Am 1975 (30)

5

36 Irving Place
   May 27<u>th</u>—
My dear Mary—

I have long had it on my conscience that I have not yet sent
you, as I desired to do, a couple of volumes which I have lately   10
put forth. I am sadly afraid that I can not justify my base
procrastination on any better ground than the ~~simply~~ simple
fact that, in order to be despatched by post, these volumes had
to be neatly enveloped & stoutly corded in brown paper, & that
my physical aversion & incapacity to tie up a parcel is so extreme   15
that it actually triumphed in this case over brotherly affection.
The parcels are not yet tied, but I have sworn a solemn oath that
they shall be before the sun goes down; & I trust they will reach
you safely & ~~at your perfect~~ [^]without falling[^] apart. I hope
also that you will feel obliged to look into the books only at your   20
perfect convenience.—I wish very much it was myself, in the
flesh, & not my stupid books, that was going out to see| [^]you.[^]
But the day for that will certainly come—I hope before very
many months. I have not seen Bob in an age, & shall have almost
to begin acquaintance with him at the beginning. Give my love   25
to him, & tell him that I am still a fond brother & that my first
loose change that has accumulated a little shall be devoted to a
pilgrimage to his dwelling. I am almost savagely impatient to see
your boy & can promise him that I will make a most delightful
uncle. You will see too that I will make an excellent brother-in-   30
law. Yours most truly
      <u>Henry James</u> jr

No previous publication

∞

219.12 procrastination • pro= | crastination

219.12 ~~simply~~ simple • [e *overwrites blotted* y]

219.15 aversion • avers= | ion

219.22 ┼ ∧ • [∧ *overwrites* .]

219.25 acquaintance • acquain= | tance

219.30–31 brother-in-law • brother | -in-law

∞

219.10 a couple of volumes • *Transatlantic Sketches* and *A Passionate
Pilgrim, and Other Tales.*

JAMES RIPLEY OSGOOD
[late spring 1875]
15   ALS Harry Ransom Humanities Research Center,
University of Texas at Austin
MS James, H. Letters; James, Henry. Works, letters A–Z box:
James, Henry letters folder

20   New York:
        36 Irving Place.
          Thursday a.m.
My dear Mr. Osgood—
        Would you be so good as to have sent to me, when it
25 appears, a copy of Tennyson's "Queen Mary"?—I intend to
review it, somewhere.
        Yours very truly
          <u>Henry James</u> jr
J. R. Osgood esq.

No previous publication

∞

220.14 [late spring 1875] • Assigned date based on HJ's temporary
residence in the late spring of 1875 at 36 Irving Place, New York; see HJ to

Mary Lucinda Holton James, 27 May [1875]; HJ to Caroline Dall, 7 June [1875]; HJ to George William Curtis, 7 June [1875]; and HJ to William Dean Howells, [23 or 30 June 1875] (pp. 219, 221–22, 222–23, 223–24, respectively). These four letters and this letter to Osgood are the only extant letters from 36 Irving Place. All are written on the same paper and are either dated by HJ or involve publishing matters that occurred at this time.

220.25 Tennyson's "Queen Mary"?—I intend to review it · HJ's review appeared as "Mr. Tennyson's Drama" in the *Galaxy*.

GEORGE WILLIAM CURTIS
7 June [1875]
ALS Yale
Beinecke Rare Book and Manuscript Library
Yale Collection of American Literature Manuscript Miscellany YCAL
MSS MISC Group 494, item F-1

N. Y. 36 Irving Place.
June 7th

My dear Mr. Curtis.

I have just been informed that I have been elected into the Century Club, & that I owe this good fortune in no small degree to your very friendly exertions on my behalf. Let me without delay thank you most cordially for your kind offices. I am afraid they cost you more time & trouble than you could conveniently spare—& I would say also a greater outlay of the art of stating things felicitously, & in a way to persuade, if I did not feel that in this point your riches were great. You may at least feel sure that your services have been warmly appreciated. I expect to find the Century a great resource, but I shall particularly value my membership if it is often my fortune to meet you there.

Believe me most truly ⅋ gratefully yours—
   <u>Henry James</u> jr

No previous publication

ᘛ

221.31 appreciated • appre= | ciated

ᘛ

221.23–24 elected into the Century Club • The Century Association was an exclusive New York private club for cultural figures. It is known to James scholars as the owner of John La Farge's portrait of HJ. Curtis and Arthur Sedgwick nominated HJ for membership, and he was elected at the association's 5 June 1875 monthly meeting. HJ remained a member until 1878.

15

CAROLINE DALL
7 June [1875]
ALS Massachusetts Historical Society
Caroline H. Dall Collection, box 6, folder 9

20

   N. Y.
   36 Irving Place.
   June 7<u>th</u>
My dear Mrs. Dall—

25   I should have sooner answered your note, had I ♭ not been during these last days, particularly occupied. I am sorry matters turned out as they did with regard to the notice of the Romance. I stand, with respect to it, quite in the position of an outsider. I have not read the book—having laid it aside when I
30 learned that a notice of it was already in print, ⅋ having since been occupied with other reading, which has taken all my time. I am therefore quite unable to measure the merits of the <u>Nation's</u> strictures or of what is justly to be replied to them. I can only say, with tolerable₁ safety, that I myself, if I had spoken

of the Romance, as you requested, would have written
otherwise. My disconnectedness with the question goes
further—for I am wholly ignorant of the authorship of the
notice—I have not even an inkling of it. I very much regret the
vexation you have suffered, but I imagine that you are not   5
learning for the first time that authorship is not a bed of roses!

Yours very truly
Henry James jr.

No previous publication

∾

222.25 ƀ not • [n *overwrites* b]

222.26 occupied • occu= | pied

222.33 strictures • stric= | tures

222.34 ¦ • [*blotted out*]

∾

222.28 Romance • See HJ to Caroline Dall, 16 April [1875] (p. 217).

WILLIAM DEAN HOWELLS   20
[23 or 30 June 1875]
ALS Houghton
bMS Am 1784 (253), folder 5, letter 37

36 Irving Place   25
        Tuesday—
Dear Howells.

Who is it that writes as well as you—almost, & yet is not
you? I have been reading the notice of T. S. in the Atlantic with
unbounded and grateful relish. It would be fatuous for me to   30
praise it, but let me at least beg you, whoever the author is, to
tell him I thank him from my heart & consider him the most
charming ~~thing~~ [ʌ]fellow[ʌ] in the world. Whoever he is, I say; &
especially if he is Lathrop!

223

Yours ever truly

<u>H. James</u> jr.

P. S. I have had it at heart ever since I heard the fact, to drop you a hint of my pleasure in learning that your'e lightened
5   of your editorial burden. Honestly, I feel a thrill of almost physical ~~satisfactin~~ satisfaction in the thought of that genius of yours now having its ease & its leisure to go & do one good thing after another, through all the coming years. Heaven's blessing attend it!

10

———

Previous publication: Anesko 219–20

∾

223.33 Whoever • Who= | ever

224.6 ~~satisfactin~~ satisfaction • [o *overwrites* n]

∾

223.21 [23 or 30 June 1875] • The following facts help date this letter: HJ's reference to the *Atlantic Monthly* review of *Transatlantic Sketches* ("T. S."), which appeared in July 1875; his reference to George Parsons Lathrop, who became associate editor of the *Atlantic* in 1875; and the 36 Irving Place address, from which HJ's only known letters, all of which use the same stationery, were written in the late spring of 1875. See HJ to Mary Holton James, 27 May [1875]; HJ to James Ripley Osgood, [late spring 1875]; HJ to Caroline Dall, 7 June [1875]; and HJ to George William Curtis, 7 June [1875] (pp. 219, 220, 221–22, 222–23, respectively).

223.29 reading the notice of T. S. in the Atlantic • *Transatlantic Sketches* was reviewed in the July 1875 *Atlantic Monthly*.

JOHN MILTON HAY
21 July [1875]
ALS Brown
John Hay Collection, MS. James 1875 Jul 21

5

20 Quincy St.
        Cambridge, Mass.
            July 21ˢᵗ
Dear Mr. Hay—
        Sometime before leaving town (which I did a few days   10
since,) I called in 42ᵈ St., to find, to my regret, that you had
already migrated for the summer. I had considerable discourse
with the worthy woman who keeps your door (& for whose
circumspection in opening it to able-bodied men in the dusky
hours I can answer,) & she intimated that you had left town   15
earlier than was natural, on account of some indisposition of
your own. I hope the remedy has been effectual, & that you are
now in the best of health; & that Mrs. Hay & your daughter share
this blessing with you.—If I had seen you, perhaps I should not
be writing to you now, & I am glad of a pretext for doing so. I   20
have had it at heart for some little time to ask you a question or
two; & perhaps it is prudent not longer to delay.
        I have a tolerably definite plan of going in the autumn to
Europe & fixing myself for a considerable period in Paris. I
should like, if I do so, to secure a regular correspondence with a 25
newspaper—non=political (I mean of course the
correspondence,) & tolerably frequent: say three or four letters a
month. When I say a "newspaper" I ~~mean~~ ₐhave₍ₐ₎ an eye, of
course, upon the Tribune. To my ambition, in fact, it would be
the Tribune or nothing. There is apparently in the American   30
public an ◇◇ essential appetite, & a standing demand, for
information about all Parisian things. It is as a general thing
rather flimsily & vulgarly supplied, & my notion would be to
undertake to supply it in a more intelligent and cultivated

fashion—to write in other words from the American (or if it doesn't seem presumptuous to say so, as far as might be from the cosmopolitan) point of view a sort of chronique of the events and interests of the day. I have thought the thing over in its

5 various bearings, & have satisfied myself that I could put it through. Indeed I have a dazzling vision of doing very good things. I should have a fair number of strings to my bow, & be able to write on a variety of topics—"social" matters, so called, h manners, habits, people &c, books, pictures, the theatre, & those

10 things which come up in talk about rural excursions & dips into the provinces₁. I should come to the matter with a considerable familiarity with a good many points in French civilization, & should, I think, always feel pretty sure of my ground. Lastly, I should be likely to produce a tolerably finished piece of writing,

15 & my letters would always have more or less the literary turn. I think I know how to observe, & may claim that I should observe to good purpose & chronicle my observations agreeably.

This very handsome account of myself is prefatory to an interrogation which you must answer at your convenience. Could

20 the Tribune make any use of these brilliant gifts? Would it enter into its economy for the coming winter (to begin with) that I should address to it the weekly masterpieces of which I have given a hint? To Two obvious reflections of course occur to me. One is that the Tribune has its regular ◊ political correspondent,

25 whose province may not be invaded. I have should have no fear of even having to warn myself against trespassing on his field; our two lines would remain naturally so distinct. The other is that perhaps Arsène Houssaye is giving, you & to continue to give, the Tribune all it wants. In this last case, of course I am

30 anticipated; but if his relations with the paper are destined within the coming couple of months to terminate ∧—& let me not seem obtrusively to assume that they are—[∧], or you are weighing the question of renewing them,—my proposition may have a certain timeliness. J'ai dit!—I hope not too diffusely. I don't know that

there is anything to add, save that my letters would of course be welcome to whatever credit my signature might bestow upon them—ᴆ that during three months or so of the year, I should be glad to date them from other places—out of the way ones, sometimes, where I might have gone it pursuit of the curious. If I had not seemed already to have blown my trumpet so lustily I would superadd that I "calculated" to produce, every way, a very good style of thing.—Such answer, more or less conclusive, as you may be good enough to give to all this will find me <u>here</u> for some time to come. I have chiefly wished, for the present, to register myself in the Tribune's books. With kind regards to Mrs. Hay, ᴆ the best wishes for the prosperity of your summer— Yours very truly—<u>Henry James</u> jr.

Previous publication: Monteiro 81–83; *HJL* 1: 476–78

∾

225.17 effectual • effect= | ual

225.21 question • ques= | tion

225.26 non=political • non | =political

225.31 ◇◇ essential • [es *overwrites illegible letters*]

225.34 supply • sup= | ply

226.1 American • Ameri= | can

226.8–9 ~~h~~ manners • [m *overwrites* h]

226.11 ¦. • [. *overwrites* ,]

226.23 ~~To~~ Two • [w *overwrites* o]

226.24 ◇ political •[p *overwrites blotted illegible letter*]

226.25 ~~have~~ should • [shou *overwrites* have]

226.28 ~~you~~ ᴆ to • [ᴆ t *overwrites* you]

∾

225.1 John Milton Hay • Indiana-born statesman and author (1838– 1905). Hay was an editorial writer for the *Tribune* from 1870 to 1875 and again in 1881.

225.18 Mrs. Hay • Clara Louise Stone (1849–1914), daughter of a Cleveland railroad magnate, married Hay in 1874.

225.18 your daughter • Helen Julia Hay (1875–1944), poet and wife of
Payne Whitney (1876–1927).

226.3 chronique • chronicle.

226.24 regular ✧ political correspondent • William Henry Huntington
(1820–85), American philanthropist and regular Paris correspondent for
the Tribune.

226.28 Arsène Houssaye • Arsène Houssaye (1815–96), French novelist
and critic.

226.34 J'ai dit! • I have spoken!

JOHN MILTON HAY

5 August [1875]

ALS Brown

John Hay Collection, MS. James 1875 Aug 5

Cambridge: Aug 5ᵗʰ.
    20 Quincy St.
My dear Mr. Hay—

I find your note of July 30ᵗʰ on my return from a short visit
to the country.—First of all let me thank you heartily for the
trouble you have taken & for your sympathy & good will. May I
ask you to render me a further service? Will you be so good as
to let Mr. Reid know that I accept his offer of $20. gold, & that I
expect to be able to write my first letter by about October 25ᵗʰ.
It is a smaller sum than I should myself have proposed, but
being, as you say, good newspaper payment, I summon
philosophy to my aid.

Your account of your own situation made me feel as if it
had been very stupid in me to lay my case before you. But
indeed it was only the day before that I had severely snubbed
Howells for intimating that you had begun a flirtation with
business, & I appealed to you with a perfect good conscience.
May I you have all the pleasures of the "avarice" you speak of, &

none of its pains—its apprehensions & alarms about your
money=bags; & may these speedily become full to bursting! I
feel as if my sails had caught a very liberal capful of wind, in this
epistolary enterprise, from your good wishes. Were I disposed
to doubt that I should put it through, I should reflect with   5
satisfaction that at any rate your perspicacity believed in it. You
fill me with regret that I should not have caught a glimpse of the
Giorgionesque daughter of your portress. Her golden hair
would have done something to console me for not finding
you.—Will you kindly add in communicating with Mr. Reid,   10
that I shall endeavor to see him before I leave America. With
many thanks, once more, & kind regards to Mrs. Hay—yours
very truly H. James jr

Previous publication: Monteiro 83–84; *HJL* 1: 478–79

∾

228.32 intimating • in= | timating
228.34 I you • [y *overwrites* I]

∾

228.24 Mr. Reid • Whitelaw Reid (1837–1912), Civil War correspondent, *New York Tribune* editor, diplomat, and Spanish-American War peace
commissioner.

JOHN MILTON HAY   25
18 August [1875]
ALS Brown
John Hay Collection, MS. James 1875 Aug 18

   Cambridge Aug. 18ᵗʰ   30
     20 Quincy St.
Dear Mr. Hay—
   I must acknowledge the receipt of your last note & thank
you for it—the more so as I have it on my conscience to say that

I shall find myself obliged to leave America a couple of weeks
later than I expected, & to begin the immortal letters at a date
correspondingly posterior. But I shall not be a day later than I
can help.—I appreciate the force of your reflections about the
5   letters proving (potentially) a (relative) gold=mine in the long
run; & if the run is long enough quite expect to be coupled
anecdotically with Milton in all allusions for ₍ₐ₎to₍ₐ₎ the £5, or
whatever it was, he received for Paradise Lost.—I am very glad
to hear you have hit upon <u>your</u> pretext for going to Paris. The
10   honor of your ingenuity awaited it! I am also delighted that
Mrs. M̶ Hay keeps abreast of the age as regards dados. If you can
purchase a second=hand one out of the Earthly Pardise, of
course you will do the right thing. The great point however is to
have one, of some sort or other, & to have mastered the art of
15   alluding to it as if you had had it for twenty years! I can talk
about them very prettily, but to this hour I am not sure that I
know what they are.—With cordial good wishes—

    Yours very truly

      H. <u>James</u> jr.

20   <u>John Hay</u> esq

Previous publication: Monteiro 84–85; *HJL* 1: 479–80

    ॐ

230.3   correspondingly • corres= | pondingly

230.11   M̶ Hay • [H *overwrites* M]

230.12   second=hand • second= | hand

230.12   Pardise • [*misspelled*]

    ॐ

230.2–3   begin the immortal letters at a date correspondingly posterior
• HJ's first letter, "Paris Revisited," dated 22 November 1875, appeared in
the *New York Tribune* on 11 December 1875.

230.12   the Earthly Pardise • Refers to William Morris's poem "The
Earthly Paradise" and to Morris's decorating company, Morris, Marshall,
Faulkner & Co.

J. R. OSGOOD AND CO.
18 August [1875]
ALS Yale
Beinecke Rare Book and Manuscript Library
Za James 12

5

Cambridge Aug. 18<u>th</u>
   20 Quincy St.
Dear Sirs.

I have just received your account of date Aug. 16<u>th</u>, for   10
the stereotyped plates of <u>Transatlantic Sketches</u>, &c: T̶ the
whole amounting to $555.07. I have received no account on the
sale of the "Sketches," & of a "Passionate Pilgrim", & I beg you
to send me one, balanced, ∧as regards my own profits,[∧] against
the amount of the present bill. I will then settle the latter, so   15
modified.

Yours very truly
   <u>H. James</u> jr.
<u>Messrs. J. R. Osgood & Co.</u>

Previous publication: *HJL* 1: 480

∞

231.10 received • re= | ceived
231.11 stereotyped • stereo= | typed
231.11 <u>Transatlantic</u> • <u>Transatlan=</u> | <u>tic</u>
231.11 T̶ the • [t *overwrites* T]

∞

231.10 your account • See HJ's 31 August [1875] letter to James Ripley
Osgood for the settling of this account (p. 233).

H. O. HOUGHTON AND CO.
24 August [1875]
ALS Houghton
bMS Am 1925 (942), folder 1, letter 1

Cambridge 20 Quincy St.
        Aug. 24<u>th</u>
Dear Sirs.
        I desire to make a request of you which I hope you will
find convenient. It would be a service if you would advance me
the balance of payment due on my story of <u>Roderick</u> <u>Hudson</u>,
now running in the Atlantic. It has been paid for up to this time
month by month, ✠ there are four numbers (one just published)
yet unpaid for. I sail for Europe in a few weeks ✠ if I might be
put into possession without delay of the outstanding four
hundred dollars I should consider it a favor.
        Faithfully yours
        <u>H. James</u> jr.
<u>Messrs</u> ~~Hurd~~ ✠ [A]H. O.[A] <u>Houghton</u>. ✠ Co.

Previous publication: *HJL* 1: 480–81

H. O. HOUGHTON AND CO.
30 August [1875]
ALS Houghton
bMS Am 1925 (942), folder 1, letter 3

20 Quincy St.
        Cambridge
                Aug. 30<u>th</u>
Dear Sirs.
        I beg to thank you extremely for your cheque for $400 —
the remainder=payment of <u>Roderick</u> <u>Hudson</u>, which I find on my

return from the country. I was aware that it was not usual with
you to advance money on MS.; & I am therefore proportionately
grateful to you for making an exception in my behalf.—

Yours very truly

H. James jr.

Messrs. H. O. Houghton & Co

Previous publication: *HJL* 1: 481

JAMES RIPLEY OSGOOD
31 August [1875]
ALS New York Public Library
Berg Collection

Cambridge Aug 31ˢᵗ.

20 Quincy St.

My dear Mr. Osgood—

I found here yesterday, on my return from a week's
absence, your note of the 23ᵈ, which, if I had been at home,
should have been sooner answered. I enclose a cheque for the
amount of your account. My profits on a Passionate Pilgrim are,
I confess, a trifle less than I had hoped.

————

As regards Roderick Hudson it would be a convenience to me
if the copy might go to press immediately. I have just
determined to sail for Europe about the 20ᵗʰ of October, & I
should like to read the whole proof before starting. The last
number of the novel comes out in the 20ᵗʰ of November: might
not the volume therefore anticipate it a little & appear during the
first days of that month? It would make, I should think, a book
of about the size of a Pass: Pilgrim, with a somewhat smaller
type. If you will let me know when I need deliver copy, I will
immediately comply.

Yours very truly
    H. James jr.
J. R. Osgood esq.

No previous publication

⌇

233.19 yesterday • yes= | terday
233.25 convenience • con= | venience
233.26 immediately • imme= | diately
233.27 determined • deter= | mined
233.29 ~~in~~ the • [th *overwrites* in]

EDMUND CLARENCE STEDMAN

15 1 September [1875]
ALS Special Collections, Colgate University

Cambridge Sept. 1st.
My dear Sir:

20   I find on my return from an absence in the country your
very gratifying and interesting letter. I am very glad that my
notice of Queen Mary gave you any pleasure & greatly ~~int~~
indebted to you for taking the trouble to express it to me. I find
it, I confess, rather confusing, even, to be complimented on the
25 article in question; especially by one who speaks on poetic
matters with authority. My pretentions, in attempting to talk
about Tennyson, were very modest, & I made no claim to express
myself as anything but, as it were, an outsider. I know him only
as we all know him—by desultory reading—& indeed from a
30 comparative & categorial examination of any great poet I would
always earnestly shrink. I know poets & poetry only as an
irredeemable proser⤧! So if I have seemed to you to hit the nail
at all on the head, in speaking of Tennyson, I am only the more
thankful for my good fortune.—I need hardly say that your own

observations strike me as very much to the ∧point[∧]—both
those in your letter & those in the enclosed sheets from your
book. The latter, on its appearance, I shall be very glad to see. I
hesitate to agree with you in your forecast of what Tennyson
will hereafter attempt & what English poetry is likely to come to. 5
Not that I have an opposite opinion, but simply because these
are questions in which I find myself much at sea—the whole
poetic mystery and its conditions being emphatically a mystery
to me. I can only say that were I myself capable of using the
instrument of flexible verse, I should go in with great goodwill 10
for the dramatic form. Your prevision two years ago of
Tennyson's putting forth a drama is very noticeable; &
noticeable also your mention of the exceptional originality of
the fable of the <u>Princess</u>.—I quite sympathise with you in your
wonder that Browning should have never felt the intellectual 15
comfort of "a few grave, rigid laws." But Browning's badness I
have never professed to understand. I limit myself to vastly
enjoying his goodness.

    With many thanks & good wishes I remain, my dear Sir,
        Yours very truly 20
        <u>Henry James jr.</u>

Previous publication: *HJL* 1: 481–82

    ☙

234.20 country • coun= | try

234.22–23 ~~int~~ indebted • [d *overwrites* t]

234.28 anything • any= | thing

234.31 earnestly • earn= | estly

234.32 ~~⟋~~! • [! *overwrites* —]

235.10 instrument • instru= | ment

    ☙

234.14 Edmund Clarence Stedman • American businessman, poet,
essayist, critic, and editor (1833–1908).

234.21–22 my notice of <u>Queen Mary</u> • "Mr. Tennyson's Drama."

235.2–3 your book • *Victorian Poets* (1875).

235.11–12 Your prevision two years ago of Tennyson's putting forth a drama • HJ probably refers to Stedman's "Alfred Tennyson."

235.14 the fable of the <u>Princess</u> • Tennyson's *The Princess: A Medley* (1847). See Stedman's *Victorian Poets:* "I leave 'The Princess,' deeming it the most varied and interesting of his works with respect to freshness and invention" (167).

H. O. HOUGHTON AND CO.

7 October [1875]

ALS Houghton

bMS Am 1925 (942), folder 1, letter 4

20 Quincy St. Cambridge

————

Oct 7<u>th</u>

Dear Sirs. — It would be a great favor if you could let me have each day <u>considerably more</u> proof of "Roderick Hudson." I am afraid otherwise I shall not be able to finish revising before the 17<u>th</u>, on which day I leave Cambridge for Europe. ᵃ About two-thirds (or a little less) of the volume remain to be seen thro' the press in these coming ten days. I shall need at this rate to see ◊ upwards of 30 pages a day, instead of the usual 12. I have not yet had proof of the XII<u>th</u> part of <u>R. H.</u> from the <u>Atlantic</u> — so that if you will have that put thro' with as little delay as possible it will also be a service. — I delivered copy for the press only up to one half of part X. Having the sheets of the Atlantic in your hands it will save time if you will please to use them simply as they stand for the remainder. I can easily make the few needful alterations ᵒⁿ in the proof of the reprint. — The matter of giving me more proof is, as you see, very urgent.

Yours very truly
        H. James jr.
Messrs. H. O. Houghton & Co

Previous publication: *HJL* 1: 483–84

∾

236.20 considerably • con= | siderably
236.22 a About • [A *overwrites* a]
236.24-25 ⊕ upwards • [u *overwrites illegible letter*]
236.25 instead • in= | stead
236.32 on in • [in *overwrites* o]
236.32 reprint • re= | print

H. O. HOUGHTON AND CO.   15
[13 October 1875]
ALS Houghton
bMS Am 1925 (942), folder 1, letter 6

20 Quincy St. Wednesday—   20
Dear Sirs.—
        I yesterday revised the proof of the Atlantic's last part of
"Roderick Hudson," which I suppose you will directly send to
~~press for printing~~ ₍ₐ₎to be composed₍ₐ₎ the plates. I would like
here to suggest a small change. This last ~~p~~ Part is numbered XII.   25
Please divide it ₍ₐ₎in the plates₍ₐ₎ into XII & XIII. Let the division
come where I marked on the Atlantic proof a red cross—that is
about a third of the way down the slip numbered 5, & at the
words (which shall begin chap. XIII) "Roderick on the homward
walk that evening . . ." Pray substi= for the title of the chapter in   30
the magazine (Switzerland) the following in the volume: "The
Princess Casamassima. And pray transfer in the volume the title
Switzerland to chapter XIII. This I think I have made plain.
        Yours very truly

<u>Henry James</u> jr

Messrs. ~~Hurd~~ & [∧]H. O.[∧] Houghton & Co

(For Proof-Reader.)

Previous publication: *HJL* 1: 482–83

∽

237.25 p̶ Part • [P *overwrites* p]

237.29 Roderick • Rod= | erick

237.29 homward • [*misspelled*]

237.30 substi= • substi= |

∽

237.16 [13 October 1875] • The content of this letter suggests it was written on a Wednesday after HJ's 7 October [1875] letter to H. O. Houghton and Company (pp. 236–37) and before HJ left Cambridge for England (Sunday, 17 October 1875, according to his 13 October [1875] letter to George Abbot James, p. 238); 13 October is the only intervening Wednesday.

20   GEORGE ABBOT JAMES

13 October [1875]

ALS Houghton

bMS Am 1094.1 (151), letter 51

25   Cambridge Oct. 13ᵗʰ

Dear George—I have been waiting to answer your note till I should have finished labelling & ticketing the hours that are left me before I sail. They are so few in number (I leave Boston Sunday p.m.) that I am afraid I can't make a solemn meal with

30   you. But I will call θ at your office on Saturday, as nearly ~~at~~ as possible ~~as~~ at 12½; & at least shake hands with you. Many thanks for your offered hospitality. Excuse this brutal brevity, & believe me, with kind regards to Mrs. James & [∧]a[∧] blessing on the boy—

Yours faithfully
<u>H. James jr.</u>

No previous publication
ᖇ

238.30 ~~o~~ at • [a *overwrites* o]

238.30 ~~at~~ as • [s *overwrites* t]

238.31 ~~as~~ at • [t *overwrites* s]

238.32 hospitality • hospi= | tality

ᖇ

238.33 Mrs. James • Elizabeth Cabot Lodge James.

238.33–34 the boy • Ellerton James (1872–1926).

H. O. HOUGHTON AND CO.   15
15 October [1875]
ALS Houghton
bMS Am 1925 (942), folder 1, letter 5

Cambridge, ~~J~~ Friday Oct. 15<u>th</u>   20
Messrs. H. O. Houghton & Co.
    Dear Sirs—
        I enclose copy for title page & contents of "Roderick
Hudson"; & with many thanks for the rapidity with which you
have enabled me to see the plates through the press, I remain   25
    Yours very truly
        <u>Henry James</u> jr.

No previous publication
ᖇ

239.20 ~~J~~ Friday • [F *overwrites* J]

239.23 Roderick • Rode= | rick

Biographical Register

This register is intended to help readers of *The Complete Letters of Henry James* keep track of the many people James mentions in his letters. It lists family members and friends and public, literary, and artistic figures of James's days whom the editors consider now to be relatively obscure. Well-known people whom James mentions—for instance, Dickens, President Grant, Prime Minister Gladstone—are omitted, as are canonical authors of James's past, like Shakespeare and Molière. Well-known contemporary authors and artists such as Henry Adams, William Dean Howells, and Fanny Kemble do appear in this register when the editors have deemed that they were significant to James's life or work. Excluded from this register are the names of people James mentions whom we have been unable to identify.

ADAMS, HENRY (1838–1918), American author, historian, man of letters, and simultaneously Harvard professor and editor of *The North American Review* (1870–77). HJ first met Adams in 1870 and was a friend during their Cambridge days with Adams's wife, Marian "Clover" Hooper.

AGASSIZ, ANNA RUSSELL (MRS. ALEXANDER) (1840–73). Her husband, Alexander Agassiz, was a Harvard marine biologist who made his fortune in copper mining.

ALDRICH, THOMAS BAILEY (1836–1907), New Hampshire–born and Boston-based novelist, poet, editor, and frequent *Atlantic Monthly* contributor. As editor of the *Atlantic Monthly* from 1881 to 1890, Aldrich published some of HJ's work.

ANDREW, EDITH (1854–1921), daughter of Eliza Jones Hersey Andrew and John Albion Andrew.

ANDREW, ELIZA JONES HERSEY (MRS. JOHN ALBION) (1826–

98), widow of John Albion Andrew (1818–67), former governor of Massachusetts (1861–65), and mother of Elizabeth "Bessie" Loring Andrew, Edith Andrew, and John Forrester Andrew. HJ encountered Mrs. Andrew and her children on several occasions during his 1873–74 travels in Italy.

ANDREW, ELIZABETH "BESSIE" LORING (1852–87), daughter of John Albion Andrew and Eliza Andrew.

ATKINSON, CHARLES FOLLEN (d. 1915), fellow student with WJ at the Lawrence Scientific School and later a Boston businessman; his sister was Emily Cabot Atkinson Holdredge.

ATKINSON (HOLDREDGE), EMILY CABOT. *See* Holdredge, Emily Cabot Atkinson.

BARTLETT, ALICE (b. 1845), friend of May Alcott, Louisa May Alcott, Alice Mason Sumner, and Elizabeth Boott. She authored several travel sketches (1871–73) and may have given HJ the germ of *Daisy Miller*. She married banker Henry Warren in 1878.

BELLAY, CHARLES-ALPHONSE-PAUL (1826–1900), French painter of Roman scenes and son of painter François Bellay, who died in Rome; Charles Bellay may have known Elena Lowe, Sarah Butler Wister, and HJ when they were in Rome in 1873.

BOOTT, ELIZABETH "LIZZIE" (1846–88), American painter, and her father, Francis Boott, were friends of the Temples and the Jameses. HJ was particularly close to them all their lives. She married Frank Duveneck, one of her art teachers, in March 1886. HJ supported her career as an artist and often visited Lizzie and her father, especially at their Italian home in Bellosguardo. Lizzie is thought to be a model for Pansy Osmond in *The Portrait of a Lady*.

BOOTT, FRANCIS (1813–1904), amateur composer and musician, friend of the Jameses, and father of Lizzie Boott.

BOTTA, ANNE CHARLOTTE LYNCH, wife of Vicenzo Botta and a painter and poet; HJ visited their New York home on West 39th Street.

BOTTA, VICENZO, husband of Anne Charlotte Lynch Botta and an

Italian who lived on West 39th Street in New York; their home was a literary and artistic salon (Edel 2: 189).

BRADFORD, GEORGE PARTRIDGE (1807–90), educator and reformer.

CABOT, LILLA (1848–1933), became engaged to Thomas Sergeant Perry in the spring of 1873; the couple married in April 1874. She was a talented painter.

CAETANI, MICHELANGELO, DUKE OF SERMONETA (1804–82), politician and writer.

CARROLL, MRS. CHARLES, wife of a Boston schoolmaster (born c. 1832) who worked at the Young Ladies School and the English High School.

CARSON, MRS. HJ's letter to MWJ on 17 May 1874 indicates that Mrs. Carson was engaged to Michelangelo Caetani (1804–82), Duke of Sermoneta, politician, and writer.

COULSON, HENRY JOHN WASTELL (b. 1848), an Englishman HJ met in Bad Homburg in the summer of 1873; he attended Harrow and Oxford and became a member of the Bar at the Inner Temple in 1876.

CRAWFORD, ANNIE (b. 1846), daughter of Louisa Ward Crawford Terry and Thomas Crawford; she became engaged to Baron Eric von Rabe in late 1873 and married him the next year.

CRAWFORD, MARY "MIMOLI" (b. 1851), daughter of Louisa Ward Crawford Terry and Thomas Crawford; she married Hugh Fraser.

CURTIS, ANNA SHAW (1838–1927). The eldest of five children born to Francis George Shaw and Sarah Sturgis, Anna Shaw married George William Curtis in 1856 in New Brighton, Staten Island. They had three children—Frank, Sally, and Elizabeth. She was involved in local efforts to help soldiers during the Civil War and served as president of the board of trustees for the Church of the Redeemer (where she had been married) from 1903 to 1919.

CURTIS, GEORGE WILLIAM (1824–92), American-born writer, lecturer, editor, and political activist. Born in Providence, Rhode Island, Curtis also lived in New York and in Massachusetts at Brook Farm. He traveled extensively, wrote the "easy chair" articles for *Harper's New Monthly Magazine*, and became an editor of *Harper's Weekly* in 1863, holding this position until his death. He was the chair of the Commission to Oversee the Reform of the Civil Service and president of the National Civil Service Reform League and the New York Civil Service Reform Agency. His works include *Nile Notes of a Howadji* (1851), *Potiphar Papers* (1853), *Prue and I* (1856), and *Trumps* (1861).

DALL, CAROLINE WELLS HEALEY (1822–1912), Boston feminist and author of *The Romance of the Association* and *Transcendentalism in New England: A Lecture;* she wrote about Sr. in her private journal.

DANA, SARAH "SALLY" WATSON (1814–1907), wife of Richard Henry Dana. She lived in Europe during the late 1870s.

DENNETT, JOHN R. (1837–74), literary editor of the *Nation* from 1868 to 1869, assistant professor of rhetoric at Harvard (1870–72), and a member of the editorial staff of the *Nation* until his death.

FISKE, JOHN (1842–1901), Harvard librarian, historian, philosopher, proponent of Darwinism, and neighbor of William Dean Howells.

FRASER, HUGH (1837–94), son of Sir John Fraser, KCMG, and Lady Selima Charlotte Baldwin Fraser; he was educated at Eton and entered the British diplomatic corps in 1862. Fraser married Mary Crawford in Rome on 15 June 1874. Diplomatic assignments sent them to Chile, Denmark, Guatemala, Austria, Italy, and Japan. Fraser died at his post in Tokyo and was buried in Japan's first municipal cemetery, Aoyama Reien. Mary Crawford chronicled their travels in *A Diplomatist's Wife in Japan: Letters from Home to Home* (1898) and *A Diplomatist's Wife in Many Lands* (1911).

GRAHAM, JAMES LORIMER, JR. (1835–76), a New Yorker and American consul to Florence; HJ first met him in October 1869.

GRAHAM, JOSEPHINE A. GARNER (1837–92), wife of James Lorimer Graham Jr. She was a noted philanthropist in Florence during her husband's service there. She later married Giuseppe Mateini.

GREENOUGH, FLORENCE (1852-1940), daughter of Henry Greenough and Frances Boott Greenough, sister of Fanny Greenough, and niece of Francis Boott; she married John Larkin Thorndike in 1878.

GREENOUGH, FRANCES BOOTT, sister of Francis Boott, wife of architect Henry Greenough, and mother of Fanny and Florence Greenough.

GREENOUGH, FRANCES "FANNY" (1843-1939), daughter of Henry Greenough and Frances Boott Greenough, sister of Florence Greenough, and niece of Francis Boott; she married Arthur Welland Blake in 1878.

GREENOUGH, HENRY (1807-83), architect and brother-in-law of Francis Boott; his Cambridge home was at 747 Cambridge Street, around the corner from the Jameses' home on Quincy Street.

GREENWOOD, AUGUSTUS GOODWIN (1832-74), Harvard graduate and Boston lawyer.

GRYZANOVSKI, DR. ERNST GEORG FRIEDRICH (1824-88), German diplomat, educator, and author. HJ saw Gryzanovski socially and regularly in Florence during late 1873 and 1874.

HALL, CONSTANCE "CONNIE," an English musician who resided in Florence and was a friend of Francis and Lizzie Boott.

HALL, ELISA, wife of Taylor G. Hall.

HALL, TAYLOR G., Boston acquaintance of the James family; HJ, AJ, and AK encountered him, his wife, and their cousin, Hugh Walsh, in Lausanne in August 1872.

HALLOWELL, ANNA, companion to Mary Louisa "Loulie" Shaw. On the occasion of the latter's death HJ wrote Hallowell a letter of condolence (11 February 1874).

HAY, CLARA (1849-1914), previously Clara Louise Stone, was the daughter of a Cleveland railroad magnate, Amasa Stone (1818-83), and the wife of John Milton Hay, whom she married in 1874.

HAY, HELEN JULIA (1875-1944), poet and wife of Payne Whitney (1876-1927), and daughter of Clara and John Milton Hay.

HAY, JOHN MILTON (1838-1905). Born in Indiana, Hay was a graduate of Brown University, a journalist, poet, statesman, novel and short-story writer, and biographer. HJ met Hay in 1875, when HJ desired to become the Paris literary correspondent for the *New York Tribune*. Hay was an editorial writer for the *Tribune* from 1870 to 1875 and again in 1881. His political posts included assistant secretary of state (1879-81), ambassador to England (1897-98), and two terms as secretary of state (1898-1901, 1901-05).

HILLEBRAND, KARL (1829-84), German writer and historian who married Jessie Laussot in 1879.

HOFFMANN, LYDIA "LILY" WARD (BARONESS RICHARD) VON (b. 1843), daughter of banker Sam Ward and Sr.'s old friend Anna Barker Ward. HJ socialized with the von Hoffmanns at Villa Mattei, their residence in Rome.

HOLDREDGE, EMILY CABOT ATKINSON (d. 1873). Her brother was Charles Follen Atkinson; she was the wife of George Ward Holdredge (b. 1847) and the mother of Henry Atkinson Holdredge (b. 1873).

HOLLAND, DR. JOSIAH GILBERT (1819-81), editor and one-third owner of *Scribner's Monthly* and author of such books as *Bitter-Sweet: A Poem* (1858) and *Sevenoaks: A Story of Today* (1875).

HOWELLS, ELINOR GERTRUDE MEAD (1837-1910), married William Dean Howells in 1862.

HOWELLS, WILLIAM DEAN (1837-1920), American author, editor, and literary critic who, together with HJ, is largely credited with ushering in literary realism in the United States. His and HJ's first meeting probably occurred in the summer of 1866 (Anesko 11-13). Despite their different upbringings, the two became lifelong friends. As assistant editor and then editor of the *Atlantic Monthly*, Howells accepted HJ's work for publication, and throughout their careers they exchanged literary advice.

HOWELLS, WINIFRED "WINNY" (1863-89), Howells's eldest daughter.

HUNTINGTON, ELLEN GREENOUGH (1814–93), was the second wife of Charles Phelps Huntington and sister-in-law to Francis Boott; she resided in Florence. Her family owned Villa Castellani at Bellosguardo.

HUNTINGTON, HENRY (1848–1926), son of Charles Phelps Huntington and Ellen Greenough Huntington; he later became American vice-consul in Florence.

HUNTINGTON, LAURA (b. 1849), daughter of Charles Phelps Huntington and Ellen Greenough Huntington; in 1874 she became engaged to a Swiss Italian banker named Wagnière.

HUNTINGTON, WILLIAM HENRY (1820–85), American philanthropist and regular Paris correspondent for the *Tribune*.

JAMES, ALICE (AJ) (1848–92), the fifth and youngest child and only daughter of Sr. and MWJ. She is remembered for her eloquent and candid journal, written during the last three years of her life and preserved and posthumously printed by her close friend Katharine Peabody Loring.

JAMES (EDGAR), ALICE (1875–1923), daughter of GWJ and Caroline Cary James.

JAMES, CAROLINE "CARRIE" EAMES CARY (1851–1931), daughter of Joseph Cary and Caroline Eames Cary; she married GWJ on 12 November 1873, and they had two children: Joseph Cary James (1874–1925) and Alice James Edgar (1875–1923).

JAMES, EDWARD "NED" HOLTON (1873–1954), son of RJ and Mary Lucinda Holton James, was educated at Harvard and became a lawyer and editor. HJ visited him in Seattle during the American tour of 1904–05. Ned published the *Liberator* in Paris. A contributor, Edward Mylius, was found guilty of libel after claiming in an article published by the paper that King George V had contracted a morganatic marriage. Ned was imprisoned for three years in Moabit Prison in Berlin for publishing antimonarchical propaganda, sentenced to ninety days in jail after inciting a riot and assaulting a policeman during a Sacco and Vanzetti demonstration, and later jailed on charges of committing criminal libel against President Franklin Delano Roosevelt. HJ had willed Ned £200 but later cut him from his will.

JAMES, ELIZABETH CABOT LODGE (c. 1843–1908), daughter of John Ellerton Lodge and Anna Sophia Cabot Lodge, she married George Abbot James in 1864.

JAMES, ELLERTON (1872–1926), son of Elizabeth Cabot Lodge and George Abbot James, he married Olivia Buckminster Tappan in 1899.

JAMES, GARTH WILKINSON "WILKIE" (GWJ) (1845–83), the third child of Sr. and MWJ. He served in the Civil War, during which he was badly wounded. After the war he and RJ tried to run a plantation in Florida, after which he moved to Milwaukee and into a series of jobs. In 1873 he married Caroline "Carrie" Cary, and they had two children: Joseph Cary James and Alice James Edgar.

JAMES, GEORGE ABBOT (b. 1838), met HJ during HJ's short time at Harvard Law School in 1862. Their lifelong friendship (they were not related) was maintained through decades of letters and visits by HJ to James's vacation home in Nahant, Massachusetts. HJ recalled their early friendship in *Notes of a Son and Brother* (368). George Abbot James married Elizabeth Cabot Lodge in 1864.

JAMES, HENRY, SR. (Sr.) (1811–82), was born in Albany, New York, graduated from Union College in Schenectady, New York, worked in business and law, and then studied at Princeton Theological Seminary (1835–37). Although raised in a strict Presbyterian family, he was repelled by orthodox Protestantism and gave up adherence to institutional religion. He is remembered as an author and theological philosopher and was heavily influenced by Swedenborgianism and (to a lesser extent) Fourierism. His books include *Christianity the Logic of Creation* (1857), *The Secret of Swedenborg* (1869), and *Society the Redeemed Form of Man* (1879). He and MWJ married in 1840 and had five children.

JAMES, JOSEPH CARY (1874–1925), son of GWJ and Caroline Cary James.

JAMES, MARY LUCINDA HOLTON (1847–1922), oldest daughter

of Edward Holton and Lucinda Millard Holton, married RJ on 18 November 1872; they had two children, Edward "Ned" James and Mary Walsh James Vaux, and a troubled marriage.

JAMES, MARY ROBERTSON WALSH (MWJ) (1810–82), married Sr. in 1840. She is most often described as having been a stable and comforting mother and wife, and HJ was devoted to her.

JAMES (VAUX), MARY WALSH (1875–1956), daughter of RJ and Mary Lucinda Holton James.

JAMES, ROBERTSON "BOB" (RJ) (1846–1910), the fourth and youngest son of Sr. and MWJ. He served in the Civil War and worked with GWJ on his plantation in Florida before holding a series of railroad jobs in the Midwest. In 1872 he married Mary Lucinda Holton, and they had two children, Edward "Ned" Holton James and Mary Walsh James Vaux.

JAMES, WILLIAM (WJ) (1842–1910), HJ's older brother and pioneering psychologist and pragmatist philosopher best remembered for *The Principles of Psychology* (1890), *The Will to Believe* (1897), *The Varieties of Religious Experience* (1902), and *Pragmatism* (1907). He began teaching at Harvard in 1872, three years after he had received his MD there, and retired in 1907. In 1878 he married Alice Howe Gibbens (1849–1922), and they had five children: Henry "Harry" (1879–1947), William "Bill" (1882–1961), Herman (1884–85), Margaret "Peggy" Mary (Mrs. Bruce Porter) (1887–1950), and Alexander "Aleck" Robertson (1890–1946).

KELLOGG, JULIA ANTOINETTE (1830–1914), disciple of Swedenborg and Sr. and author of *The Philosophy of Henry James* (1883); she crossed the Atlantic with WJ in October 1873.

KEMBLE, FRANCES "FANNY" ANNE (1809–93), from the Kemble family of famous British actors and a noted actress in her own right. She married Pierce Butler in 1834 and divorced him in 1848. HJ met her and her daughter, Sarah Butler Wister, in Rome in 1872 and became close friends with both of them.

KING, CHARLOTTE (COUSIN CHARLOTTE) ELIZABETH SLEIGHT MATTHEWS, daughter of MWJ's aunt Charlotte Walsh and her husband, the Reverend James Matthews. She married Clarence W. King.

LA FARGE, JOHN (1835–1910), was an American painter, stained-glass designer, and writer. He studied art under William Morris Hunt (who would later teach WJ and to some extent HJ) during his time in Newport, where he met the Jameses in 1858. La Farge had a major influence on both WJ and HJ, as he encouraged HJ to pursue writing and the study of literature and mentored WJ in the Hunt studio. In *Notes of a Son and Brother* HJ says, "John La Farge became at once [. . .] quite the most interesting person we knew" (84–85). In 1860 La Farge married Thomas Sergeant Perry's older sister Margaret. He also provided the original illustrations for *The Turn of the Screw* when it appeared in *Collier's Weekly*. HJ later recalled La Farge to Mary Cadwalader Jones as one of his oldest friends.

LANE, THE MISSES, operators of a boardinghouse in Quebec where AJ and AK were to have stayed during July 1873 and that William Dean Howells represented in *A Chance Acquaintance*.

LATHROP, GEORGE PARSONS (1851–98), American author and husband of Nathaniel Hawthorne's youngest daughter, Rose. Lathrop served as associate editor for the *Atlantic Monthly* (1875–77) and was the author of *A Study of Hawthorne* (1876), which HJ used for his *Hawthorne*.

LAUSSOT, JESSIE TAYLOR (1829–1905), musician and benefactor of Richard Wagner (with whom she was briefly involved in 1850); she married writer Karl Hillebrand in 1879.

LEFEBVRE, CHARLES-EDOUARD (1843–1917), a composer whom Sarah Butler Wister and HJ knew in Rome in 1873.

LIMBURG, ISABELLA CASS VON (1805–79), daughter of Lewis Cass (1782–1866), a brigadier general during the War of 1812, the first governor of Michigan (1813–31), and minister to France (1836–42). She married Baron Theodore Marinus von Limburg (b. 1800).

LOCKWOOD, (MRS.) FLORENCE BAYARD (1842–98), was the daughter of a prominent Delaware political family and wife of Maj. Benoni Lockwood (1834–1909).

LOMBARD, FANNY, a daughter of the James family's Cambridge friend, Mrs. Lombard.

LOMBARD, MRS., a Cambridge family friend whom the Jameses also knew when vacationing in Maine in the summer of 1871; HJ encountered her and her daughters, Essie and Fanny, in Europe in 1872–74.

LOWE, ELENA, daughter of Francis Lowe of Boston; in June 1874 she married British diplomat Gerald Perry. Sarah Butler Wister, HJ, and possibly painter Charles Bellay knew her in Rome in 1873.

LOWELL, JAMES RUSSELL (1819–91), well-known poet, American diplomat (minister to Spain [1877–80] and to England [1880–85]), and Harvard professor of modern languages (1855–76). He was the first editor of the *Atlantic Monthly* (1857–61) and in 1864 helped Charles Norton edit the *North American Review*. He and HJ later became close friends, especially when Lowell was posted in England.

LOWELL, JOSEPHINE "EFFIE" SHAW (1843–1905), widow of Civil War colonel Charles Russell Lowell and sister to Anna Shaw Curtis, wife of George W. Curtis. In 1876 she was appointed the first female commissioner of the New York State Board of Charities.

MASON, ALICE. *See* Sumner, Alice Mason (Mrs. Charles).

NORTON, CHARLES ELIOT (1827–1908), influential author, editor, and scholar, professor of the history of fine art at Harvard (1873–98), translator of Dante, editor of the *North American Review* (1864–68), and one of the founders of the *Nation*. He lived in Cambridge, at Shady Hill, near the Jameses and was an early mentor of HJ's career, publishing some of his first review articles and introducing him in 1869 to prominent cultural figures in London. Norton married Susan Ridley Sedgwick in 1862; they had six children.

NORTON, GRACE (1834–1926), Charles Eliot Norton's youngest sister. She lived most of her life with her brother, helping to raise his children, but in the early twentieth century she published several studies of Montaigne, including *Studies in Montaigne* (1904), *The Spirit of Montaigne* (1908), and *The Influence of Montaigne* (1908). She and HJ maintained a lengthy and intimate correspondence from 1868 to the end of his life.

OSGOOD, JAMES RIPLEY (1836–92), publisher of HJ's first books; he was the partner of James T. Fields in Fields, Osgood and Co., then directed James R. Osgood and Co. until 1878, when he became the partner of H. O. Houghton in Houghton, Osgood and Co. From 1880 until declaring bankruptcy in 1885, he again operated as James R. Osgood and Co.; the 1885 bankruptcy caused HJ to lose much of the revenue due to him from *The Bostonians*.

PARKES, DR., possibly Dr. Edmund Alexander Parkes (1819–76), a British physician and professor at University College and the Army Medical School.

PERKINS, MRS. STEPHEN, a friend of the Bootts and the Jameses who was residing in Bellosguardo when HJ was in Florence in the spring of 1874.

PERRY, GERALD RAOUL, British diplomat who married Elena Lowe in 1874.

PERRY, LILLA CABOT. *See* Cabot, Lilla.

PERRY, THOMAS SERGEANT (1845–1928), writer, scholar, educator, translator, and close friend of HJ for over fifty years, until HJ's death. They first met at school in Newport in 1858.

PORTER, BENJAMIN CURTIS (1843–1908), notable society portrait painter who resided in Boston and New York.

RABE, ANNIE CRAWFORD (BARONESS ERIC) VON. *See* Crawford, Annie.

RABE, BARON ERIC VON (d. c. 1885), Prussian army officer wounded in the Franco-Prussian War; he met Annie Crawford in 1873 and married her the next year, after which they resided at Lesnian, his estate in western Prussia.

REID, WHITELAW (1837–1912). A newspaper reporter during the Civil War, Reid assumed editorship of the *New York Tribune* in 1868. Reid also published books on journalism and diplomacy.

RISTORI, ADELAIDE (1822–1906), internationally famous Italian actress who toured the United States in 1860, 1867, 1875, and 1884. See HJ's "Madame Ristori."

ROSE, CHARLOTTE TEMPLE SWEENY, LADY, wife of Sir John Rose. She was the sister of Mary Temple Tweedy and Robert Temple Jr., the father of HJ's Temple cousins.

SCHÖNBERG, ERNST, fiancé of Bessie Ward, daughter of Samuel Gray Ward and Anna Hazard Barker Ward.

SEDGWICK, ARTHUR GEORGE (1844–1915), lawyer, writer, and editor for the *Nation* (1872–84) and the *New York Evening Post* (1881–85). The novelist Catharine Maria Sedgwick was his great-aunt, and his sister Susan married Charles Eliot Norton in 1862. Before he moved to New York in 1872 he lived with his sisters Sara and Theodora and their maternal aunts, Anne and Grace Ashburner, on Kirkland Street, between the Nortons' Shady Hill estate and the Jameses' house at 20 Quincy Street, Cambridge.

SERMONETA, DUKE OF. *See* Caetani, Michelangelo, Duke of Sermoneta.

SHAW, MARY LOUISA "LOULIE" (d. 1874). James family letters from the early 1870s mention Shaw and her companion, Anna Hallowell. Shaw's Boston home was on Beacon Street, and she was related to the Russells, Lowells, and Hoopers. Loulie Shaw died on 31 January 1874 after a long illness. She left a small bequest to GWJ.

SHELDON, ISAAC E. (d. 1898), son of Smith Sheldon, founder of Sheldon & Co., which owned the *Galaxy* from 1868 to 1878.

SPANGENBERG, JOHANNA (d. 1876), ran the Dresden boardinghouse where WJ resided in 1867 and visited in 1874.

STEDMAN, EDMUND CLARENCE (1833–1908), American journalist, popular poet, banker, literary critic, and literary anthologist.

STORY, EDITH (c. 1844–1907), daughter of sculptor William Wetmore Story. She later married the Florentine marquis Simone Peruzzi, a descendant of the Medicis.

STORY, EMELYN ELDREDGE (1821–94), wife of William Wetmore Story.

STORY, JULIAN RUSSELL (1850–1919), American artist and son of William Wetmore Story.

STORY, WILLIAM WETMORE (1819–95), American sculptor. His best-known piece, *Cleopatra*, was immortalized in Hawthorne's *The Marble Faun*. HJ's 1903 biography of Story, *William Wetmore Story and His Friends*, recounts his art and life in Palazzo Barberini in Rome.

SUMNER, ALICE MASON (MRS. CHARLES) (1838–1913), widow of William Sturgis Hooper, she married Senator Charles Sumner in 1866; they divorced in 1873, and Mason resumed her maiden name. She was a friend of Alice Bartlett, and HJ saw both of them often in Rome in 1873.

TAPPAN, CAROLINE STURGIS (1819–88), author and friend of the Jameses and of the Emersons; she was Loulie Shaw's aunt, and Ellen Sturgis Hooper Gurney and Marian "Clover" Hooper Adams were her first cousins.

TAYLOR, MRS., wife of Edgard Taylor and mother of Jessie Laussot.

TERRY, LOUISA CUTLER WARD CRAWFORD (MRS. LUTHER) (1823–97), wife of expatriate American painter Luther Terry, widow of American sculptor Thomas Gibson Crawford, sister of Julia Ward Howe and Washington lobbyist Sam Ward, and mother of Annie Crawford, Mimoli Crawford, novelist Marion Crawford, Margaret Terry (b. 1862), and Arthur Terry (b. 1864).

TERRY, LUTHER (1813–90), American expatriate painter with whose family HJ socialized during the winter of 1873; at that time Terry resided in the Odescalchi Palace near the Trevi fountain in Rome. He married Louisa Cutler Ward Crawford in 1861.

TWEEDY, EDMUND (ca. 1812–1901), a friend of Sr., a follower of Fourier, and a contributor to the *Harbinger*; his wife, Mary Temple

Tweedy, was the paternal aunt and guardian of HJ's Temple cousins. They lived in Pelham, New York, and had a house in Newport.

TWEEDY, MARY TEMPLE (d. 1891), the paternal aunt of HJ's cousins, the Temples; she was the sister of Robert Emmet Temple (1808–54), who married Sr.'s sister, Catharine James (1820–54), in 1839; after the deaths in 1854 of Robert and Catharine Temple, Mary Tweedy and her husband, Edmund, took in the orphaned Temple children, Robert "Bob," William, Katharine "Kitty," Mary "Minny," Ellen "Elly," and Henrietta. HJ visited often with the Tweedys while they were in Rome and Bad Homburg in 1873, and WJ visited them in Germany in 1874.

WALSH, ALEXANDER ROBERTSON (UNCLE R.) (1809–84), MWJ's oldest brother and Sr.'s business agent. He lived in New York.

WALSH, CATHARINE (AUNT KATE, AK) (1812–89), sister of HJ's mother. She remained a constant and usually present member of the James family until her death. She lived and traveled with her sister's family and became something of a second mother to the children. Catharine is usually described as having been much more outgoing and opinionated than her quieter sister. In 1853 she married Capt. Charles H. Marshall, but the union lasted for only twenty-eight months. She died after a fall in her home in March 1889.

WARD, ANNA HAZARD BARKER (c. 1813–1900), an intimate friend of Sr. during the 1840s and 1850s and wife of Samuel Gray Ward (1817–1907), New York and Boston banker and U.S. partner of the Barings Bank. Her brother William H. Barker married Sr.'s sister Jeannette James.

WARD, ELIZABETH "BESSIE," daughter of banker Sam Ward and Sr.'s old friend Anna Barker Ward and sister of Lydia "Lily" Ward von Hoffmann; she became engaged to Ernst Schönberg.

WARD, LYDIA "LILY." *See* Hoffmann, Lydia "Lily" Ward (Baroness Richard) von.

WARD, SAMUEL GRAY (1817–1907), American banker and partner of the Barings Bank; his wife was Anna Hazard Barker Ward (c. 1813–

1900), and his daughters were Lydia "Lily" Ward von Hoffmann and Elizabeth "Bessie" Ward.

WARING, VIRGINIA, possibly VIRGINIA CLARK WARING (b. c. 1835), wife of sanitation engineer George E. Waring.

WASHBURN, FRANCIS "FRANK" TUCKER (1843–73), a friend of WJ. Graduated from Harvard (1864), attended Harvard Divinity School, and became a Unitarian minister.

WATERMAN, THOMAS (1842–1901), American physician who taught anatomy and physiology at Harvard in place of WJ while he was abroad in 1873–74.

WHITWELL, MRS. AND MISS. HJ and WJ knew a Bessie and a May Whitwell, one of whom may have been the Miss Whitwell of Boston whom HJ, AJ, and AK saw in Berne in the summer of 1872 and whom HJ saw again in Rome in the winter of 1873. The Whitwells traveled to Egypt with Emerson in 1872–73.

WISTER, OWEN (1860–1938), son of Sarah Butler and Dr. Owen Wister. He was the author of *The Virginian, Salvation Gap and Other Western Classics, When West Was West, Padre Ignacio, Lin McLean, Red Men and White*, and other writings.

WISTER, DR. OWEN JONES (1825–96), husband of Sarah Butler Wister.

WISTER, SARAH BUTLER (1835–1908), Philadelphia literary critic, daughter of Fanny Kemble and Pierce Butler, wife of Dr. Owen Wister, and mother of novelist Owen Wister; she and HJ met in Rome in December 1872 and became lifelong friends.

Genealogies

The James Family

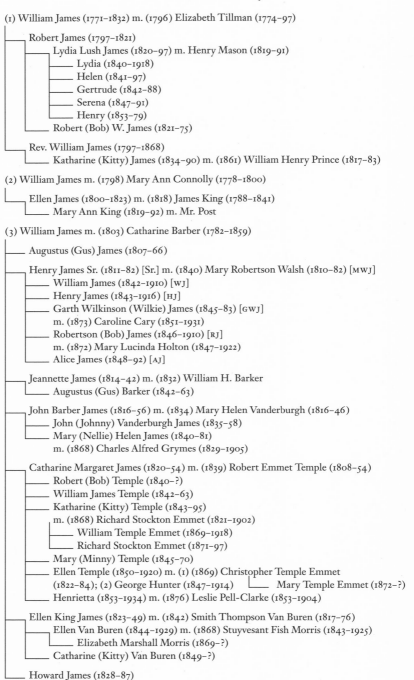

(1) William James (1771–1832) m. (1796) Elizabeth Tillman (1774–97)

Robert James (1797–1821)
Lydia Lush James (1820–97) m. Henry Mason (1819–91)
Lydia (1840–1918)
Helen (1841–97)
Gertrude (1842–88)
Serena (1847–91)
Henry (1853–79)
Robert (Bob) W. James (1821–75)

Rev. William James (1797–1868)
Katharine (Kitty) James (1834–90) m. (1861) William Henry Prince (1817–83)

(2) William James m. (1798) Mary Ann Connolly (1778–1800)

Ellen James (1800–1823) m. (1818) James King (1788–1841)
Mary Ann King (1819–92) m. Mr. Post

(3) William James m. (1803) Catharine Barber (1782–1859)

Augustus (Gus) James (1807–66)

Henry James Sr. (1811–82) [Sr.] m. (1840) Mary Robertson Walsh (1810–82) [MWJ]
William James (1842–1910) [WJ]
Henry James (1843–1916) [HJ]
Garth Wilkinson (Wilkie) James (1845–83) [GWJ]
m. (1873) Caroline Cary (1851–1931)
Robertson (Bob) James (1846–1910) [RJ]
m. (1872) Mary Lucinda Holton (1847–1922)
Alice James (1848–92) [AJ]

Jeannette James (1814–42) m. (1832) William H. Barker
Augustus (Gus) Barker (1842–63)

John Barber James (1816–56) m. (1834) Mary Helen Vanderburgh (1816–46)
John (Johnny) Vanderburgh James (1835–58)
Mary (Nellie) Helen James (1840–81)
m. (1868) Charles Alfred Grymes (1829–1905)

Catharine Margaret James (1820–54) m. (1839) Robert Emmet Temple (1808–54)
Robert (Bob) Temple (1840–?)
William James Temple (1842–63)
Katharine (Kitty) Temple (1843–95)
m. (1868) Richard Stockton Emmet (1821–1902)
William Temple Emmet (1869–1918)
Richard Stockton Emmet (1871–97)
Mary (Minny) Temple (1845–70)
Ellen Temple (1850–1920) m. (1) (1869) Christopher Temple Emmet (1822–84); (2) George Hunter (1847–1914)   Mary Temple Emmet (1872–?)
Henrietta (1853–1934) m. (1876) Leslie Pell-Clarke (1853–1904)

Ellen King James (1823–49) m. (1842) Smith Thompson Van Buren (1817–76)
Ellen Van Buren (1844–1929) m. (1868) Stuyvesant Fish Morris (1843–1925)
Elizabeth Marshall Morris (1869–?)
Catharine (Kitty) Van Buren (1849–?)

Howard James (1828–87)

The Norton Family

Catharine Eliot (1793-1879) m. (1821) Andrews Norton (1786-1853)

- Catharine Jane Norton (1824-77)
- Charles Eliot Norton (1827-1908) m. (1862) Susan Ridley Sedgwick (1838-72)
  - Eliot Norton (1863-1932)
  - Sarah (Sally) Norton (1864-1922)
  - Elizabeth (Lily) Gaskell Norton (b. 1866)
  - Rupert Norton (1867-1914)
  - Margaret Norton (1870-1947)
  - Richard Norton (1872-1918)
- Grace Norton (1834-1926)

The Sedgwick Family

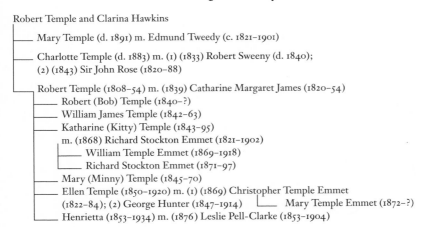

Theodore Sedgwick (1780-1839)   Anne Ashburner (1807-94)
m. (1808) Susan Anne Livingston Ridley (1788-1867)
- Theodore Sedgwick (1811-59) m. (1835) Sarah Morton Ashburner (1812-56)
  - Susan Ridley Sedgwick (1838-72)
    m. (1862) Charles Eliot Norton (1827-1908)
      - Eliot Norton (1863-1932)   Grace Ashburner (1814-93)
      - Sarah (Sally) Norton (1864-1922)
      - Elizabeth (Lily) Gaskell Norton (b. 1866)
      - Rupert Norton (1867-1914)
      - Margaret Norton (1870-1947)   Sam Ashburner (b. 1816)
      - Richard Norton (1872-1918)   m. (1845) Annie Barstow (1820-95)
  - Sarah Price Ashburner Sedgwick (1839-1902)   Annie Ashburner
  - Arthur George Sedgwick (1844-1915)   (1846-1909)
  - Maria Theodora Sedgwick (1851-1916)

The Temple Family

Robert Temple and Clarina Hawkins

- Mary Temple (d. 1891) m. Edmund Tweedy (c. 1821-1901)
- Charlotte Temple (d. 1883) m. (1) (1833) Robert Sweeny (d. 1840); (2) (1843) Sir John Rose (1820-88)
- Robert Temple (1808-54) m. (1839) Catharine Margaret James (1820-54)
  - Robert (Bob) Temple (1840-?)
  - William James Temple (1842-63)
  - Katharine (Kitty) Temple (1843-95)
    m. (1868) Richard Stockton Emmet (1821-1902)
      - William Temple Emmet (1869-1918)
      - Richard Stockton Emmet (1871-97)
  - Mary (Minny) Temple (1845-70)
  - Ellen Temple (1850-1920) m. (1) (1869) Christopher Temple Emmet (1822-84); (2) George Hunter (1847-1914)   Mary Temple Emmet (1872-?)
  - Henrietta (1853-1934) m. (1876) Leslie Pell-Clarke (1853-1904)

The Robertson and Walsh Families

Alexander Robertson (1733–1816) m. Mary Smith

    Hellen Robertson (d. 1818) m. John Richardson Bayard Rodgers (d. 1833)

        Alexander Robertson Rodgers (b. 1807) m. Mary Ridgely Darden (d. 1888)

          Katherine (Katie) Rodgers (b. 1841)

          Henrietta (Nettie) Dorrington Rodgers (1843–1906)

    Mary (great-aunt Wyckoff) Robertson (1778–1855) m. Albert Wyckoff (1771–1840)

      Helen Rodgers Wyckoff (1807–87) m. Leonard Perkins (d. 1869)

      Henry A. Wyckoff (1815–90)

              Hugh Walsh (1745–1817) m. (1775) Catharine Armstrong (1755–1801)

    Elizabeth Robertson (1781–1847)

    m. (1806) James Walsh (c. 1780–1820)

      Alexander Robertson Walsh (1809–84)

        m. (1838) Emily Brown (1816–81)

          Emily Belden Walsh (b. 1844)

          m. (1867) Thomas Cochran Jr.

      Mary Robertson Walsh (1810–82) [MWJ]

        m. (1840) Henry James Sr. (1811–82) [Sr.]

          William James (1842–1910) [WJ]

          Henry James (1843–1916) [HJ]

          Garth Wilkinson (Wilkie) James (1845–83) [GWJ]

          Robertson (Bob) James (1846–1910)[RJ]

          Alice James (1848–92) [AJ]

      Catharine (Aunt Kate) Walsh (1812–89) AK

      m. Charles H. Marshall

      Hugh Walsh (1816–59)

      m. Elizabeth Hall

        Hugh McKenzie Walsh

      James William Walsh (1819–72)

      m. Margaret Ruth Lawrence

    Catharine Walsh (1785–1829)

    m. (1805) David Andrews

      Catherine Walsh Andrews (1806–65)

        m. Joseph Ripley

        Helen Ripley

    Charlotte Walsh (1789–1816)

    m. Rev. James Matthews

      Charlotte Elizabeth Sleight Matthews m. C. W. King

        William Vernon King

        Annie King

        Arthur King

The Barber Family

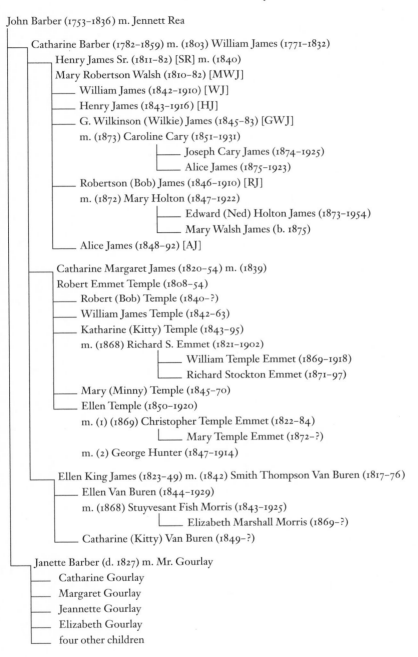

John Barber (1753–1836) m. Jennett Rea

Catharine Barber (1782–1859) m. (1803) William James (1771–1832)

Henry James Sr. (1811–82) [SR] m. (1840)
Mary Robertson Walsh (1810–82) [MWJ]

William James (1842–1910) [WJ]

Henry James (1843–1916) [HJ]

G. Wilkinson (Wilkie) James (1845–83) [GWJ]
m. (1873) Caroline Cary (1851–1931)

Joseph Cary James (1874–1925)

Alice James (1875–1923)

Robertson (Bob) James (1846–1910) [RJ]
m. (1872) Mary Holton (1847–1922)

Edward (Ned) Holton James (1873–1954)

Mary Walsh James (b. 1875)

Alice James (1848–92) [AJ]

Catharine Margaret James (1820–54) m. (1839)
Robert Emmet Temple (1808–54)

Robert (Bob) Temple (1840–?)

William James Temple (1842–63)

Katharine (Kitty) Temple (1843–95)
m. (1868) Richard S. Emmet (1821–1902)

William Temple Emmet (1869–1918)

Richard Stockton Emmet (1871–97)

Mary (Minny) Temple (1845–70)

Ellen Temple (1850–1920)
m. (1) (1869) Christopher Temple Emmet (1822–84)

Mary Temple Emmet (1872–?)

m. (2) George Hunter (1847–1914)

Ellen King James (1823–49) m. (1842) Smith Thompson Van Buren (1817–76)

Ellen Van Buren (1844–1929)
m. (1868) Stuyvesant Fish Morris (1843–1925)

Elizabeth Marshall Morris (1869–?)

Catharine (Kitty) Van Buren (1849–?)

Janette Barber (d. 1827) m. Mr. Gourlay

Catharine Gourlay

Margaret Gourlay

Jeannette Gourlay

Elizabeth Gourlay

four other children

General Editors' Note

We intend *The Complete Letters of Henry James* to be as useful to as broad a range of readers as possible, given the limitations of print reproduction. One cannot anticipate what biographical or historical details or stylistic idiosyncrasies contained in any given letter may be of value to users of the edition. The general editors of this edition, therefore, believe that our duty is "to be as complete as possible," as James wrote in another context ("Art of Fiction" 408). By being as complete as possible, we enable the opportunity for study of any aspect of James's letters. An inclusive edition of the letters enriches by its range and detail our understanding of James's life and the lives of his correspondents, his use of language, and his importance to our cultural legacy.

The goal of this edition is to provide an inclusive, reliable, available, and easily read scholarly and critical text for all extant letters, telegrams, and notes written by Henry James. We aim to establish the letter text, thus evidence of the compositional process represented by it, with the greatest precision possible in a format that is easy to read and understand. It may be important to some readers, for example, to see that James's "Whom" in his 9 January [1874] letter to William Dean Howells appears in holograph as "Who" with the *m* inserted. Understanding James's change of "Who" to "Whom" gives a small insight into the moment of composition, to James's wavering at that moment between "Who" and "Whom." Likewise, James's adjustment of "N" to "Absolutely nothing," which one could reasonably speculate indicates an intensification of meaning in the 3 June [1874] letter to his mother from the initially conceived "Nothing" to the final "Absolutely nothing," offers a window to James's compositional methods and strategies. Such readability in combination with representational precision helps us to produce a reliable edition.

Where reliability (in terms of the meaningful details of the historical document itself) is in tension with readability, we give priority to reliability. Informing this view is a conviction that historical documents are fundamentally different from "literary texts" such as poems and novels and therefore must be edited and published differently. We do not correct slips or other errors in the letters, preferring instead to render what James wrote whenever possible.

The manuscripts of James's letters show that James was a spontaneous letter writer who wrote rapidly, for they contain a substantial number of changes and corrections. The position and apparent sequence of James's cancellations, corrections, and insertions indicate that he adjusted, shaped, and sharpened his meaning as he wrote, working just ahead of his pen, when he caught an error or clarified meaning at all. Those changes, made as he drove himself to answer letter after letter received and to open new paths of communication, reveal James's mind in action. They also record the way in which James responded to individual correspondents and rhetorical situations. As we considered the changes—both what James rejected and what he accepted—as well as the representation of those changes, it became evident that those adjustments were themselves interesting because James obviously made the particular change for a reason. And such changes could hold an interest all their own, just as they would for those who read the original letters. In the same way shifts and turns of meaning are signaled by changes, so too do mistakes and errors of carelessness and other idiosyncrasies carry meaning. To omit those details would be to misrepresent the letter James wrote and his correspondent read. Thus, we sought an approach to editing the letters that would enable us to represent what James wrote, that is, what appears on the letter page and what the letter recipient read so that readers of this edition might use the edited letters more nearly as they would James's own letters. The most suitable approach we found is plain-text editing, developed by Robert H. Hirst for *Mark Twain's Letters* and adapted for this edition.

We rationalize our decision to present the letters in a plain-text style, in part, in terms of G. Thomas Tanselle's point that "the posting of a letter is equivalent to the publication of a literary work, for each activity serves as the means by which a particular kind of communication is directed to its audience" ("The Editorial Problem" 204). Henry James indicated his preference for a "definitive" letter as soon as he sealed an envelope and sent it through the mail. We see no reason, then, to alter the meaningful elements of what James wrote and a letter's recipient read. In "Recent Editorial Discussion and the Central Questions of Editing" Tanselle elaborated the concept by arguing that "[r]eaders are not normally prevented from understanding a text by oddities and inconsistencies of punctuation and spelling, and when these irregularities are characteristic of the author what is the point of altering them? It is hard to see why editors think they are accomplishing anything by straightening out the details of spelling and punctuation in a letter or journal simply for the sake of tidying it up" (58).

As much as we hope that this edition can function to communicate to readers a substantial amount of the meaning of James's originals, no edition of letters can represent all details of the original documents. The plain-text approach to editing and representing the letter does not attempt to render a facsimile of the letter text. It enables us to represent meaningful details of the text of the historical document. At the same time, by using commonly understood editorial symbols in combination with a record of emendations and other textual notes, we provide the reader with a highly reliable and readable edition. By including in the edited text cancellations, insertions, and other changes seen in the manuscripts and typescripts and by representing these manuscript details with similar ones in the typography, plain-text editing enables users to read the edited letters nearly as they would the originals without having to reconstruct changes entirely by way of an apparatus or specially memorized editing marks or by having to decipher James's handwriting. By representing textual details of the letters rather than the letter writer's final decisions only, plain-text editing enables readers to see when and where in a letter James changed his mind or altered an emphasis.

Our aim is to help our readers experience something of the moment of composition, which only a careful examination of the manuscript can offer fully. Our position on this aspect of the editorial rationale is based on Tanselle's critique of modernization and his argument that editors of historical documents should preserve a writer's deletions and, by extension, other meaningful features of the holograph in a scholarly edition, for then "the editor allows the reader to have the same experience" as the original reader of the historical document ("Editing" 50–51). A letter differs from texts such as poems and novels in the way that it should be read and understood because in a letter there is no "final" or published text other than the one that the writer sealed in an envelope and put into the mail (Tanselle, "The Editorial Problem" 204). "Drafts" and "revisions" in the form of authorial changes may be contained in a single letter text rather than in a series of separate drafts.

The texts of the letters that comprise this edition are reproduced essentially as they were written and sent, without correction or normalization, including cancellations, as long as that text can be intelligibly transcribed with typographical features available to the editors via the page designers. If what might be a significant feature of the manuscript can be transcribed and included in the edition, it has been. Infrequently in some letters either the recipient, a family member who gathered and reviewed the letters, or an editor added a comment. None of these interventions is represented in the edited letter texts, which aim to give James's letters as James wrote and sent them.

Reading particular idiosyncratic elements of Henry James's handwriting is a challenge because many of the letter forms—for example, *h* and *b*, *a*, *u*, *o*, and *v*, as well as *F* and *J*—often look alike. To distinguish them, one must first remember the range of ambiguous letter forms and then consider their possible combinations in the context of an entire word or individual words in a phrase or sentence—only then can one begin to read James's hand accurately.

An example of understanding the context of a particular letter form appears in James's [7], 8, 9 March 1870 missive to William James, in which he wrote: "i.e. that poor Jno. La Farge were with me sharing my enjoyment of this English scenery—enjoying it that is, on his own [. . .]" The next word is either "hook" or "book" because of the similarity of James's *h* to his *b* (*CLHJ, 1855–1872* 2: 315). An investigation of both "on his own hook" and "on his own book" uncovered the contemporary colloquialism "by one's own hook," the definition for which suited James's sense perfectly. So we rendered the word.

An unfamiliar proper name may pose a problem if one lacks an immediate context in which to understand critical letter forms. For example, because James's majuscule *I* and *T* were formed alike at the time, we couldn't know if James was referring in his 28 November 1871 letter to George Abbot James to "Mr. I. Cook, Tailor, London" or "Mr. T. Cook" (*CLHJ, 1855–1872* 2: 425). We did find listed in the 1870 *Post Office London Directory* a "Thomas William Cook, Tailor, 8 Clifford st., Old Bond st. W" (772) and no mention of any other tailor named Cook, so we adopted the reading "T. Cook." A similar problem occurred in the typed letter copy of James's 29 July [1874] to Sarah Butler Wister (the original has been lost). In that letter the transcriber gave the following: "I cut out of the Galignani the other day, to send you, a paragraph on Miss Lane's marriage, at Venice, but have stupidly lost it." Our problem was that we had no knowledge of a "Miss Lane" and could find out nothing about a person who seemed from the context to be so well known by James and Mrs. Wister. We wondered whether the transcriber had mistaken "Lane" for another name, perhaps "Lowe"; James and Mrs. Wister knew Elena Lowe. James's letter forms for *ow* could be misread as *an*. The only way to know for sure, however, would be to read the article that James cut from the *Galignani*. We located a copy of the 9 July 1874 *Galignani's Messenger*, which reports on page 3 the 20 June 1874 marriage in Venice of Elena Lowe, "daughter of the late Francis Lowe, Esq., of Boston," and "Gerald Raoul Perry, Esq.," British consul to the Island of Reunion and son of Sir William Perry, "for many years H. B. M.'s Consul-General at Venice."

There are instances of James's handwriting for which we have not been able to find neat solutions. Special problems include words that may or may not end in a final *s*, words in the middle of a sentence that may or may not be capitalized, and compound words like "anything," "somewhere," and "everyone" that may be one or two words. Understanding James's habits regarding capitalization in a particular letter, knowing his good knowledge of English grammar, and mapping his letter-spacing habits provide ways to understand other difficulties of James's hand.

Knowledge of usage frequencies, surveyed through electronic searches for particular word combinations across several thousand transcribed letters, also helped rationalize our decisions when we were faced with two possibilities. For example, James closed his 18

February 1870 letter to Grace Norton by writing vertically across the complete penultimate page: "believe me dear Grace—unutterably [or "unalterably"?] yours." The fourth and fifth letters of this word are both crossed, but because James is regularly very imprecise about crossing his *t*'s, we could not be sure by the usual ways of analysis that he wrote double *tt* or *lt*; there are countless other examples of *lt* combinations that can only be read as such and where both letters are crossed. Furthermore, *u* and *a* often look alike, so we cannot be certain that the third letter is one or the other. Either reading, "unutterably" or "unalterably," fits the context of the closing. We decided to render "unutterably" after we made a search for both words in our electronic files of all the letters up through 1875 (*CLHJ, 1855–1872* 2: 301). "Unalterably" does not appear at all in any of these letters, whereas "unutterably" appears five times. Therefore, we felt that it was not atypical of James to use the word "unutterably" and, as a result, that this would be the more likely reading. Unfortunately, Grace Norton's letters to James do not survive, and none of his other letters to her offers a further clue.

One significant feature is cancellation. James frequently cancels material with one or more lines. When these are legible, we represent them as struck-through text (~~cancel~~, ~~cancel~~, etc.). We represent illegible canceled letters with the mark we use to indicate illegible single letter characters, ◇, struck through: ◈. When a series of canceled characters with space on both sides is illegible to the point that we cannot determine the number of characters, we represent it with a black rectangular box: ■.

James also canceled words and letters within words by overwriting them. This we represent by giving the overwritten word or part of a word as struck-through text followed by the word that results after the overwriting. James would also blot out letters or words before the ink dried and then sometimes overwrite the blot. In the letter texts we indicate blotting as struck-through text. Since the precise nature of James's change is never entirely obvious from how we have represented overwriting and blotting out, all cases of overwriting and blotting receive an explanation in the textual commentary.

When a literal representation of a cancellation of a single character in the original letter is easily readable, we prefer that representation. For example, in his 15 September [1873] letter to William James, James wrote "trunks" and then canceled the final *s* by crossing it out. We represent this as "trunk~~s~~" (p. 51.1). While it is true that James in essence canceled the entire word, "trunks," and replaced it with "trunk" when he crossed out the final *s*, representing the change as "~~trunks~~ trunk" would not, in our judgment, aid readability and would also be a less accurate representation of the manuscript.

In all cases we preserve James's spelling and punctuation. Such preservation not only shows James's use of American, English, French, Italian, and other word forms, his attention or lack of attention to certain words, but also may suggest that in certain instances James might have misspelled a word deliberately to create a pun or other humorous effect. His use of "<u>tiss</u>" for "kiss" in his 13 January [1874] letter to his sister, Alice, "shill" rather than "shall" in his 17 May 1874 letter to his mother, "injoyment" for "enjoyment" in his 14 August [1873] to his parents, and "Curnarder" for "Cunarder" indicates typical puns that depend on a special language of intimacy ("tiss") or mimicry of American speech ("shill," "injoyment," "Curnarder"). James also used variant spellings that are less common in the early twenty-first century (e.g., "shew," "despatch," "fulness," and "dulness"), and we preserve these variant spellings, as we do those in other languages. James would, on occasion, inadvertently misspell words. Inadvertent misspellings are indicated as such in the corresponding textual commentary so that it is clear to our readers that the slip was James's. Variant spellings in English and other languages receive no commentary. Where James misspells one word into a correct spelling of another word, such as "cease" in "If I were at home I would cease mother round her delicate waist and lift her to ethereal heights in celebration of this ~~fact~~ latest" (14 August [1873] to his parents), we give no misspelling note, since the problem is a misuse (here also probably a pronunciation pun) rather than a misspelling. We provide no textual commentary on James's misspellings of proper names unless comprehension is otherwise severely compromised. We do, however, provide the correct spelling of the name in the explanatory notes. James's use of Italian presents special problems. Standard spelling of nineteenth-century Italian in some cases may be less certain than spelling of English or French words. There is also evidence that James uses dialectic and archaic forms that may not be incorrect in terms of their spelling (e.g., 8 March [1875] to Elizabeth Boott) but are used awkwardly or syntactically incorrectly as they would be by many nonnative speakers and writers. Consistent, then, with our annotation of James's misspellings in other languages, we annotate a word as a misspelling only when we are certain that James's spelling deviates from accepted contemporary usage.

We indicate inadvertent repetition of a word caused by a line or page break by a note in the textual commentary. We do not gloss inadvertent omissions of words or midline repetitions, and readers should assume these to be James's.

We report all cases of end-line hyphenation in the textual notes.

James's use of the apostrophe is irregular and does not always conform to today's conventions. We cannot know in any instance if James's errors were the result of carelessness, convention, or a poor understanding of the appropriate uses of apostrophes. Whatever the reasons, we believe that it is important not to correct or standardize his use of the apostrophe. When there is doubt about the placement of an apostrophe, we give James the benefit of the doubt and represent that placement according to his best usage. Where there is no doubt of his placement, we show it as it appears in his hand.

James often but not always linked the personal pronoun "I" to the following word, especially in the combinations "I had" and "I have." Having concluded that this link is not meaningful and that representing James's habit of linking the words would make reading the printed letter awkward, we have silently inserted a space in these instances. For the same reasons, we have also systematically and silently inserted a space in James's signature between "James" and "jr." when James, as he often did, linked them.

James very rarely wrote out "and." He instead wrote an abbreviated ampersand like the one used by contemporaries such as Samuel Clemens, Charles Eliot Norton, and William James. Consistent with our presenting James's abbreviated words and names as he wrote them in his letters, we represent James's abbreviated ampersand with the symbol *&*.

Recurrent stylistic idiosyncrasies are meaningful. One such idiosyncrasy is James's way of emphasis by underlining once, twice, three times, sometimes with a flourish, occasionally with a circle around or a wavy line beneath a word or phrase, for a particular degree of emphasis. We render those forms of emphasis as James did. Just as we work to represent the meaning inherent or, perhaps, explicit in the range of cancellations, so do we represent as literally as possible the meanings inherent in the range of James's means of showing emphasis.

Since we do not follow James's line endings, line breaks are recorded in the textual commentary when a break could help to explain an awkwardness in a letter. For example, in his [7], 8, 9 March 1870 letter to William James, Henry James wrote "income—" at the end of one line and began the next with "—let it lie warm." Yet the meaning of the dashes (should they be rendered as a pair of hyphens or as two long dashes to indicate two words separated by a line break?) was not clear. Thus, we wanted to preserve the possible importance of the line break in a textual note to give interested readers the opportunity to decide for themselves (*CLHJ, 1855–1872* 2: 313).

James tends in these early letters to avoid indentation to mark a subject change in his letters. Instead, like many of his generation, James relied on a dash for a range of meanings. He used it following a period to mark a new subject. He used it within a sentence to mark a parenthetical thought. He used it between sentences to mark a shift but not a subject change. In addition, James did not seem to relate the length of the dash to its meaning. Thus, a dash marking emphasis cannot be distinguished in terms of its length from one marking a transition between subjects. Because James seems not to have related meaning to length, because we couldn't be sure in every case—or even in most cases—of a dash's particular function, and because we thought it likely that not all of James's own correspondents could have understood his idiosyncratic meaning, we represent all such dashes as em dashes and thus represent them without distinguishing their function. Our readers will have to determine for themselves, just as James's did, whether a dash between sentences indicates a new paragraph, as it were, or not. Here, as elsewhere, we remain consistent with James's own practice in his letters.

We follow James's indentations in terms of their relation to each other (see Hirst). Thus, we give James's shortest indentation one standard indentation space. We give his next longest one two, next longest after that three, and so on. Where James places a line or series of lines against the right margin of his paper, so do we.

We represent material inserted interlineally by James (usually signaled in his letters with a caret) with a caret preceding the insertion and a bracketed caret to mark the end of the insertion. When James inserted material interlineally but omitted a caret, we supply in square brackets the initial caret to mark the start of the inserted material. A second bracketed caret marks the end of the interlineal insertion. In our transcriptions interlineal insertions always appear after the cancellations above which James placed them, even in cases when James placed the caret to the left of the deletion. In so doing, we favor in our transcriptions a temporal rather than a spatial representation of James's text. Intralineal insertions are noted in the textual commentary.

When nearing the end of his letter and also the end of available blank space on his page, James would, in the convention of his time, finish his letter in the margin of a page or across a page. This we note.

The header to each letter provides the full name of the correspondent on the first line, the full date on the second line, the form of the source text (ALS, TLC, etc.) and the name of its repository on the third line, and, if applicable, the catalog number of the source text on the fourth line. Square brackets in the first line indicate a woman recipient's married name if she wasn't married at the time of the letter's writing and is better known to history or in James's biography by her married name (thus, Lilla Cabot [Perry] but not Elizabeth Boott [Duveneck]). Square brackets in the second line indicate our insertion of dates not written on the letter itself. Square brackets in the header's fourth line are a part of the archival information.

James regularly leaves letters partially or wholly undated in terms of day, month, or year. When James omits the day and/or the month dates from his letters, we date them conjecturally through an examination of the letter and envelope. We explain in a note the reason for our dating. When James omits the year date, we determine it through an examination of the letter and the envelope, when it is available. When that evidence differs from a year date arrived at by earlier scholars, we explain in a note the reason for our dating. Our aim in dating letters is to arrive at the best date or range of dates possible given the evidence provided in the letter (and occasionally the stationery) itself. Of course, all such dating is to one degree or another conjectural.

The articulation of multiple dates over which a letter was written deserves a few words of explanation. We give the dates of a letter written over the course of more than one day, when each day is indicated in the letter itself either by an actual date written or when the letter gives evidence that there were starts and stops in composition, with a comma separating the dates on which the letter was written (e.g., 25, 26 April [1873]). When the letter gives a temporal cue of time separating the writing of sections of the letter ("yesterday," "last night," "two days ago") but the date of the writing is not written in the letter, the implied dates are given in square brackets (16, [17] November [1873]). When it is clear from evidence in the letter that James began writing the letter late one day and finished it without a marked break on the next, the dates are separated by an en dash.

We use the ✉ sign in the letter's header to indicate the presence of an envelope with a given letter. That ✉ sign recurs prior to previous publication information to signal a description of the address and postal cancellation stamp(s).

We translate foreign phrases that we judge might not be familiar to many of our readers. We offer these translations in the informational notes.

Our approach to annotation in general is to provide information that will help our readers understand not only some of what we judge James's reader might have known but also, when it will help provide a useful context, what we know about people, places, and subjects to which James referred. While no set of notes will satisfy every reader, if we err, we prefer to err on the side of providing too much information, as it were, rather than too little. Overall, we hope that our notes provide a way for readers to develop for themselves insights into James's letters, life, and time. Biographical information gleaned from combinations of sources for birth and death records such as the *Dictionary of National Biography* and national census and marriage data and other standard reference works is not cited in the notes or in the biographical register. All other sources of information are given.

The Complete Letters of Henry James, 1872–1876, volume 2, contains seventy-eight letters, of which twenty-eight are published for the first time. Each letter is followed by previous publication information or a note that there is no previous publication. In addition, there is a record of one letter from HJ to Mrs. Samuel (Anna Barker) Ward dated 4 January 1874. The record was written by Edel and is now in the Leon Edel Papers, Department of Rare Books and Special Collections, McLennan Library, McGill University, Montreal, Quebec, Canada. The letter no longer exists, as Edel writes on the record: "[This letter was destroyed in Donald O'Brien fire] [I had never taken a copy of it]."

The full version of this general editors' note is given in the first volume of *The Complete Letters of Henry James, 1855–1872* (xlix–lxviii).

Works Cited

Peviously Published Letters

Anesko   Anesko, Michael. *Letters, Fictions, Lives: Henry James and William Dean Howells*. New York: Oxford University Press, 1997.

CLHJ,   James, Henry. *The Complete Letters of Henry James, 1855–*
1855–1872   *1872*. Ed. Pierre A. Walker and Greg W. Zacharias. 2 vols. Lincoln: University of Nebraska Press, 2006.

CLHJ,   James, Henry. *The Complete Letters of Henry James, 1872–*
1872–1876   *1876*. Ed. Pierre A. Walker and Greg W. Zacharias. Vol. 1. Lincoln: University of Nebraska Press, 2008.

CWJ 1–12   James, William, and Henry James. *The Correspondence of William James*. Ed. Ignas Skrupskelis and Elizabeth Berkeley. 12 vols. Charlottesville: University of Virginia Press, 1992–2004.

HJL 1–4   James, Henry. *Henry James Letters*. Ed. Leon Edel. 4 vols. Cambridge MA: Belknap–Harvard University Press, 1974–84.

Horne   James, Henry. *Henry James: A Life in Letters*. Ed. Philip Horne. New York: Viking, 1999.

Lubbock 1–2   James, Henry. *The Letters of Henry James*. Ed. Percy Lubbock. 2 vols. New York: Scribner's, 1920.

Monteiro   James, Henry, and John Hay. *Henry James and John Hay: The Record of a Friendship*. Ed. George Monteiro. Providence: Brown University Press, 1965.

SL 2   James, Henry. *Henry James: Selected Letters*. Ed. Leon Edel. Cambridge MA: Belknap–Harvard University Press, 1987.

WHSL   James, William, and Henry James. *William and Henry James: Selected Letters*. Ed. Ignas Skrupskelis and Elizabeth Berkeley. Charlottesville: University of Virginia Press, 1997.

Additional Works Cited

Aldrich, Thomas Bailey. *Prudence Palfrey.* Serialized in the *Atlantic Monthly* 33 (Jan. 1874): 1–13; (Feb. 1874): 144–58; (Mar. 1874): 257–68; (Apr. 1874): 385–402; (May 1874): 513–28; (June 1874): 672–84.

Baedeker, Karl. *Italy. A Handbook for Travellers by K. Baedeker. First Part: Northern Italy, Leghorn, Florence, and Ancona, and the Island of Corsica.* 3rd ed. Leipsic: Baedeker, 1874.

———. *Italy. Handbook for Travellers by K. Baedeker. First Part: Northern Italy, including Leghorn, Florence, Ravenna, the Island of Corsica and Routes through France, Switzerland, and Austria.* 4th ed. Leipsic: Baedeker, 1877.

———. *London and Its Environs; Including Excursions to Brighton, the Isle of Wight, etc.* 2nd ed. Leipsic: Baedeker, 1879.

Boott, Elizabeth. Letter to Henry James, 13 June 1874, bMS Am 1094 (32). Houghton Library, Harvard University.

Boott, Francis. Letter to Henry James, 14 June [1874], bMS Am 1094 (33). Houghton Library, Harvard University.

Bradford, Richard H. *The Virginius Affair.* Boulder: Colorado Associated University Press, 1980.

Brosses, Charles de. *Lettres familières écrites d'Italie en 1739–1740.* Paris: Perrin, 1885.

Crawford, Mary [Mrs. Hugh Fraser]. *A Diplomatist's Wife in Japan: Letters from Home to Home.* London: Hutchinson, 1898.

———. *A Diplomatist's Wife in Many Lands.* New York: Dodd, 1911.

Dall, Caroline Wells Healey. *The Romance of the Association; or, One Last Glimpse of Charlotte Temple and Eliza Wharton: A Curiosity of Literature and Life.* Cambridge MA: Wilson, 1875.

———. *Transcendentalism in New England: A Lecture.* Boston: Roberts, 1897.

Edel, Leon. *Henry James.* 5 vols. Philadelphia: Lippincott, 1953–72.

Edel, Leon, and Dan H. Laurence. *A Bibliography of Henry James.* 3rd ed. Oxford: Oxford University Press, 1982.

Emerson, Ralph Waldo (ed.). *Parnassus.* Boston: Houghton, 1874.

Ferrari, Giuseppe. *Filosofia della rivoluzione.* London, 1851.

———. *Machiavel juge des révolutions de notre temps.* Paris: Joubert, 1849.

———. *La révolution et les réformes en Italie.* Paris: Amyot, 1848.

Feydeau, Ernest. *Théophile Gautier: Souvenirs intimes.* Paris: Plon, 1874.

Gautier, Théophile. *Histoire du romantisme, suivie de notices romantiques et d'une étude sur la poésie française 1830–1868 avec un index alphabétique.* Paris: Charpentier, 1874.

Goldsmith, Oliver. *The Traveller, or A Prospect of Society: A Poem.* London: Newbery, 1764.

Habegger, Alfred. *The Father: A Life of Henry James, Sr.* New York: Farrar, 1994.

Harlow, Virginia. *Thomas Sergeant Perry: A Biography, and Letters to Perry from William, Henry, and Garth Wilkinson James.* Durham: Duke University Press, 1950.

Haskell, Daniel C., comp. *The Nation Volumes 1–105, New York, 1865–1917: Index of Titles and Contributors.* 2 vols. New York: New York Public Library, 1951–53.

Hirst, Robert H. "Editing Mark Twain, Hand to Hand, 'Like All D——d Fool Printers." *Papers of the Bibliographic Society of America* 88.2 (1994): 157–88.

Holland, J[osiah] G[ilbert]. *Bitter-Sweet: A Poem.* New York: Scribner's, 1858.

———. *Sevenoaks: A Story of Today.* New York: Scribner's, 1875.

Hooper, Ellen. "The Wood-Fire." *Dial* 1.2 (1840): 193.

Howells, William Dean. *A Chance Acquaintance.* Serialized in the *Atlantic Monthly* 31 (Jan. 1873): 17–28; (Feb. 1873): 181–96; (Mar. 1873): 339–56; (Apr. 1873): 431–48; (May 1873): 563–78; (June 1873): 693–704.

———. *A Chance Acquaintance.* Boston: Osgood, 1873.

———. *A Foregone Conclusion.* Serialized in the *Atlantic Monthly* 34 (July 1874): 1–15; (Aug. 1874): 145–60; (Sept. 1874): 345–61; (Oct. 1874): 475–88; (Nov. 1874): 534–50.

———. *A Foregone Conclusion.* Boston: Osgood, 1875.

———. *Poems.* Boston: Osgood, 1873.

———. Rev. of *A Passionate Pilgrim, and Other Tales,* by Henry James. *Atlantic Monthly* 35 (Apr. 1875): 490–95.

———. "Roundabout to Boston." *Harper's [New Monthly] Magazine* 91 (Aug. 1895): 438.

James, Henry, Jr. "Adina." *Scribner's Monthly* 8 (May–June 1874): 33–43, 181–91.

———. [Unsigned] "Art [The Duke of Montpensier's Pictures at the Boston Athenaeum]." *Atlantic Monthly* 34 (Nov. 1874): 633–37.

———. [Unsigned] "Art [Pictures by Wilde, Boughton, J. Appleton Brown, Mrs. W. J. Stillman, and Egusquiza]." *Atlantic Monthly* 35 (Jan. 1875): 117–19.

———. "The Art of Fiction." *Longman's Magazine* 4 (Sept. 1884): 502–21.

———. "The Art of Fiction." *Partial Portraits.* London: Macmillan, 1888. 375–408.

———. [Unsigned] "The Autumn in Florence." *Nation* 18 (1 Jan. 1874): 6–7.

———. "An Autumn Journey: Leaves from a Note-Book." *Galaxy* 17 (Apr. 1874): 536–44.

———. "Benvolio." *Galaxy* 20 (Aug. 1875): 209–35.

———. *The Bostonians.* London: Macmillan, 1886.

———. [Unsigned] *"Bric-à-Brac Series: Personal Reminiscences by [Thomas] Moore and [William] Jerdan.* Edited by R. H. Stoddard." *Nation* 20 (1 Apr. 1875): 229.

———. [Unsigned] "[Captain J. A. Lawson's Literary Fraud, Wanderings in the Interior of New Guinea]." *Nation* 20 (24 June 1875): 425.

———. "A Chain of Italian Cities." *Atlantic Monthly* 33 (Feb. 1874): 158–64.

———. [Unsigned] "[Charles Kingsley]." *Nation* 20 (28 Jan. 1875): 61.

———. [Unsigned] *"A Christian Painter of the Nineteenth Century: Being the Life of Hyppolite Flandrin."* *Nation* 21 (26 Aug. 1875): 137–38.

———. "The Churches of Florence." *Independent* 9 July 1874: 4.

———. [Unsigned] "[Théophile Gautier's] *Constantinople.*" *Nation* 21 (15 July 1875): 45.

———. [Unsigned] "Correspondence of William Ellery Channing, D.D., and Lucy Aikin, from 1826 to 1842." *Atlantic Monthly* 35 (Mar. 1875): 368–71.

———. [Unsigned] *"Days near Rome."* *Nation* 20 (1 Apr. 1875): 229.

———. [Unsigned] "[Prosper Mérimée's] *Dernières nouvelles.*" *Nation* 18 (12 Feb. 1874): 111.

———. [Unsigned] "The Drama [*The School for Scandal* at the Boston Museum]." *Atlantic Monthly* 34 (Dec. 1874): 754–77.

———. [Unsigned] "[T. L. Kington-Oliphant's] *The Duke and the Scholar, and Other Essays.*" *Nation* 21 (30 Sept. 1875): 216.

———. [Unsigned] "Dumas and Goethe." *Nation* 17 (30 Oct. 1873): 292–94.

———. [Unsigned] "[Louisa M. Alcott's] *Eight Cousins: Or the Aunt-hill.*" *Nation* 21 (14 Oct. 1875): 250–51.

———. [Unsigned] *"Essays—Aesthetical."* *Nation* 20 (3 June 1875): 383.

———. "Eugene Pickering." *Atlantic Monthly* 34 (Oct.-Nov. 1874): 397–410, 513–26.

———. [Unsigned] "An Ex-Grand Ducal Capital." *Nation* 17 (9 Oct. 1873): 239–41.

———. [Unsigned] *"Ezra Stiles Gannett, Unitarian Minister in Boston,*

1824–1871. A Memoir, by His Son, William C. Gannett." *Nation* 20 (1 Apr. 1875): 228–29.

———. [Unsigned] "[Thomas Hardy's] *Far from the Madding Crowd.*" *Nation* 19 (24 Dec. 1874): 423–24.

———. [Unsigned] "Flaubert's *Temptation of St. Anthony.*" *Nation* 18 (4 June 1874): 365–66.

———. "Florentine Architecture." *Independent* 18 June 1874: 3–4.

———. "A Florentine Garden." *Independent* 14 May 1874: 3–4.

———. "Florentine Notes." *Independent* 23 Apr. 1874: 2–3.

———. "Florentine Notes." *Independent* 30 Apr. 1874: 2–3.

———. "Florentine Notes." *Independent* 21 May 1874: 1–2.

———. [Unsigned] "[William Dean Howells's] *A Foregone Conclusion.*" *North American Review* 120 (Jan. 1875): 207–14; *Nation* 20 (7 Jan. 1875): 12–13.

———. [Unsigned] "[Albert Rhodes's] *The French at Home.*" *Nation* 21 (5 Aug. 1875): 91–92.

———. "From a Roman Note-Book." *Galaxy* 16 (Nov. 1873): 679–86.

———. [Unsigned] "*Fruit Between the Leaves.*" *Nation* 21 (1 July 1875): 15–16.

———. "*Frülingsfluthen. Ein König Lear des Dorfes. Zwei Novellen.* Von Iwan Turgéniew." *North American Review* 118 (Apr. 1874): 326–56.

———. [Unsigned] "Gautier's *Winter in Russia.*" *Nation* 19 (12 Nov. 1874): 321–22.

———. [Unsigned] "*A Group of Poets and Their Haunts.*" *Nation* 20 (10 June 1875): 399–400.

———. *Hawthorne.* English Men of Letters Series. London: Macmillan, 1879.

———. [Unsigned] "[Andrew A. Paton's] *Henry Beyle.*" *Nation* 19 (17 Sept. 1874): 187–89.

———. [Unsigned] "Homburg Reformed." *Nation* 17 (28 Aug. 1873): 142–44.

———. [Unsigned] "*Home Sketches in France, and Other Papers.*" *Nation* 20 (10 June 1875): 400.

———. [Unsigned] "[J. W. De Forest's] *Honest John Vane: A Story.*" *Nation* 19 (31 Dec. 1874): 441–42.

———. "Howells' *Poems.*" *Independent* 8 Jan. 1874: 9.

———. [Unsigned] "[Julian Hawthorne's] *Idolatry: A Romance.*" *Atlantic Monthly* 34 (Dec. 1874): 746–48.

———. [Unsigned] "In Belgium." *Nation* 19 (3 Sept. 1874): 151–52.

———. [Unsigned] "In Holland." *Nation* 19 (27 Aug. 1874): 136–37.

———. [Unsigned] "[Sir Samuel Baker's] *Ismailia: A Narrative of the Expeditions to Central Africa for the Suppression of the Slave Trade, Organized by Ismail, Khedive of Egypt.*" *Nation* 20 (4 Feb. 1875): 81–82.

———. "An Italian Convent." *Independent* 2 July 1874: 3–4.

———. *Italian Hours.* London: Heinemann, 1909.

———. [Unsigned] "[Frances Elliot's] *The Italians: A Novel.*" *Nation* 21 (12 Aug. 1875): 107.

———. [Unsigned] "[Jules Sandeau's] *Jean de Thommeray; Le Colonel Evrard.*" *Nation* 18 (12 Feb. 1874): 95.

———. [Unsigned] "John Coleridge Patteson." *Nation* 20 (8 Apr. 1875): 244–45.

———. [Unsigned] "Lady Duff Gordon's Letters." *Nation* 20 (17 June 1875): 412–13.

———. "The Last of the Valerii." *Atlantic Monthly* 33 (Jan. 1874): 69–85.

———. [Unsigned] "[George Eliot's] *The Legend of Jubal, and Other Poems.*" *North American Review* 119 (Oct. 1874): 484–89.

———. Letter to parents, 9 November [1875], bMS Am 1094 (1829). Houghton Library, Harvard University.

———. "The Letters of Madame de Sabran." *Galaxy* 20 (Oct. 1875): 536–46.

———. "The Letters of Prosper Mérimée." *Independent* 9 Apr. 1874: 9–10.

———. [Unsigned] "Livingstone's Last Journals." *Nation* 20 (11 Mar. 1875): 175–76.

———. [Unsigned] "Macready's Reminiscences." *Nation* 20 (29 Apr. 1875): 297–98.

———. [Unsigned] "Madame Ristori." *Nation* 20 (18 Mar. 1875): 194–95.

———. [Unsigned] "[Victor Cherbuliez's] *Meta Holdenis.*" *North American Review* 117 (Oct. 1873): 461–68.

———. [Unsigned] "*Miss Rovel.*" *Nation* 20 (3 June 1875): 381.

———. "Mme. de Mauves." *Galaxy* 17 (Feb.–Mar. 1874): 216–33, 354–74.

———. [Unsigned] "[Mr. Frank Duveneck]." *Nation* 20 (3 June 1875): 376–77.

———. [Unsigned] "[Mr. George Rignold as Macbeth]." *Nation* 20 (27 May 1875): 362.

———. [Unsigned] "Mr. Greville's Journal." *Nation* 20 (28 Jan. 1875): 62–63.

———. "Mr. Tennyson's Drama." *Galaxy* 20 (Sept. 1875): 393–402.

———. [Unsigned] "Nadal's Impressions of England." *Nation* 21 (7 Oct. 1875): 232–33.

———. [Unsigned] "New Novels." *Nation* 21 (23 Sept. 1875): 201–03.

————. [Unsigned] "Nordhoff's Communistic Societies." *Nation* 20 (14 Jan. 1875): 26–28.

————. "A Northward Journey." *Independent* 20 Aug. 1874: 6; 27 Aug. 1874: 4.

————. *Notes of a Son and Brother.* New York: Scribner's, 1914.

————. [Unsigned] "Notes on the Theatres." *Nation* 20 (11 Mar. 1875): 178–79.

————. "Old Italian Art." *Independent* 11 June 1874: 2–3.

————. [Unsigned] "[Francis Parkman's] *The Old Régime in Canada.*" *Nation* 19 (15 Oct. 1874): 252–53.

————. "On Some Pictures Lately Exhibited." *Galaxy* 20 (July 1875): 89–97.

————. [Unsigned] "[Gilbert Haven's] *Our Next-Door Neighbor: A Winter in Mexico.*" *Nation* 21 (8 July 1875): 29–30.

————. "Paris Revisited" (dated 22 Nov.). *New York Tribune* 11 Dec. 1875, 3: 1–2.

————. *A Passionate Pilgrim, and Other Tales.* Boston: Osgood, 1875.

————. [Unsigned] "[Paul Veronese and Jean-François Millet]." *Nation* 20 (17 June 1875): 410.

————. [Unsigned] "Personal Reminiscences of Cornelia Knight and Thomas Raikes, Bric-à-Brac Series." *Nation* 20 (24 June 1875): 428.

————. [Unsigned] "[A Portrait by Copley]." *Nation* 21 (9 Sept. 1875): 166.

————. [Unsigned] "[Portraits by Mr. Frank Duveneck]." *Nation* 21 (9 Sept. 1875): 165–66.

————. [Unsigned] "[Theodore Martin's] *The Prince Consort.*" *Nation* 20 (4 Mar. 1875): 154–55.

————. "Professor Fargo." *Galaxy* 18 (Aug. 1874): 233–53.

————. [Unsigned] "Professor Masson's Essays." *Nation* 20 (18 Feb. 1875): 114–15.

————. [Unsigned] "[Bayard Taylor's] *The Prophet: A Tragedy.*" *North American Review* 120 (Jan. 1875): 188–94.

————. [Unsigned] "Ravenna." *Nation* 19 (9 July 1874): 23–25.

————. [Unsigned] "[P. V. N. Myers's] *Remains of Lost Empires: Sketches of the Ruins of Palmyra, Nineveh, Babylon, and Persepolis, etc.*" *Nation* 20 (28 Jan. 1875): 65–66.

————. *Roderick Hudson.* Serialized in the *Atlantic Monthly* 35 (Jan. 1875): 1–15; (Feb. 1875): 145–60; (Mar. 1875): 297–313; (Apr. 1875): 422–36; (May 1875): 515–31; (June 1875): 644–58; 36 (July 1875): 58–70; (Aug. 1875): 129–40; (Sept. 1875): 269–81; (Oct. 1875): 385–406; (Nov. 1875): 553–70; (Dec. 1875): 641–55.

————. *Roderick Hudson.* Boston: Osgood, 1875.

————. "A Roman Holiday." *Atlantic Monthly* 32 (July 1873): 1–11.

————. "Roman Neighborhoods." *Atlantic Monthly* 32 (Dec. 1873): 671–80.

————. "Roman Rides." *Atlantic Monthly* 32 (Aug. 1873): 190–98.

————. [Unsigned] "Sainte-Beuve's English Portraits." *Nation* 20 (15 Apr. 1875): 261–62.

————. [Unsigned] "Sainte-Beuve's First Articles." *Nation* 20 (18 Feb. 1875): 117–18.

————. "Siena." *Atlantic Monthly* 33 (June 1874): 664–69.

————. [Unsigned] "[Ouida's] *Signa: A Story.*" *Nation* 21 (1 July 1875): 11.

————. [Unsigned] "[Sir Arthur Help's] Social Pressure." *Nation* 20 (18 Mar. 1875): 193–94.

————. [Unsigned] "[Émile Montégut's] *Souvenirs de Bourgogne.*" *Nation* 19 (23 July 1874): 62.

————. [Unsigned] "[H. Willis Baxley's] *Spain. Art Remains and Art Realities: Painters, Priests, and Princes, etc.*" *Nation* 20 (20 May 1875): 350–51.

————. "The Sweetheart of M. Briseux." *Galaxy* 15 (June 1873): 760–79.

————. [Unsigned] "Swinburne's Essays." *Nation* 21 (29 July 1875): 73–74.

————. [Unsigned] "Taine's Notes on Paris." *Nation* 20 (6 May 1875): 318–19.

————. [Unsigned] "[Stopford A. Brooke's] Theology in the English Poets." *Nation* 20 (21 Jan. 1875): 41–42.

————. "[Ernest Feydeau's] *Théophile Gautier, Souvenirs intimes* [and] *Histoire du Romantisme, Suivie de Notices Romantiques, etc.* Par Théophile Gautier." *North American Review* 119 (Oct. 1874): 416–23.

————. [Unsigned] "Thomson's Indo-China and China." *Nation* 20 (22 Apr. 1875): 279–80.

————. [Unsigned] "Three French Books [Vicomte Henri de Bornier's] *La Fille de Roland*; [Alphonse Daudet's] *Fromont Jeune et Risler Aîné*; and [H. Wallon's] *Jeanne D'Arc.*" *Galaxy* 20 (Aug. 1875): 276–80.

————. *Transatlantic Sketches.* Boston: Osgood, 1875.

————. [Unsigned] "[John Latouche's] *Travels in Portugal.*" *Nation* 21 (21 Oct. 1875): 264–65.

————. [Unsigned] "Tuscan Cities." *Nation* 18 (21 May 1874): 329–30.

————. [Unsigned] "Victor Hugo's *Ninety-Three.*" *Nation* 18 (9 Apr. 1874): 238–39.

————. [Unsigned] "[Harriet Beecher Stowe's] *We and Our Neighbors: Records of an Unfashionable Street.*" *Nation* 21 (22 July 1875): 61.

————. *William Wetmore Story and His Friends.* 2 vols. Edinburgh: Blackwood, 1903.

James, Henry, Sr. Letter to Henry James, 8 Aug. [1873], bMS Am 1092.9
   (4201). Houghton Library, Harvard University.

James, Mary Walsh. Letter to Henry James, 1 July [1873], bMS Am 1093.1
   (48). Houghton Library, Harvard University.

———. Letter to Henry James, 4 Aug. [1873], bMS Am 1093.1 (49).
   Houghton Library, Harvard University.

———. Letter to Henry James, 12 Sept. [1873], bMS Am 1093.1 (50).
   Houghton Library, Harvard University.

———. Letter to Henry James, 22 Sept. [1873], bMS Am 1093.1 (51).
   Houghton Library, Harvard University.

———. Letter to Henry James, 8 Dec. 1873, bMS Am 1093.1 (52). Houghton Library, Harvard University.

———. Letter to Henry James, 17 Mar. [1874], bMS Am 1093.1 (53).
   Houghton Library, Harvard University.

———. Letter to Henry James, 3 Apr. [1874], bMS Am 1093.1 (54).
   Houghton Library, Harvard University.

———. Letter to Henry James, 18 May [1874], bMS Am 1093.1 (55).
   Houghton Library, Harvard University.

———. Letter to Henry James, 6 July [1874], bMS Am 1093.1 (56).
   Houghton Library, Harvard University.

James, William. "Vacations." *Nation* 17 (7 Aug. 1873): 90–91.

Kellogg, J[ulia] A. *The Philosophy of Henry James . . . A Digest.* New York:
   Lovell, 1883.

Kingsley, Charles. "The Sands of Dee." *Poems.* New York: Macmillan,
   1907. 246.

Lathrop, George Parsons. *A Study of Hawthorne.* Boston: Houghton, 1876.

Laugel, Auguste. "Feydeau's Life of Gautier." *Nation* 18 (14 May 1874):
   313–14.

Lecocq, Alexandre-Charles, M. Clairville, Victor Koning, and M. Sirau-
   din. *La fille de Madame Angot: An Opera Bouffe in Three Acts.* London:
   S. French, 1873.

Livingstone, David. *The Last Journals of David Livingstone in Central
   Africa, from 1865 to His Death.* 2 vols. London: Murray, 1874.

Lowell, James Russell. "Agassiz." *Atlantic Monthly* 33 (May 1874): 586–97.

Maher, Jane. *Biography of Broken Fortunes: Wilkie and Bob, Brothers of
   William, Henry and Alice James.* Hamden: Archon, 1986.

Martin, Theodore. *The Life of His Royal Highness the Prince Consort.* 5 vols.
   London: Smith, Elder, 1875–1880.

McMahon, Helen. *Criticism of Fiction in* The Atlantic Monthly, *1857–1898.*
   New York: Bookman, 1973.

Mérimée, Prosper. *Dernières nouvelles.* Paris: Lévy, 1874.

———. *Lettres à une inconnue.* Paris: Lévy, 1874.

Moore, Rayburn. "The Letters of Alice James to Anne Ashburner, 1873–78: The Joy of Engagement," *Resources for American Literary Study* 27.1 (2001): 17–64; 27.2 (2001): 196–236.

Morris, William. *The Earthly Paradise: A Poem.* London: Ellis, 1868.

Murray, John. *Handbook for North Germany, from the Baltic to the Black Forest, and the Rhine, from Holland to Basle.* 19th ed. London: Murray, 1877.

———. *A Handbook for Visitors to Paris.* 5th ed. London: Murray, 1872.

Norton, Charles Eliot. Letter to Henry James, 5 Dec. 1873, bMS Am 1094 (379). Houghton Library, Harvard University.

Pater, Walter. *Studies in the History of the Renaissance.* London: Macmillan, 1873.

Perry, Thomas Sargeant. [Unsigned] Rev. of *Prosper Randoce,* by Victor Cherbuliez. *Atlantic Monthly* 33 (Apr. 1874): 497.

Pitman, Marie J. Davis. *European Breezes.* Boston: Lea and Shepard, 1882.

———. *Wonder World Stories: From the Chinese, French, German, Hebrew, Hindoostanee, Hungarian, Irish, Italian, Japanese, Russian, Swedish, and Turkish.* New York: Putnam's, 1877.

Post Office London Directory, 1870. London: Kelly, 1870.

Stedman, Edmund Clarence. "Alfred Tennyson." *Scribner's Monthly* 8 (May 1874): 100–08; (June 1874): 160–70.

———. *Victorian Poets.* Boston: Osgood, 1875.

Swingle, Charles Manning. *The Keep-Well Book with Something of the Philosophy of Well-Being.* Cleveland: Self-published, 1914.

Tanselle, G. Thomas. "The Editing of Historical Documents." *Studies in Bibliography* 31 (1978): 1–56.

———. "The Editorial Problem of Final Intention." *Studies in Bibliography* 29 (1975): 167–211.

———. "Recent Editorial Discussion and the Central Questions of Editing." *Studies in Bibliography* 34 (1981): 23–65.

Tennyson, Alfred, Lord. *The Princess: A Medley.* London: Moxon, 1847.

———. *Queen Mary: A Drama.* London: King, 1875.

Thoreau, Henry David. *Walden, or, Life in the Woods.* Boston: Ticknor and Fields, 1854.

Turner, James. *The Liberal Education of Charles Eliot Norton.* Baltimore MD: Johns Hopkins University Press, 1999.

[Unsigned] Rev. of Emerson's *Parnassus. Atlantic Monthly* 35 (Apr. 1875): 495–96.

[Unsigned] Rev. of *Prosper Randoce*, by Victor Cherbuliez. *Galaxy* 17 (Apr. 1874): 573–74.

[Unsigned] Rev. of *Transatlantic Sketches*, by Henry James. *Atlantic Monthly* 36 (July 1875): 113–15.

Valery, Antoine-Claude-Pasquin. *Curiosités et anecdotes italiennes*. Brussels: Société belge de librairie, 1843.

———. *Voyages en Corse*. Paris: Bourgeois-Maze, 1837.

———. *Voyages historiques et littéraires en Italie*. Brussels: Hauman, 1825.

Whitmore, William Henry. Unsigned review of *The Romance of the Association* by Caroline Dall. *Nation* 20 (13 May 1875): 334–35.

Wordsworth, William. *Lyrical Ballads*. London: T. N. Longman and O. Rees, 1800.

Index

This index includes the names of every person to whom James addressed a letter ("letters to"), every person mentioned in a letter, every place from which a letter was sent ("letters from"), every place mentioned, every piece of art or architecture, and every article or book HJ indicated that he read, wrote, reviewed, or thought about writing.

Page numbers in bold indicate entries in the Biographical Register. Page numbers in italics indicate illustrations.

The Complete Letters of Henry James

The Complete Letters of Henry James, 1855–1872
    Volume 1 (1855–1869)
    Volume 2 (1869–1872)
The Complete Letters of Henry James, 1872–1876
    Volume 1 (1872–1873)
    Volume 2 (1873–1875)